WOMEN OF THE
SPANISH-AMERICAN WAR
Fighters, War Correspondents, and Activists

CHERYL MULLENBACH

Guilford, Connecticut

An imprint of Globe Pequot, the trade division of
The Rowman & Littlefield Publishing Group, Inc.
4501 Forbes Blvd., Ste. 200
Lanham, MD 20706
www.rowman.com

Distributed by NATIONAL BOOK NETWORK

British Library Cataloguing in Publication Information available

Library of Congress Cataloging-in-Publication Data

Names: Mullenbach, Cheryl, author.
Title: Women of the Spanish-American war : fighters, war correspondents, and activists / Cheryl Mullenbach.
Other titles: Fighters, war correspondents, and activists
Description: Guilford, Connecticut : Lyons Press, [2022] | Includes bibliographical references. | Summary: "While it's mindboggling to fathom anyone labeling a war 'splendid,' a high-ranking American official used that term to describe the Spanish American War in 1898. If any slivers of splendor existed in the grim brutalities of war, they were frequently on display in the remarkable actions of brave women who nursed their fallen warriors, reported conditions on the battlefields, fought on behalf of fervently-held causes, and protested questionable actions of their governments. Today most Americans are aware of Teddy Roosevelt and the Rough Riders. Even casual historians recall the chant 'Remember the Maine, to hell with Spain!' The role of horses and mules in the war have sparked attention. And the exploits of several dogs have been documented. However, in the quest for shining examples of splendor, high motives, and magnificent intelligence and spirit during the Spanish American War, the accomplishments of some extraordinary individuals have been overlooked and deserve recognition. Women of The Spanish-American War brings to light their stories of relentless courage and selflessness"—Provided by publisher.
Identifiers: LCCN 2022001929 (print) | LCCN 2022001930 (ebook) | ISBN 9781493056484 (cloth) | ISBN 9781493056491 (epub)
Subjects: LCSH: Spanish-American War, 1898—Women. | Nurses—United States—History—19th century. | Spanish-American War, 1898—Participation—Female. | Spanish-American War, 1898—Journalists. | Women journalists—United States—History—19th century. | Women revolutionaries—Cuba—History—19th century.
Classification: LCC E725.5.W7 M85 2022 (print) | LCC E725.5.W7 (ebook) | DDC 973.8/95—dc23/eng/20220118
LC record available at https://lccn.loc.gov/2022001929
LC ebook record available at https://lccn.loc.gov/2022001930

♾ The paper used in this publication meets the minimum requirements of American National Standard for Information Sciences—Permanence of Paper for Printed Library Materials, ANSI/NISO Z39.48-1992.

For Richard Wohlgamuth

It has been a splendid little war, begun with the highest motives, carried on with magnificent intelligence and spirit. —U.S. Secretary of State John Hay, 1898–1905

Contents

ACKNOWLEDGMENTS

Special thanks go to several individuals who contributed invaluable professional insight and guidance or simple down-to-earth doggedness in assisting me with research. Thank you to Dr. Bruce Fehn, Eugene E. Fracek (Dakota), Dr. Jacqueline Jones, Dr. Gene Morales, and Teresa Prados-Torreira. RaeAnn Swanson-Evans provided thoughtful, professional expertise as a historian—a priceless gem. Surely Latin has served me well over the years, but I would have been lost without crucial Spanish and German translations from Leo Etcheto, Miguel Garate, and Martha Chancellor. My sincere gratitude goes to Vicky Lopez for her incomparable perspective on the life of Clemencia Lopez. A heartfelt thank you to Joyce Christine Colon, Irene S. Magallon, and Cherry Ganancial in the Philippines and Kevin Taylor at the National Archives—even a pandemic failed to derail him from following up on my quest for primary source materials.

1

Not So Little and Far from Splendid

"OH, TRUE FRIEND OF MOTHERS, TELL US WHAT TO TEACH OUR SONS? 'My country, right or wrong?' Is that all? Is that the best the sons of those who have four times fought for their country can teach us? Oh, that my eyes were fountains of tears, that I might weep 'for the lost honor of my beloved country, and for the wasted lives of those who died to save what the wickedness of men in high places' has thrown away!" The words of this mother reflected the sentiments of many Americans in 1898 as young men and women boarded trains and ships to serve their country in faraway tropical lands—places many had little knowledge of other than newspaper and magazine articles and rousing political speeches intended to rally support for the direction politicians and military leaders led the nation's young and old. Confusion, uncertainty, patriotism, and humanitarianism sprinkled with skepticism for the nation's plunge into war against a European monarchy holding onto its last remnants of prominence as a world power in Cuba, the Philippines, Guam, and Puerto Rico percolated in the collective conscious of America.

The reasons for going to war with Spain in 1898, as well as the end results, were subjects of controversy and scrutiny before, during, and long after the loss of lives and disruption of families had tapered off. For those mothers, fathers, spouses, siblings, and other family members who had lost loved ones in the "splendid little war," the heartache and grief lingered beyond the sensational headlines and beguiling chants and slogans.

Coffins of Spanish-American War Dead COFFINS OF SPANISH WAR DEAD, ARLING-
TON, VIRGINIA, 1898, RETRIEVED FROM THE LIBRARY OF CONGRESS, HTTPS://WWW.LOC.GOV/
ITEM/2007682428.

While it's mind-boggling to fathom anyone labeling a war "splendid," a high-ranking American official used that term to describe the Spanish-American War in 1898. What about the war was splendid? Certainly not the loss of lives, disruption of families, or uncertainty of life in Cuba and the Philippines. The ordinary men, women, and children who were most impacted by the conflict might have chosen a different word to describe their experiences. If any slivers of splendor existed in the grim brutalities of war, they were in the remarkable actions of brave women who nursed their fallen warriors, reported conditions on the battlefields, fought on behalf of fervently held causes, and protested questionable actions of their governments. Armed with relentless courage and selflessness, many women served as examples of splendor, high motives, and magnificent intelligence and spirit during the Spanish-American War and the Philippine-American War.

American ambassador to Great Britain John Hay was reportedly a well-respected and popular representative of the United States in London, where he and his wife lived in one of the finest houses in town. They were frequently seen in the most coveted social circles and were "regular first-nighters" at the preeminent theaters. It was said he cut quite a figure when, with a nod to British tradition, he appeared at official functions dressed in knee breeches and silk stockings.

Hay had been selected by President William McKinley to fill the ambassador's post in London in 1897. The lifelong Republican had made a name for himself in the literary field as a newspaper editorial writer and the author of several works, including a biography of Abraham Lincoln and a poem titled "Little Breeches," but he preferred to be recognized for his previous stint as private secretary to President Abraham Lincoln.

The United States and Spain went to war in April 1898 while Hay was serving as ambassador, and a truce was called in August 1898, when Hay was called back home to America to become secretary of state. At the time of his selection, Hay was described as "keen and incisive in speech . . . every sentence says exactly what Col. Hay means it to say. He utters nothing carelessly." It was in July that the future secretary had written to his friend Theodore Roosevelt from the comfort of his charming residence in London proclaiming that the military actions in Cuba and Philippines constituted a "splendid little war." Of course, Hay was writing to a man who in 1897 had said, "I should welcome almost any war, for I think this country needs one."

Despite the enthusiasm for war championed by Hays, Roosevelt, and others, the march to armed conflict was obstructed for a time by roadblocks, including a conflicted public saddled with powerful but fading memories of the Civil War and a reluctant president who said in his inaugural address, "War should never be entered upon until every agency of peace has failed." A veteran of the Civil War, McKinley expressed his distaste for war: "I have been through one war. I have seen the dead piled up, and I do not want to see another." Ultimately, the barriers were overcome as a host of individuals and ideologies converged to lead the nation to war with Spain on April 25, 1898.

Expansionism and imperialism had become critical issues to Americans in the months leading up to the war. The idea that the country should expand its boundaries had been part of the American lexicon and psyche almost since its inception—resulting in the conquest of indigenous lands and the continued policies of westward movement. In 1839, John O'Sullivan, writing for *The United States Magazine and Democratic Review*, defined a vision for the United States to become a nation "destined to manifest to mankind the excellence of divine principles." And in 1845, the same publication included an article outlining America's goal for the "fulfillment of our manifest destiny to overspread the continent allotted by Providence for the free development of our yearly multiplying millions." The policy became known as Manifest Destiny, a belief that "the United States should expand across the continent to the Pacific Ocean." Imperialism, an extension of that notion, was a policy in which stronger nations extended their influence over weaker territories. By 1898, considerable portions of Africa and Asia had been colonized by European nations. Americans looked to this and thought it was time for the United States to get into the business of acquiring overseas lands. America's imperialistic tendencies were driven by a variety of factors, including a desire for military strength and preparedness and a need for raw materials and new markets for agricultural and manufactured products. A racist belief in the cultural and racial superiority of White Americans also drove the move toward imperialism. There were rabid and vocal advocates in support of and opposition to each of those elements of American imperialism in 1898.

In 1890, the U.S. Congress's naval appropriations reflected a movement to make the navy "an instrument of diplomatic and military power extending American interests over a significant portion of the globe." The move had been partly influenced by men like longtime naval officer Alfred T. Mahan, who after nearly forty years in the military had become an exceptionally powerful advocate for expansion and the building of a strong navy. His book *The Influence of Sea Power upon History*, published in 1890, had earned him widespread recognition among American leaders as well as Europeans. He was a sought-after speaker and commanding writer. If he failed to attract the average American man and woman through his books and public appearances, he likely grabbed the attention of some of the nation's impressionable young folks—"the shapers of the next thirty years"—when his work appeared in a weekly publication, *The Youth's Companion,* a "family paper of America" featuring writers who "add[ed] their ablest efforts to charm, instruct and help readers." It was a British writer who described Mahan as "the man who must be held chiefly responsible for the warlike spirit which is making itself manifest all over the world" and that his words were "as oil to the flame of 'colonial expansion.'" It was partly because of the urging of Mahan and others that the United States expanded and strengthened its navy, building warships such as the USS *Maine,* which would eventually play a significant role in the decision to go to war with Spain.

Over the course of the nineteenth century, American farmers and factory workers had built the nation into a formidable producer of agricultural and manufactured goods. While this was a good thing, economists and policymakers recognized the possibility of overproduction and began to look beyond the borders of the United States for additional markets. The nation was recovering from the economic depression of 1893, and no one wanted to see a situation in which a surplus of goods caused factories to shut down, putting Americans out of work. As one statesman put it, there was "a crying need of . . . more markets and larger markets for the consumption of the products of the industry and inventive genius of the American people."

And while the United States was already exporting products, including oil, grain, livestock, and cotton, to foreign markets in 1897, the nation's leaders continued to eye the potential presented by millions of consumers in places like Latin America and Asia, especially China. In addition, these markets could be sources for needed raw materials, such as rubber and tin. There were already well-established American businesses in Cuba and Hawaii, including mines, railroads, and sugar and tobacco plantations. And although some American business owners viewed expansion outside American borders as competition, it began to make sense to many Americans that the country would be well served by further expansion and acquisition of overseas colonies, and Spain's colonies in the Pacific and the Caribbean might just quench that thirst for both. If that meant going to war with Spain, so be it.

Some Americans justified war with Spain and annexation of Cuba as a solution to the spread of yellow fever in the United States. The disease had long been a killer in Cuba, and over the years, it had found its way to southern states in America. Refugees from Cuba were in part blamed for infecting southern communities. One American congressman said that Cuba, with its perpetual unsanitary conditions, was "like having an open cesspool opposite one's front door." American ownership of the island would ensure the elimination of the disease. (As it turned out, more Americans died during the war from disease—contracted in American military camps as well as in war zones—than from battle wounds.)

Americans' interest in Cuba and the Philippines was driven by humanitarian concerns as well as commercial and health factors. By 1898, Cubans had tried to overthrow the Spanish more than once, and the Filipinos had fought against Spanish rule for years as well. Some saw Spain's treatment of their territories comparable to England's relation to its American colonies in 1776. Others couldn't help but compare the circumstances of enslaved Cubans, who had been freed by Spain in 1886, to African Americans, who had been enslaved in America until the enactment of the Thirteenth Amendment in 1865. Many Americans viewed the situations in Cuba and the Philippines as humanitarian crises in need of attention. But there was a dark side to the humanitarian rallying cry for some. Massachusetts Senator Henry Cabot Lodge put it into words when he referred to these areas of the world as "waste places of the earth" as he championed the need for the "advancement of the race"—meaning the White race. Racism and belief in the superiority of Western civilization were foundational beliefs propelling American imperialism. It had driven westward expansion and the conquest of indigenous lands in the U.S. West in the past, and the concept was now applied to Cuba and the Philippines.

As President McKinley, Congress, politicians, and other policymakers debated the wisdom of engaging in war with Spain, they weighed a variety of factors. An important consideration was the mood of the

Print shows Uncle Sam as a teacher of students labeled Cuba, Puerto Rico, Hawaii, and the Philippines. An African American boy cleans windows, and an Indian boy reads an upside-down book. A book on the teacher's desk is titled *U.S. First Lessons in Self-Government*. LIBRARY OF CONGRESS PRINTS AND PHOTO-GRAPHS DIVISION, WASHINGTON, D.C., LC-DIG-PPMSCA-28668.

public—specifically voters. Were Americans willing to sacrifice young men's lives for economic or humanitarian causes? It was a burning question. And although women couldn't vote, would mothers welcome an opportunity to send their sons off to die in distant lands to secure the country's status as a first-class military power? As one twentieth-century historian put it, "The Philippines might as well have been the moon." At any rate, leaders who wanted to justify war may have gauged support based on those Americans who most energetically waved flags or sang patriotic songs louder than their pacifist neighbor. And if reluctant Americans needed convincing, those bellicose leaders turned to other tactics that would make it difficult for peace-loving people to resist war.

An exchange published in the Asheville, North Carolina, *Daily Citizen* newspaper in April 1898 exemplified opposing views held by people in those days just before the nation went to war. Back in 1891, Captain Thomas Walton Patton, a Civil War veteran, visited Cuba, and the

Asheville paper ran sections of a letter he wrote from Havana. In April 1898, as the nation's statesmen contemplated war with Spain over Cuba, the paper reprinted the letter. Patton's words and the paper's decision to republish them reinforced the beliefs of American cultural and racial superiority.

The captain's letter began in a complimentary style describing the remarkable natural beauty as he approached Cuban shores, but his tone quickly pivoted as he met the first Spaniards, "the most disgusting specimens" of the land. "The only feature that has come up to our expectations is its filth," the captain wrote about Havana, adding that although he had been warned to expect "the dirtiest city on the face of the globe," he thought the description "falls far short of the fact." The streets did not meet the captain's approval—"roughly paved, where the paving can be seen through the masses of mud and filth." His annoyance with the people extended to their use of the Spanish language, which made it nearly impossible for English speakers to express their wants. At Guanobacoa, Patton met "filthy, God-forsaken, wicked" people unlike any he had met anywhere in the world. The American had a solution for the ills he witnessed in Cuba: the United States must purchase the island. According to him, under new ownership, Cuban cities would become charming resorts, the Protestant faith ("a better and purer religion") would acquire a foothold, and the Spaniards "would either change their beastly nature, or go back to that beastly country which gave them that nature." And the United States would build "the grandest naval station imaginable."

Patton's writings prompted a letter to the editor from Helen Morris Lewis, and she didn't hold back, reminding readers of past and continued racial injustices in American society—extermination of Indians and denial of full civil rights for Blacks. "The integrity of our political government and the spotlessness of our Christian morality, he presumes, would soon purify the degradation and pollution in which Cuba by Spanish rule is now submerged," Lewis wrote about Patton's ideas. She recommended that before the United States looked to overtaking Cuba and solving its problems, the country should "look into our own affairs" and observe the "evils" that existed in America before "we concern ourselves with foreign affairs." Lewis predicted that the United States would deal with the Cubans much as it had "already dealt with the American Indians—by wiping them off the face of creation." She added, "We might also problemize over them as we do the negro." Lewis lamented that Patton and others like him were "buckling on their armor and preparing for war" while magazines and newspapers were "shouting themselves hoarse for bloodshed." As she concluded, those who were eager to bring about the war would not be the ones to suffer; rather, it would be "the flower of American manhood" who would be sacrificed.

In the months leading to war, the typical American man likely turned to the fellow sitting on the bar stool next to him, the typical woman listened to a worried mother with fighting-age sons at the church sewing circle, and both may have clung to the preachings of the minister at the Sunday church service as they sought news and opinions about the nation's foreign affairs. And they most certainly looked toward newspapers and magazines to learn about happenings in a distant land called the Philippines and a not-so-far-away island called Cuba. Just as Asheville's residents weighed the opinions of Captain Patton and Helen Morris Lewis in their local newspaper, other Americans in cities, towns, and rural communities across the country were influenced by editorials, headlines, and letters to the editor in local newsletters, magazines, and newspapers.

The widely read *McClure's* magazine published well-researched pieces about the potential cost of war from an emotional as well as financial perspective, including essays about the "nationalistic zeal that swept the country" and the "hard choices confronting McKinley" as he grappled with issues that would eventually lead to war. Two newspapers, the *New York World* owned by Joseph Pulitzer and the *New York Journal* owned by William Randolph Hearst, competed to win readership in an age when print media dominated. The two tycoons could only get richer if the nation went to war. The more sensational the headlines, the more newspapers sold. Frequently, reporters ignored facts to create more sensational reading. These reporters focused on the Spaniards' behavior in Cuba and the Philippines in the months leading up to war. The term "yellow journalism" became a well-known phrase used to describe the habit of some newspapers to exaggerate or outright misrepresent facts solely to sell papers. By the time the American public had been exposed to outrageous reports

9

by unscrupulous reporters and publishers, some peace-loving Americans were second-guessing their commitment to a nonviolent solution to the concerns in Cuba and the Philippines. It became nearly impossible for the American public to separate fact from fiction, but a common theme and misconception seemed to be that Spaniards were a bad lot. A favorite subject reflecting yellow journalism was a Spanish general who had been sent to Cuba in 1896 to quell the unrest of Cubans who had revolted against Spanish rule. General Valeriano Weyler earned his nickname "The Butcher" through his brutal tactics, including the rounding up of Cubans into concentration camps—*reconcentrados.*

In February 1898, Americans on both sides of the fence were outraged when they learned that the Spanish minister to the United States, Enrique Dupuy de Lôme, had insulted the president in a letter ultimately published in newspapers across the country. The letter contained explosive details in which the minister called McKinley "weak and catering to the rabble" and criticized the president for repeating in "natural and inevitable coarseness" press accounts about General Weyler. Already fuming over de Lóme's letter, Americans were horrified when on the night of February 15 an American warship, the USS *Maine*, sent to bring American citizens home in the event of war, exploded as it sat in Cuba's Havana harbor. More than 260 sailors were killed, and others were injured. Although at first the cause of the tragedy was unclear, anyone who was looking for a reason for a war with Spain found their rationale. McKinley called for an investigation that lasted about a month but ended with a conclusion that the *Maine* had been "destroyed by the explosion of a submarine mine." Those who were eager for war propagated the chant, "Remember the Maine, to hell with Spain." (There has never been consensus on what caused the explosion.)

On April 11, President McKinley delivered a speech to Congress outlining his reasons for recommending military intervention in Cuba, including "the cause of humanity," protection for the Cuban people, "the very serious injury to the commerce, trade, and business of our people," and "menace to our peace." On April 20, Congress passed a joint resolution authorizing the use of force in Cuba with the Teller Amendment attached, which was meant to reassure Cubans that the United States

War Maps of Cuba, Puerto Rico, and the Philippines, 1898 BOSTON PUBLIC LIBRARY, NORMAN B. LEVENTHAL MAP CENTER COLLECTION.

had no interest in annexing their island.[1] On April 25, the United States declared war on Spain. The American military sprang into action.

By May 1, the U.S. Asiatic fleet under Commodore George Dewey destroyed the Spanish fleet in Manila Bay in the Philippines without losing a single American life, and Dewey became "the most popular man in America." "Not one Spanish flag flies in Manila Bay," Dewey telegraphed his superiors. Newspapers around the world reported Dewey's heroic accomplishments: the *New York Times*: "Manila in Dewey's Grasp"; London's *Daily News*: "a terrible conflict ensued"; *Belfast News-Letter* (Northern Ireland): "brilliant achievement"; Sacramento, California, *Record-Union*: "wild excitement." Printers sold Dewey portraits; Ritchie's Dry Good Store in St. Johnsbury, Vermont, advertised Dewey souvenir fans for twenty-five cents; and Uhl's department store in Somerset, Pennsylvania, offered a gold-lined souvenir spoon of the war hero with any purchase over $2. Iowa's 51st Infantry Volunteers adopted a dog mascot, naming him Dewey, and took him to the Philippines with them, where the canine showed no fear of flying bullets. In Kansas, a distracted

---

1. However, after the Spanish were defeated, the United States set up a military government in Cuba with an American governor overseeing the writing of a Cuban constitution that included the Platt Amendment placing limits on Cuba's right to enter treaties and allowing the United States to intervene in Cuban affairs. The Platt Amendment was in place until 1934. While the Teller Amendment addressed the relationship between Cuba and the United States, it did not include the Philippines and Puerto Rico. In 1902, Congress passed the Philippine Government Act, which provided that an appointed governor and a legislature ruled the Philippines. In 1946, the Philippines became independent. The Jones Act of 1917 gave Puerto Ricans U.S. citizenship.

Reverend O. J. Nelson gave up trying to write his sermon and instead penned this poem:

> Dewey our hero
> Remember his name;
> He came to Manila;
> Had revenge for our Maine.

But Dewey's swift and relatively effortless success in Manila Bay turned out to be the easiest part of the war in the Philippines, where the Filipino people had endured nearly four centuries of Spanish "exploitation and misrule." By the 1890s, three Filipino men had emerged as resistance leaders. José Rizal, a well-educated writer and advocate for peaceful reform, was arrested and executed by firing squad in 1896. Andres Bonifacio founded an underground resistance group, the Katipunan. When Emilio Aguinaldo displaced Bonifacio as leader of the Katipunan in 1897, he had Bonifacio executed for subversion. Aguinaldo took control of the revolutionary movement and continued the struggle for independence, fighting at first alongside the Americans to defeat the Spanish.

As Americans celebrated Dewey's victory in the Philippines in early May, the nation's soldiers, sailors, and marines prepared for military action in Cuba. To augment the regular military, President McKinley had called for 125,000 volunteers, and people across the United States answered his call. Thousands of zealous men formed local regiments, and women also expressed interest in joining the fight. The *Times-Picayune* (New Orleans, La.) reported that "officials at Washington are said to be pestered to death with the importunities of patriotic daughters who want to go to the front." A medical doctor from Washington, D.C., Alice Lee Moqué, was eager to form a regiment of women. "There are women as hale and hearty, as brave and fearless, as daring and patriotic, as strong and enduring, as any male who ever marched in trousers," she said.

Cuba had been under Spanish domination for centuries when America and Spain declared war. The Cuban people had resisted their Spanish rulers long before the Americans arrived. Slavery had been part of Spanish rule since the 1500s, and slave uprisings occurred periodically.

Alice Lee Hornor Moqué *HARRISBURG TELEGRAPH*, MARCH 9, 1897, WIKIMEDIA COMMONS.

In 1886, slavery was abolished. Between 1868 and 1878, Cuban revolutionaries fought unsuccessfully for independence from Spain in the Ten Years' War. Several key leaders took control of the renewed revolt in the 1890s. Antonio Maceo, a "brilliant, charismatic black rebel" known as "the Bronze Titan," was killed in December 1896. Máximo Gómez came out of retirement in 1895, having fought in the Ten Years' War, to become a commander of the freedom fighters at the age of fifty-nine. And General Calixto García, also a veteran of the Ten Years' War, rejoined the fight in 1898 at age sixty-five. José Martí returned from exile in Spain.

Days after America declared war on Spain, revolutionary leaders Gómez and García met with the Americans to confirm their commitment to work together to defeat the Spanish and to plan military strategy. Navy Admiral William T. Sampson and Commodore Winfield Schley began to establish blockades of several ports in Cuba, including Havana. On June 10, about 600 U.S. Marines engaged the Spaniards at Guantánamo Bay, which the Americans secured as a base for operations after five days of fighting. By June 22, thousands of Americans were in Cuba fighting alongside Cuban revolutionaries. Some of the White Americans were surprised to observe that many of their Cuban comrades, officers as well as regular soldiers, were Black. The army was around 60 percent Black, and 40 percent of the officers were Black. African Americans had served in the U.S. military throughout its history despite limiting quotas, restrictions to supporting roles, and segregation of units. Racism and discrimination in the American military simply reflected American society. And for some White American soldiers, Black fighters—American and Cuban—deserved little respect. However, together, the Cubans and Americans fought at El Caney as fighting converged around the city of Santiago. At Kettle Hill and San Juan Hill, Theodore Roosevelt and his Rough Riders under the command of Colonel Leonard Wood and the African American 9th and 10th cavalries, cemented their place in history. (Caroline Anthony, head nurse at the hospital in Siboney, told a reporter at the time that patients who had witnessed the events at San Juan Hill told her "the colored troops saved the Rough Riders from annihilation."[2])

On July 3, Spanish ships unsuccessfully attempted to escape the American blockade tangling with Commodore Winfield Schley's USS *Brooklyn*, ultimately causing the destruction of the Spanish fleet in the Caribbean. By August 12, the Spaniards had signed a cease-fire agreement.

---

2. According to Robert F. Jefferson Jr. in *Brothers in Valor*, six African Americans received the Medal of Honor for service during the war: Dennis Bell, Fitz Lee, William H. Thompkins, George H. Wanton, Edward L. Baker, and Robert Penn.

Under the peace treaty signed in December and ratified by the U.S. Congress in February 1899, the United States acquired Guam and Puerto Rico, and Spain relinquished control of Cuba and sold the Philippines to the United States for $20 million.

The signing of the peace treaty in December 1898 led to discontent for some. While Spain set Cuba free under the treaty, it became an "American protectorate for a period to be determined by the United States." The Cuban revolutionaries resented the Americans, who had "pretended that the Cuban rebel army did not exist." Left out of the peace process, General Gómez voiced his dismay about the final decisions: "None of us thought that it would be followed by a military occupation of the country by our allies. This cannot be our fate after years of struggle."

And while the Americans had used the Spanish occupation of the Philippines as justification for war, they were motivated also by the economic value seen in ownership of the islands. Located in the middle of current and potential trade destinations including Japan, China, and Indonesia, the Philippines was viewed as a valuable commercial asset— creating opportunities for America to access new markets in Asia. And with the signing of the peace treaty between the United States and Spain, fighting continued between the Americans and the Filipinos. It had become clear the Americans had no intention of giving the Filipinos self-rule, so Aguinaldo and his fighters along with various other groups turned their resistance toward the Americans in what became known as the Philippine-American War. Over the course of three years, Americans and Filipinos waged a war using traditional military methods as well as guerrilla warfare. American newspapers carried reports of terrible atrocities committed by Filipino revolutionaries, although often the accounts were unconfirmed. In March 1901, Aguinaldo was captured by the Americans. Guerilla fighters continued the resistance movement against the Americans, but in July 1902, President Theodore Roosevelt declared the war in the Philippines over. While the fighting had subsided, controversy surrounding the war continued, especially as Americans learned, through a 1902 U.S. Senate investigation, about atrocities that had been committed by the American military. American service members testified describing acts they had witnessed. A former soldier testified that "the town was fired on . . . two old men came out. . . . They had a white flag. They were shot down. At the other end of town we heard screams, and there was a woman there; she was burned up, and in her arms was a baby." Another described a practice called the "water cure" used to get information from captured Filipinos: "It was given by means of a syringe. Two men . . . obtained two syringes, large bulbs, a common syringe, about two feet of common hose pipe on either end. One was inserted in his mouth and other up his nose. And as the water did not seem to have the desired effect . . . a cup of salt was thrown into the water. . . . Then one man, an American soldier, who was over six feet tall . . . struck this native in the pit of the stomach as hard as he could. . . . It seemed as if he didn't get tired of striking him."

In America, many were unhappy with the situations in Cuba and the Philippines. The Anti-Imperialist League had formed in 1898 to challenge the undemocratic practice of denying self-rule to the people in the newly acquired areas. Many Americans agreed with the Kentucky mother who wrote, "How can the country that has bathed the land in the blood of the best of her sons to wash away the sin of slavery, have a right to buy ten millions of men, and butcher them by the thousand because they will not kiss the hand of their new masters? . . . It is such mockery to say all men have equal right to 'life, liberty, and the pursuit of happiness.'"

As Secretary of State John Hay and other American statesmen celebrated the expeditious execution and conclusion of the splendid little war and looked to a future with the United States as a newly minted world power, others came to terms with the aftermath of the war at a more personal level. Countless Filipinos continued to fight and die for their independence while grieving for their fellow Filipinos who had given their lives for the cause. Cubans welcomed the financial and human contributions to schools and orphanages from generous American organizations while questioning the continued presence of the American military on their island. Michigan soldiers mourned the death of nurse Ellen May Tower, who had contracted typhoid fever while caring for sick soldiers in the war. "A sweeter, nobler woman never lived," one soldier said. The family and friends of Sergeant Charles Burnsen, a Minnesota soldier who was shot through the head and died on August 16 according to the casualties list published in the *St. Paul Globe*, struggled to scrub that horrible image from their memories.

2

Nurses

Heroes in Skirts

EVELYN BELDEN, WHO HAD RECENTLY RETURNED TO HER HOME IN Sioux City, Iowa, after a monthlong visit to Camp Thomas in Chickamauga, Georgia, in the summer of 1898, told a newspaper reporter, "Whatever you hear that is bad about the division hospital—do not discount it. There were maggots on the living men, I myself brushed flies from a soldier's unprotected face, which were so numerous as to almost obscure his features." Evelyn had visited the camp to see for herself the army facility to which her son had been sent with the 52nd Iowa Volunteers in 1898. The camp and the hospital certainly didn't meet her maternal standards or public health ideals at the time. When nurses arrived at the Georgia camp from the Presbyterian Hospital of New York, they found "fifty thousand men lived in deplorable conditions, teeming with the triple scourge of typhoid, malaria, and measles." News that the military's division hospital was a hellhole continued to filter out to the public. Word began to spread around the country about conditions at other training camps, and families were disgruntled about their boys living in such circumstances. Similar conditions at camps and hospitals, at home as well as in Cuba, became sources of concern. While families expected their soldiers to face injury or even death in battle, the idea that military camps in the United States were a danger seemed unnecessary.

At first, Surgeon General George Sternberg, the officer in charge of the army's medical department, persisted in relying on the army hospital corps, composed of servicemen, to handle the medical needs of the military during the conflicts in Cuba and the Philippines. But as conditions at the training camps in the United States where volunteer and regular army soldiers had gathered became increasingly serious—as in Camp Thomas—and as epidemics threatened the camps, he relented. In April, Congress had authorized him to hire female contract nurses, which he did, at first limiting them to base and general hospital facilities and not allowing them at field and division hospitals. Eventually, this changed, and as Sternberg said, "I did not care whether I had Red Cross nurses, or White Cross nurses or nurses of no cross; what I wanted was to know that when a dozen or twenty nurses were needed they would be forthcoming."

Initially, each regiment of men from the individual states arrived at the training camps, located in Chickamauga; Falls Church, Virginia; and Jacksonville, Florida, with its own medical personnel. However, it wasn't long before the distinct regimental medical units were consolidated into a division hospital at each camp. In theory, the division hospitals were mobile and in battle would collect the sick and wounded, taking them to large base or general hospitals for treatment. Some division hospitals—like the one at Camp Thomas, where Evelyn Belden saw such horrendous conditions—were poorly organized and understaffed, lacked equipment, and were in an abysmal state early in the war. A nurse described the conditions she witnessed: "It was certainly a most harrowing sight to see the long narrow cots filled with what had been strong splendid men, hollow eyed, emaciated, muttering in the delirium of fever, sores in which dead flies were encrusted filled their mouths, making swallowing almost impossible." Finally, in late July, Sternberg established two large hospitals to deal with incoming wounded from the war zones and to ease conditions at the U.S. military camps' division hospitals. One was a 1,000-bed facility at Fort Monroe, Virginia, and the other a 750-bed facility at Camp Thomas in Chickamauga that Evelyn Belden described as "covering fifteen acres and composed of 200 tents, 13 pine pavilions, iron bedsteads and fitted out in fine condition." In addition, Sternberg's decision to employ female contract nurses helped the situation. However, while some politicians and military officials realized the value in hiring female nurses, the idea was controversial and subject to public scrutiny as evidenced in a letter to the editor in the *San Francisco Examiner* in June: "A soldiers' camp is no place for women, whether they wear the badge of the Red Cross, the poke bonnet of the Salvation Army or the bewitching shirt waist and sailor hat of the ordinary girl. They are all women, and of the weaker sex."

Dr. Anita Newcomb McGee, representing the Daughters of the American Revolution (DAR), was hired by Sternberg to oversee the selection of nurses out of the thousands who expressed interest. Something had to be done to weed out the less qualified applicants, as one report admitted that "their qualifications ranged from having served one season successfully in light opera to twenty years of successful experience as a trained nurse." The DAR used specific criteria in their selection process. The women hired as contract nurses were between thirty and fifty years of age, trained in the nursing field, and of reputable character and enjoyed good health. African American nurses would be considered. And the female nurses, who became known as the DAR hospital corps, would receive $30 a month plus one ration per day. In addition to the nurses secured by the DAR, nurses came from a variety of other sources: the American Red Cross's Clara Barton (who had been doing humanitarian work in Cuba before the war and who ultimately nursed soldiers on the battlefield in addition to in hospitals), the Associated Alumnae of Trained Nurses Association, the Tuskegee Training School for Nurses, the American National Red Cross Auxiliary No. 3 for the Maintenance of Trained Nurses (not to be confused with the American Red Cross), and several religious orders of Catholic nuns. In some instances, local organizations or independent hospitals contributed nurses to the war effort—as the Presbyterian Hospital of New York did for Camp Thomas. In Portland, Oregon, Jane B. Creighton formed the White Cross Society, which sponsored nurses to the Philippines. And in addition to army nurses, the U.S. Navy hired contract nurses.

The first contract nurses were sent to Key West Military Hospital in Florida in May. Early in July, six nurses contracted by the navy were on their way to Cuba on a hospital ship, the *Relief*. By mid-July, yellow fever was reported among the troops in Santiago, Cuba, and as it became increasingly widespread, the need for nurses who were immune to the disease intensified. The hunt for immune nurses focused on the southern United States, where the fever was "more or less prevalent at certain seasons of the year" and survivors were believed to be immune. There was also the racist view that Black people were immune to certain types of fevers. In August, military camps in the United States were also becoming infected with contagious diseases in record numbers. Female nurses were serving in Cuba, Puerto Rico, and the Philippines as well as camps and hospitals in the United States.

The life of a contract nurse could be challenging because the physical environments where they served were dirty, disorganized, short of supplies, and breeding grounds for deadly diseases. Despite the army's preference for male doctors, nurses, and attendants, they were in short supply; some were poorly trained, and many of those men resented women in their departments. One male officer at Fort Monroe was not subtle in his reaction to working with female nurses: "There is nothing for women to do on a military base . . . in plain words, 'you are not wanted.'" African American women faced their own unique trials, as they at times faced racism that had been institutionalized in the 1896 U.S. Supreme Court decision *Plessy v. Ferguson* and Jim Crow legislation that legalized separate public accommodations based on race. As one newspaper reported in late July, "Patriotism at thirty dollars a month doesn't seem to include broadmindedness." On one of the hospital ships transporting nurses to Cuba, some of the White contract nurses from New Orleans refused to share space with two Black nurses. "The fact that their colored sisters held diplomas quite equal to their own had no effect; they positively refused to share their quarters," the newspaper reported. The problem was solved when the Black women agreed to separate quarters. According to the newspaper, "The colored women seem to have been of finer material." A similar situation occurred on another transport ship where some southern contract nurses complained to the major that they could not share accommodations with the Black nurses on board. Fortunately for the dissatisfied nurses, the major was a southerner and "appreciated their position," promising to find separate quarters for the Black women. The White nurses were pacified—but only for a time. When they learned that the male contract nurses were being paid $60 a month and three rations per day, they threatened to break their contracts and return home. This time, they went to see a colonel who was well known for his diplomacy and had "a smile that would melt a Spanish bullet." Flashing that devastating smile at the grumbling nurses, he told them how greatly the government needed their services, and he promised to see what could be done about the salary differences. The women left the colonel believing that he was "the nicest man they had ever met." And on further consideration, they had this to say about breaking their contracts: "We're sort of angels of mercy and we can't back out now." Sometimes, the contract nurses endured other inconveniences on the transports that took them to their duties in Cuba, such as a lack of cooking utensils or bedding. And there was the time that twenty-five Red Cross nurses were assigned to their sleeping quarters only to find that their beds were hammocks and, worse, located on the level directly below the stalls where the mules and horses were quartered.

By the time the peace treaty between Spain and the United States was signed in December 1898, many of the individuals who had opposed women as nurses had been converted. Early in January 1899, the *New York Sun* reported that the war had "proved the utility of the woman nurse" despite the decision to employ female nurses causing "an endless amount of perplexity." But as the paper reported, "Everywhere their conduct met with unqualified approval from the surgeons, while their devotion and self-sacrifice proved an inspiration to their patients." A male surgeon at the military hospital at Fort Monroe admitted, "I am satisfied that whatever success we may have had in the treatment of our sick and wounded, has been in a great measure due to the skill and devotion of the female nurses." And female nurses continued to serve in the Philippines, where American soldiers and Filipino freedom fighters fought until 1902, treating wounds and tropical diseases. The contributions women made as nurses in these wars were officially recognized when the army nurse corps was established as part of the U.S. Army in 1901. And in 1905, a memorial to the nurses who had died in service in the war was dedicated in Arlington National Cemetery.

A colonel in the U.S. Army voiced what others felt when he told one of the women who had served as a nurse, "When you first arrived we did not know what to do with a contingent of women in the camp, now we are wondering what we should have done without you."

NAMAHYOKE SOCKUM CURTIS: "A PLEASANT TALKER AND LADY OF INTELLIGENCE"

Samuel M. Parish, agent with the Chicago real estate firm Barnes & Parish, should have been more vigilant in investigating the background of the well-dressed woman who rented the apartment at 3517 State Street in the fall of 1894. She offered impressive references from prominent Chicagoans, including meatpacking giant Philip D. Armour, journalist Moses P. Handy, and George R. Davis, director of the world's fair held in Chicago in 1893. The woman, whom he "supposed at the time was white," inspected the flat, handed over $20, and moved in the next day. Nothing in her appearance indicated to him that she had "negro blood" flowing through her veins. It wasn't until a few days later that Samuel got word from neighbors and the landlord that "colored persons" were moving into the apartment. "She appeared to me to be a white woman," he said later when asked about his inexcusable mistake. When her husband and other family members showed up, it became obvious the family did not belong in the neighborhood. A neighbor who ran a restaurant in the building complained the new tenants hurt her business. The landlord said they had to go. Samuel visited three times, trying to convince them they should leave the flat. He offered to refund their money, and he promised to find another house for them "in a different locality." He explained that he had "no prejudice against colored people" but that they had entered the rental agreement under false pretenses—the woman failing to disclose her race and that she was married. He had no recourse—he began proceedings to have them evicted.

Namahyoke Sockum Curtis and her husband Dr. Austin M. Curtis fought back when the landlord accused her in court of fraud by not revealing her race when she entered the rental agreement. During the court proceedings, there was much discussion about Namahyoke's appearance—"a woman of culture and some beauty" and "a woman fair and comely"—and also talk about her ancestry—"full-blooded Indian" and "pure negro." Dr. Curtis defended his wife: "The only charge made by the prosecution is that Mrs. Curtis obtained the lease by deception. In other words, she did not go about with a placard announcing her antecedents." The landlord replied, "The agents were under instructions not to lease to negroes, and therefore the contract is void." Finally, the judge rendered a verdict: "It is the fundamental law of this country that all men, regardless of race, color, wealth, or poverty, must absolutely stand upon an equality before the law. The law will not assume that colored people are an injury to property . . . the failure to reveal color does not of itself constitute a fraud. I shall have to hold that the landlord must abide by his lease."

Namahyoke was born in California and spent her childhood there, and, as the racist landlord feared, Namahyoke's lineage included African American and Indian ancestors. She married Dr. Austin Curtis, a well-known and highly respected physician from

Namahyoke Sockum Curtis COURTESY OF THE MOORLAND-SPINGARN RESEARCH CENTER, HOWARD UNIVERSITY ARCHIVES HOWARD UNIVERSITY, WASHINGTON, D.C.

Chicago. Namah had indeed known the prominent White businessmen who wrote letters of recommendation for her, as she was on the planning committee for the "Colored American Day" at the 1893 World's Columbian Exposition. When her husband was being considered for the coveted position of surgeon in chief of Freedmen's Hospital in Washington, D.C., the *Washington Bee* newspaper speculated that his wife was responsible for his success in gaining the position, as she "made a lively campaign for him." The paper described Namahyoke as a "a pleasant talker and a lady of intelligence." Austin and Namahyoke arrived in the nation's capital in March 1898 just a month before the United States declared war on Spain.

"Rotting carcasses of dead animals piled among heaps of decomposing garbage, dung and filth. . . . American cavalry horses trotted across open sewers clogged with foul water and human excrement." These were the conditions that greeted the Americans when they entered the city of Santiago, Cuba, after the occupying Spanish forces were defeated in mid-July. With a death rate of more than 200 a day, disposal of the bodies was a serious problem. The Americans decided the only solution was to burn the corpses—eighty bodies high—over grates constructed with railroad tracks and layered with dry grass. Gallons of kerosene were used to douse the bodies, and soon they were no more than ashes. "It was the only thing to be done, for the dead threatened the living and a plague was at hand," the American military commander explained. Not only were civilians suffering, American forces were in dire straits—from disease. In the days immediately after the battle for Santiago, it was reported that half of the American troops suffered from malaria and dysentery as well as typhoid and yellow fever. Disease had become a serious problem in Cuba as it was in army camps in the United States. More men were dying from disease than from battle. The situation was desperate. Namahyoke Curtis, the woman who had earned the respect of some of Chicago's most powerful businessmen, had refused to bend to the will of a racist landlord, and had campaigned to have her husband appointed head of a prestigious hospital in the nation's capital, stepped up to help alleviate the suffering.

Reluctantly, Surgeon General George Sternberg had agreed to hire women nurses to supplement the all-male army hospital corps in the United States, and as the threat of tropical ailments such as yellow fever, malaria, and typhoid became more serious in Cuba, Sternberg looked to another source for help—Black women who were willing to treat soldiers with contagious diseases. And he turned to Namahyoke Sockum Curtis, described by a Washington newspaper as a "very accomplished lady and full of business," to help find and recruit these women.

❦

A Kansas newspaper announced to its readers that yellow fever, a "worse foe than Spaniards," had attacked the American army in Cuba, but citizens could be reassured because the government had employed "colored nurses," as they "are less susceptible to the disease." The *Kansas City Journal* reported on July 13 that officials were enlisting a force of "colored nurses" for service in Santiago. According to the report, "colored persons are believed to be even less susceptible to the ravages of the fever than those of white blood who have gone through a yellow fever scourge successfully."[3]

Although not a trained nurse herself, Namahyoke was hired for special duty in the medical department of the U.S. Army in July 1898 at a salary of $60 per month and was sent to Tampa, Florida, to begin her work as a recruiter of immune nurses. Charged with lining up twenty-five nurses, Namahyoke set out on her mission, traveling to southern cities in search of a select team of courageous women. She made stops in Tallahassee, Florida, and Mobile, Montgomery, and Birmingham, Alabama. The July 17 New Orleans *Time-Democrat* announced that Namah had arrived in the city and was holding examinations at the office of Dr. Newman, dean of the "colored college on St. Charles avenue"—New Orleans University. According to the paper, there had been a rush of applicants for the positions, and there would be little trouble filling the quota. Some of the nurses would be in service of the Red Cross, while others would be sent to posts assigned by the government. Requirements were straightforward: anyone accepted must have had yellow fever or have nursed through an epidemic at some time, and the applicants must show certificates from a doctor stating they were good nurses. (There were conflicting reports as to the level of training some of the nurses had acquired.)

Namahyoke's recruitment efforts took place about the same time an army doctor came to town to recruit male contract nurses. Setting up his headquarters at the St. Charles Hotel, the doctor reported that applicants had turned out in "droves" and that he had already hired twenty-two candidates. At that point, Namahyoke had hired eight female nurses and was continuing to take applications, offering the women a salary of $30 per month. But when she heard that the male nurses hired by the army doctor were being offered twice that amount, she contacted her supervisors in Washington to inquire about the discrepancy. Although she was known

---

3. There is no evidence that Black people are immune to yellow fever. Historian Mariola Espinosa concludes in her article "The Question of Racial Immunity to Yellow Fever in History and Historiography," "As there is no evidence supporting the belief of black immunity to yellow fever, it is time for historians to discard it."

for her persuasive personality, she couldn't convince the army to pay the female nurses a salary equitable to their male counterparts. She was successful, however, in fulfilling her directive to hire nurses for a dangerous assignment in a war-torn island where inhabitants were dying from tropical diseases—at a time when the medical community possessed little in the way of conclusive evidence about how best to treat victims.

The *Los Angeles Herald* reported that Namahyoke had succeeded in lining up far more than the initial request for twenty-five immune nurses and that she was resuming her recruitment efforts after traveling with her new hires to Tampa, Florida, where they would board a transport to their assignments in Cuba. The nurses would join other contract nurses hired by a variety of groups, including the Daughters of the American Revolution and the American Red Cross.

Many of the newly arrived medical personnel went to Santiago to tend to the ever-increasing cases of yellow fever, typhoid, and malaria. The work was grueling for the nurses, who worked unbelievably long shifts under overwhelming conditions. While some patients arrived at the hospital in the back of an ox cart or on a stretcher carried by their comrades, it wasn't unusual for patients to walk to the hospital—sometimes for miles—complaining of a headache and soon to become delirious with fever and chills. Mouths agape and filling with flies, eyes rolled back into the head, and with only a faint flutter of pulse, the sick soldiers lingered for days, and many ultimately did not survive. Nurses and doctors blamed the disease on conditions the soldiers had endured during the first week of battle in early July, when they slept for days in trenches soaked with endless rains. Some blamed mosquitoes, filthy drinking water, and insufficient food.

Authorities tried to isolate yellow fever victims at the town of Siboney. Soldiers suspected of having yellow fever were immediately removed from the regular hospitals and transported to Siboney, where they were tended in a special hospital with nurses who were thought to be immune. Fannie Brigham Ward, a reporter for the *Washington Times* newspaper, wrote about two soldiers who had been brought to the hospital in Santiago by fellow soldiers who held the sick men up. Both men slumped "into a pitiful heap on the floor" when released from the arms of their comrades. Within moments, a hospital worker greeted them: "In God's name, what are these yellow fever men doing here? Out with them quick as you can." Nurses thought to be immune were called to hurry the fainting men outside down a long pier, along a street, and across another pier to the "suspect building"—a small boathouse used to temporarily house men suspected of having yellow fever until they could be loaded onto a boat for Siboney. There, the sick men waited until the boat arrived, and when it did, they were loaded into the vessel, along with a yellow fever corpse lashed onto a board, for their journey to Siboney. "A sadder sight I hope never to see than that boatload of the sick and the dead—the outstretched corpse in its sheet the most conspicuous object, and the living men in their mud-stained uniforms and gray slouch hats, trying to keep up a brave front on their way to almost certain death," Fannie wrote.

"Siboney! How that name will haunt the memory of many a brave American soldier!" a veteran of Siboney wrote in a Washington newspaper in late September 1898. "The death rate in the hospital was awful—terrific. Men died by the dozens, aye, scores, not in ones or twos. Malaria, dysentery, dengue and typhoid fevers took off men who had escaped Mauser bullets." At the graveyard, "from ten to fifteen yawning holes were always kept open and ready for the patients who were sure to fill them." Only two coffins were available, so they were used over and over. As a patient died, he was placed in a coffin with a blanket over the top, and at the grave, the dead soldier was lifted from the coffin, rolled up in his blanket, and buried. The coffin was taken back to the hospital "for further duty," the veteran explained. "Yes, decidedly, Siboney was an awful hell-hole."

This was the environment the nurses recruited by Namahyoke were stepping into when they arrived in Cuba in July and August 1898. It took a toll on the men and women who served. At least two of the individuals recruited by Namahyoke died after becoming ill in Cuba. Isabella R. Bradford, from New Orleans, serving at Santiago, died on August 26, and Minerva Turnbull, an African American nurse, died after being released from her nursing contract "on account of ill health." She had contracted typhoid fever while in service and succumbed on a train at Baton Rouge, Louisiana, on September 18, 1898.

By September, many of the women who had been hired as contract nurses were returning to the United States. The *Brooklyn Eagle* newspaper in New York sent a reporter to interview a group of African American nurses who had spent the night at a Red Cross facility after arriving on the transport ship *Vigilancia* the night before. They were a disgruntled group due to the conditions they had endured on the trip north from Siboney, where they had worked in the yellow fever camp. They had nothing to eat on the transport except army rations of beans and bacon—something they were happy to have until they discovered there was more appetizing food on board—if they were willing to hand the cooks and stewards a bribe. The women who were lucky enough to have a few dollars did just that. Fifteen cents got them a biscuit or some soup. One nurse spent all she had—$3.30—for food. And that was another thing: some of the nurses had not received their pay and were wondering when they would see their two months' salary—$60. When the captain of the *Vigilancia* heard about the scheme to extort money for food, he put an end to it, telling the nurses they were entitled to all the food they desired and did not have to pay for it. As for their missing salaries—that remained a mystery.

Namahyoke's duties did not end in the fall of 1898, when many of her nurses returned to resume their normal lives. Once again, she was employed by the U.S. Army; according to military records, she was sent to Camp Wikoff, Montauk Point, New York, as a contract nurse for the month of September with a salary of $30. She also was called on by some in the African American community in Washington, D.C., to do something about a blatant injustice that played out in the city in the spring of 1899 as city leaders planned the biggest celebration since the end of the war.

The Peace Jubilee, a three-day celebration slated for May 23–26, 1899, in the nation's capital, was months in the making. Designed to celebrate the conclusion of the war, the festivities would honor the men and women who had served and families who had sacrificed during the Spanish-American War. As plans evolved, African American leaders in the city became aware that the contributions of the thousands of Black men and women who had served were to be ignored. In April, the popular African American newspaper the *Washington Bee* called on Black leaders to insist on representation. While a few Black men served on some of the minor planning committees, the executive committee included only White men. "It would be manifestly unjust to ignore the colored people and thus to falsely instruct the rising generation," the paper declared. Asking education officials to insist on participation and letting readers know that even White nurses who had served were being honored, the paper posed the question, "What is to become of the colored nurses who were sent into Cuba by Mrs. Curtis of the Freedmen's Hospital? Will they not be represented at the Peace Jubilee?" The questions were answered when three days of floats, parades, pyrotechnic displays, and band concerts featuring patriotic music ended at a cost of $60,000. The contributions of the Black community were ignored.

SARAH JANE ENNIES: "HEROINE OF SANTIAGO"

"I, Sarah Jane Ennies, the undersigned, do hereby agree to remain two years, from date, a pupil of school and hospital and to be subordinate to the authorities governing the same."

Sarah J. Ennies affixed her name to the contract Freedmen's Hospital offered her as a student at their nursing school in Washington, D.C., in 1896. She had pursued a rather rigorous application process to enter the program administered through a partnership with Howard University. The requirements were straightforward. The program was open to African American women between the ages of twenty-one and thirty-five, unmarried or widowed, enjoying good health, and possessing a disposition and temperament favorable to a career in nursing. A letter from a clergy was required stating the applicant was of good moral character. The hospital made their wishes clear: "women of superior education and cultivation will be preferred." If the applicant was accepted into the program, she was subject to a monthlong probation period, demonstrating her proficiencies in reading, writing, and simple arithmetic, including fractions and percents. Her lodging, boarding, and laundry services were provided, but she must provide her own clothing. She could be terminated for misconduct, inefficiency, or neglect of duty. After passing the probation period, the student began her two-year schooling in earnest, serving as an assistant in various departments at the hospital while attending lectures offered by doctors, surgeons, and nursing superintendents. She learned techniques at patients' bedsides. She was provided a simple blue gingham uniform with white apron, cap, and linen collar and cuffs and worked from 7:30 a.m. to 7:30 p.m. with an hour for dinner, rest, and exercise. Students were given a half day on Sundays and a half day during the week as free time. A two-week vacation was allowed during the summer, and when a student was sick, she must make up the time. And although students were paid $5 per month, they never received any of it—the money served as their tuition. At the end of the two years, successful students earned a diploma certifying their educational achievements. Sarah Ennies received her diploma in January 1898, only a few months before the United States went to war with Spain.

Born in Saint Thomas, West Indies, around 1870, as an adult, Sarah moved with her husband to the United States. In 1895, a deadly sea disaster thousands of miles from her home in America changed the course of her life. The German passenger liner *Elbe* left its port in Bremershaven on Tuesday afternoon, January 29, 1895, steaming its way to New York by way of Southampton, England, with more than 300 passengers and crew on board. About thirty miles from the coast of Holland in the North Sea on January 30, the crew spotted an approaching steamer heading straight toward the *Elbe*. Unable to change course, the German ship was struck by a British liner, the *Crathie*, and although it was very dark at the time of the collision, the *Crathie*'s crew managed to extract the liner from its resting place in the *Elbe* and continued on its way. Within twenty minutes of the collision, the *Elbe* "lifted its bow high in the air and then slowly and silently sank, taking with it its human freight." Among the crew who perished on that frigid January night was a ship's steward, whose wife Sarah waited for his return in the United States. Sarah J. Ennies became a widow on January 30, 1895. Shortly after receiving word of her husband's death, Sarah applied to Freedmen's Hospital Training School for Nurses and began the next chapter in her life.

On her graduation from the Freedmen's program, Sarah took a position as a private nurse working for a wealthy Washington family, but by July 1898, she was on her way to Cuba. It's impossible to know Sarah's thoughts as she boarded the ship carrying her to the war, but she must have known her life would change dramatically.

Sarah's arrival in Cuba on July 12 came at a critical time. On the morning of July 1, American forces with the aid of Cuban freedom fighters had embarked on what turned out to be seventeen days of intense fighting to take the city of Santiago from the Spaniards. Both land and sea battles resulted in victory for the Americans, but fierce fighting took place along the way as the Americans landed on Cuban shores at Daiquiri and Siboney and made their way westward to Santiago. Trekking through the Cuban countryside on their advance to Santiago in the sultry days of summer with equipment, artillery, and provisions, the Americans endured dense forests, narrow jungle trails, incessant rain, and land crabs, all the while dodging bullets from Spanish sharpshooters. While the enemy snipers posed a deadly threat, Cuba's steamy weather and irksome creatures made for some very unpleasant conditions.

MRS. ENNIS, THE SANTIAGO NURSE.

Sarah Ennies *REPUBLICAN NEWS* (LAPORT, PA), JUNE 1, 1899.

"For three hours a great, cold torrent swept down from the clouds drenching the soldiers to the skin . . . sending rivers of mud and red water swirling along the narrow road . . . and through the filthy flood the army streams along, splashing in the mud," a reporter embedded with the soldiers recalled. "An hour before the heat was so intense that men reeled and swooned."

And there were the land crabs. By some accounts the size of a man's hand, by others "as big as the seat of a big chair," these multicolored, brilliantly hued creatures delighted in tormenting the men. "After a weary day's tramping I fell asleep on the ground and was awakened by the clammy embrace of half a dozen" of the creatures, a soldier reported. He debated which was more unpleasant—the crabs or the sociable but less aggressive green lizards that occasionally dropped from the trees.

But the movement of men, animals, and equipment was only the prelude to strategic encounters planned at key places on the way to Santiago—El Caney, San Juan Hill, and Kettle Hill. The men were eager to begin the serious work of war. "One thought which seemed to run like an electric current through the army was anxiety to get to the front," a reporter wrote. "The possibility of disease, exposure and hunger does not trouble. They want to fight."

On the morning of July 1, all-out assaults began with 5,000 Americans attacking the tiny village of El Caney, where Spanish soldiers were entrenched surrounded by barbed-wire fences and trenches dug to protect the Spanish riflemen. Expecting the capture of El Caney to wrap up in two to three hours, American military leaders were surprised to find they had greatly miscalculated. The Spaniards were defeated but only after ten hours of exhausting fighting. As the Americans entered the village to survey the damage, Captain Arthur H. Lee provided a vivid picture of what they found: "The trench around the fort was a grewsome sight, floored with dead Spaniards in horribly contorted attitudes and with sightless, staring eyes. Others were littered about the slope, and these were mostly terribly mutilated by shell fire. Those killed in the trenches were all shot through the forehead, and their brains oozed out like white paint from a color-tube." At the end of the first day, more than 400 American and Spanish lives had been lost and more than 1,500 wounded.

Over the next days, skirmishes continued with significant battles taking place at San Juan Heights and Kettle Hill. On July 3, the Americans declared a decisive victory when naval forces destroyed the Spanish navy in Santiago harbor; however, the Spanish still occupied the city of Santiago. On July 13, the day after Sarah Ennies arrived to begin her duties, face-to-face negotiations began between the Americans and Spanish. Finally, on July 17, the Spaniards agreed to capitulate—not surrender. (To the dismay of the Cuban freedom fighters, they were excluded from the negotiations and the capitulation ceremony.) As the Americans approached the formerly occupied city, they witnessed terrible conditions. A reporter described a scene: "Along the road were carcasses of horses . . . shallow graves along the road had been scratched open by vultures and the odor was horrible." Many of the citizens had abandoned the city and fled to El Caney, creating a humanitarian crisis as sickness and starvation consumed old men, women, and children.

Medical professionals at hospitals in nearby towns and cities offered follow-up treatment. Wounded soldiers arrived at hospitals from the battlefields in a range of conditions and through various forms of transportation. When a soldier was wounded in battle, he was initially treated in the most rudimentary fashion using whatever materials were at hand near the battle site. With bandages in short supply, the wounds were often dressed using makeshift bindings fashioned from the soldier's shirt or pants, leaving him vulnerable to the elements. When Will Apitz, a Kansas boy with the American troops at the battle for Santiago, looked down to find a bullet had struck his right hand, tearing a hole in it and blowing off two fingers, he knew his shooting days were over. He walked twelve miles to a hospital at El Caney to have his wounds dressed and was treated by Clara Barton and her Red Cross nurses. It was not unusual for wounded men to walk to the nearest field hospital. Stretchers had been abandoned early on during the march from the transports that delivered the men to Cuban shores. Ambulances were in short supply, so walking may have been safer and more comfortable than the other choice—a springless army wagon pulled by mules. A writer from *McClure's* magazine described the situation after a battle near El Caney. The army wagons were "loaded with the sadly moaning and pitifully mutilated bodies of those who had fallen in the gallant charge." The ride in the wagons over rugged roads was excruciating for the injured men, many receiving deep wounds from the rough splinters protruding from the floor and sides of the wagon. Crossing creeks without the benefit of bridges and running into obstacles in the dark made the trip unbearable, all the while dodging enemy bullets in open areas. Many dead bodies were pulled from the mass of injured when the wagon arrived at the hospital. Many who survived the ordeal were "delirious and shrieking with horror" as they were unloaded.

Santiago Refugees Near El Caney, 1898 LIBRARY OF CONGRESS PRINTS AND PHO-
TOGRAPHS DIVISION, WASHINGTON, D.C., LC-USZ62-68355 (BLACK-AND-WHITE FILM COPY
NEGATIVE).

As a contract nurse at the U.S. General Hospital in Santiago, Sarah
took on the duties of dealing with the aftermath of battle as well as nursing soldiers suffering from contagious diseases. She worked under military surgeon Lawrence C. Carr. A former Spanish military hospital had
officially become the U.S. General Hospital. With a 300-bed capacity,
the spacious rooms and the location—eight acres high on a hill overlooking the bay—made the building attractive to the Americans as a medical
facility. Carr had arrived in Santiago in July and immediately went to
work preparing the old building for use by his large staff of doctors and
nurses. New sewage and water systems and bathrooms were installed with
hot and cold water, an operating room with a skylight was prepared, and
a tiled and glazed roof was completed, making the building secure from
drenching rains. Carr's duties included taking control of the yellow fever

epidemic that was killing American soldiers and Cuban civilians. As an African American contract nurse, Sarah's duties at the hospital included tending yellow fever victims. On July 12, the very day Sarah left for Cuba, the *Kansas City (MO) Journal* published an article about the threat of yellow fever around Santiago. According to the newspaper, only African American nurses had been hired for this special assignment in Cuba because "colored persons are believed to be even less susceptible to the ravages of the fever than those of white blood who have gone through a yellow fever scourge successfully." (Sarah's army records indicate she had not ever had yellow fever at the time of her hire.)

Sarah's military supervisors graded her work as a head nurse "first class," "excellent," and "thoroughly satisfactory and competent." In February 1899, she was given a raise, making her salary $50 per month. In July, she was reassigned to a camp hospital at Boniato, where she tended soldiers with the 5th Infantry until August. Her next assignment was a short stint at Cristo, Cuba, after which she took her first leave. In September while serving in Boniato, Sarah had sent a letter to Dr. Anita Newcomb McGee, acting assistant surgeon general of the U.S. Army. "I was glad to go as I thought I was more needed," she wrote about her transfer to Boniato from Santiago. "At our camp all the yellow fever patients are now convalescing. . . . I have had no time off but if I can be spared I will ask for some time off in the fall." She was granted her wish, taking the month of November off with pay. On her return, Sarah was assigned again to Santiago where she treated yellow fever patients until December 11, when she was again given leave. On January 11, 1900, Sarah's contract with the army was annulled. The reason for her termination, according to army records, was her "secret marriage with Private Edward Brooks, 24th Infantry."

Newspapers at the time reported on the activities of female nurses. And, while usually not bothering to name them, the fact that "colored nurses" were in Cuba was reported. Sarah was one of the few who was identified and whose work was lauded. Reporting her arrival in Cuba on July 12, 1898, newspapers across the United States shared a little of Sarah's history with readers—her husband being lost in the *Elbe* tragedy, her enrollment in and graduation from the Freedmen's Hospital nursing program, and her decision to become a contract nurse after working as a private nurse in Washington. According to the reports, Sarah was a popular nurse and a hard worker, as many as 110 soldiers having been assigned to her care and proudly proclaiming all recovered—with the exception of one. Sarah was described as a nurse with "untiring energy and devotion" and someone who had earned the "esteem of officer and privates." It was said she had never taken a day off for illness or any other reason. Little of Sarah's life story and experiences in the war remains for her legacy. However, headlines from the time help to establish her place in history:

"A Popular Army Nurse"

"Beloved by Soldiers: Splendid War Record of Mrs. Sarah J. Ennis [sic], a Colored American Army Nurse"

"A Heroine of Santiago"

Sarah had written about her time in Cuba as "one of the happiest of my experiences of a nurse," adding, "all my superior officers have treated me kindly and in return I have tried to show my appreciation by performing my duties to the best of my ability." She concluded that she hoped "to continue as long as one of our noble soldiers need my services."

DELLA WEEKS: "FOREVER IN THEIR HEARTS"

The students at Jennie Steele Huegle's private school in Des Moines, Iowa, were not typical in some respects. For one thing, the school operated from 7:00 to 9:30 every night, and students ranged in age from seven to forty-five. They represented a variety of ethnic backgrounds—Russian, Swedish, Danish, and Italian—with limited English-speaking skills. Adult students learned reading, writing, and arithmetic, while the younger students also studied history and geography. They were hard-working shopgirls, clerks, print shop apprentices, hotel maids, and factory workers who were seeking to learn English and improve themselves after working ten- or twelve-hour days. Some of the younger students tended their young siblings during the day while their parents worked. So when the students at the school came up with the idea to hold a night of entertainment to raise money for Della Weeks, a local nurse who wanted to travel with Iowa's 51st Infantry Volunteers in the summer of 1898, perhaps they felt a kinship to the woman who seemed to face overwhelming obstacles.

Although she was not a graduate of a nursing program, Della was an experienced nurse who was determined to accompany the soldiers to Camp Merritt in northern California and eventually to the Philippines. She had appealed to officials in Washington, asking permission to serve the regiment wherever they went, but officials were slow to respond, and when they finally did, it was to deny Della's wish. The citizens of Des Moines stepped in. The idea that their sons, brothers, and husbands could benefit from a hometown girl looking after their medical needs appealed to many. A committee quickly formed and began a campaign to raise money to send Della with the boys. In addition to the money raised by Jennie's students, local banks, department stores, hardware stores, newspapers, lumber companies, churches, and a university contributed to the cause. In a short time, enough money had been raised to purchase train tickets for Della to California, where the 51st had already settled in, awaiting orders to the Philippines.

Della arrived in late June at Camp Merritt, where the 51st Regiment's Second Lieutenant Fred L. Baker met his fellow Iowan for the first time. "Della Weeks arrived here Thursday afternoon. She will be a good addition to the regiment; but the boys have not got acquainted with her yet," Baker wrote home to his family. About the same time, Della wrote home to Des Moines that the boys of the 51st were well and relatively comfortable in the army camp, where she saw little sickness among the troops. However, within a month, much had changed; many of the men of the 51st made Della's acquaintance. As the Iowa boys waited for orders for the Philippines, weeks dragged on, and more and more men in the camp suffered from a variety of maladies. Pneumonia, diphtheria, meningitis, measles, and typhoid fever sent many soldiers to the hospital, and some died from their illnesses.

Described as a "wee morsel of a woman, light footed and steady of hand," Della tirelessly nursed the sick men in California. It didn't take long for the men to recognize Della and to appreciate her commitment to them. One soldier claimed her dedication to hard work "would make stone-breaking seem light in comparison." Another wrote, "Every man in the regiment, from officers down, would lay down his life for Nurse Weeks." When Della, pointing to a recovering soldier, told a reporter the fellow had pulled through and was about to report back to camp, the young man disputed her words. "I didn't pull through; you pulled me through," he said.

Throughout July and August as the Iowa boys trained and drilled in preparation for the Philippines, Della continued to serve their needs—as a nurse but also stepping in to help in any way she could. She purchased coal for the cookstove, where she made broth for the sick men. Using the money raised by the people of Des Moines, she bought medicines that the military didn't provide. She wrote letters to family members back in Iowa reassuring them that their sons were doing well. She worked from seven in the morning until nine or ten at night—all with no pay. All her efforts as a nurse were strictly voluntary. The money sent from Des Moines—$200—was specifically intended for the boys, and Della was vigilant about this. "If we could all get women like Miss Weeks to assist us, we could accomplish ten times as much," a surgeon from South Dakota said about the Iowa regiment's nurse. "She is worth twice her weight in gold," John H. Ruecker with Iowa's Company H said.

By October, the men of the 51st were getting restless, eager to get to the war in the Philippines, but sickness continued to plague the soldiers at their camp in California. Typhoid fever created havoc, as one report listed 350 cases of sickness in the hospitals near the camp. It was during this time that Della's tireless devotion to the men "endeared her to the soldiers," keeping her "forever in their hearts." Della helped the men when the "deepest gloom" settled over the 51st at the death of Private J. E. Ritter, followed by four more fellow Iowans. But the men celebrated when Mary Monett traveled from Des Moines to marry her sweetheart Fred Baker just before he shipped out for the Philippines.

At the end of August, Della had received word that she was to be offered an appointment as an army nurse with a monthly salary of $30. The fund-raising committee back in Des Moines was thrilled and thought

Della would be too. However, they learned that Della had no intention of accepting the army's offer because it did not guarantee she would remain with Iowa's 51st Regiment. When the Des Moines committee learned that Della had declined the offer, they were furious and threatened to withdraw their support of Della's work in California. Della reconsidered and by late September had agreed to the army's offer with the stipulation that she would stay with the Iowa boys—wherever they were stationed. Late in October the 51st learned they would begin their journey to the Philippines on the transport ship *Pennsylvania* on November 3, due to arrive in the Philippines on December 7.

After receiving permission to travel to the Philippines, Della learned that she could not travel on the same transport as the soldiers—no women allowed. Her journey on the steamer *St. Paul* took her by way of Honolulu, Hawaii, to Manila, the Philippines. About thirty nurses were on board. Most were members of an organization called the White Cross Society, formed in Portland, Oregon, by Jane B. Creighton at the beginning of the war. The steamer carried hundreds of packages and bundles of letters for the fighting men in the Philippines. Thanksgiving dinner was served on board the ship, the menu consisting of chicken, turtle soup, fillet of sole, creamed spinach with egg, mince pie, oranges, nuts, and figs. After a coaling stop in Honolulu, the ship and its valuable cargo would arrive in Manila in time for Christmas.

At first, Della worked at the 1st Reserve Hospital in Manila; in March 1899, she was assigned to the Corregidor Convalescent Hospital, located about thirty miles from Manila, and her salary was raised to $50 per month.

Corregidor Island, consisting of a series of rugged hills, was used as a retreat for sick and wounded patients brought from the hospitals of Manila. Patients were transported by boat down the bay from Manila— a three-hour journey. About 200 native Filipinos lived on Corregidor, and Della's hospital held several hundred patients. An Iowa newspaper reported that "many good men owe their lives to their stay there." Della wrote to her mother back in Iowa that Corregidor was much cooler than Manila. One observer reported that Della was doing "noble work," busy from early morning until late into the night.

Filipino Ward, 1st Reserve Hospital, Manila LIBRARY OF CONGRESS, LC-USZ6-1813, STROHMEYER & WYMAN, 1899.

Back in Iowa, a group of women had formed the Mothers' Prayer Circle of the 51st Iowa, a support squad for women whose sons served in the Philippines. Meeting weekly, the women prayed for the safety of their sons, and when news reached Des Moines that one of the boys had been injured, the members comforted the mother of the wounded soldier. And as time wore on, the inevitable occurred. News of fatalities in the Iowa regiment began to come in from the Philippines, and the women of the Mothers' Prayer Circle grieved alongside some of their heartbroken members. When the *Daily Iowa Capitol* newspaper published a list of deaths in the 51st, the women consoled the mother of John Turner, who had died of smallpox; the mother of John Reed, who had died of measles;

the mother of Walter Hutchinson, who had died of typhoid fever; and the mother of Walter Wagner, who had died from a head wound inflicted by an enemy bullet. And when news was received that one of the boys of the 51st had committed suicide, the women tried to ease his mother's heart-wrenching pain.

In March 1899, the Mothers' Prayer Circle became aware of a threat to their sons that they saw as more dangerous than sickness or death, and they decided to go straight to the top in their crusade to protect their sons. A news report indicated plans were under way to establish a regimental canteen for the boys of the 51st. Profits from the canteen would be put to good use supplementing the mess hall. But the mothers knew what a canteen meant—alcoholic refreshments would be sold—a "useless form of temptation" in the words of the women. The members dashed off a letter to Colonel John C. Loper, commander of the 51st Iowa, hoping to convince him to quash plans for the canteen. They received a letter from Kittie V. Loper, the colonel's wife, who had accompanied the soldiers to the Philippines. She explained her husband was quite sick, recovering in the Corregidor hospital under the care of Della Weeks, and Kittie was replying in his place. She assured the Iowa mothers that her husband was ever vigilant in guarding the welfare of his men. He had put an end to gambling among the men, and he had done all he could to put a halt to the canteen idea before he was sidetracked by his illness. If plans for the canteen went ahead in his absence, the colonel would be most displeased. Kittie took the opportunity to assure the mothers that their sons were highly regarded among the other regiments, quoting an officer: "The Iowa boys are all right; when they shoot, something must fall." Surprisingly, Kittie voiced her opinion about the overall war effort in the Philippines. Her decidedly critical remarks must have caused some consternation at the highest levels of the military, as she accused high-ranking commanders of questionable practices. "The lives of our brave boys are being constantly sacrificed to add jewels to the crowns of these same officers . . . they are killing our volunteer men in attempting to accomplish in a few weeks what they should accomplish in years," Kittie wrote.

Only a few months later, in July 1899, Della made comments that also created quite a stir. Writing to a friend in Iowa, she described the situation in Corregidor. "If the boys are not sent home soon, there will not be many to come home. So many are sick," she wrote. Issuing a report including her statistics for the month of May, Della indicated 234 men from the 51st Iowa were sick, including many from "heat prostration." This directly conflicted with the U.S. government's official report—sixteen sick men in the 51st. "Miss Weeks must have the desire to be made a martyr," a newspaper reported military leaders saying, while other critics called her "a traitor." Some accused Della of inflating her numbers by reporting sickness and injuries no matter how trivial. Others came to Della's defense, claiming that "through the thoughtfulness of a girl nurse," accurate information had been revealed. Suggesting the president and other government officials had released untruthful statistics, a newspaper reported, "No good purpose could have been served by the secrecy." Furthermore, the paper accused government officials of hiding the realities of conditions among the troops, as the truth would hurt recruiting efforts for new volunteers, declaring such actions by the War Department as "brutal to the last degree." The newspaper concluded, "The war does not belong to the officials. They are neither supplying the men nor the means. The citizens of the country are the interested parties, and all the officials have to do is to find the will of the majority and to obey that will."

By the autumn of 1899, when the 51st was scheduled to return to Iowa, Della also wanted to return home. Once again, she was barred from traveling with the soldiers. Instead, she went by a mail steamer, the *Cape Sydney*. Arriving in San Francisco on October 27, the men of the Iowa regiment, who were waiting for permission to return to Iowa, were delighted to see their "hero in skirts." By mid-November, the 51st and Della were all back home in Iowa, greeted with celebrations and cheering crowds. Della, the nurse who was determined to serve the soldiers of the 51st wherever they ventured, had come full circle, bringing the boys home to their families.

ESTHER VOORHEES HASSON: "BRAVEST OF BRAVE"

In July 1897, W. G. Alling, a hardworking physician, traveled by boat from New York to the White Mountains, where he looked forward to spending a monthlong vacation with his family. He would join his wife and infant son, who had gone earlier in the season, and his older son, Willis, a well-known and popular organist, was traveling with the doctor. The Alling family had purchased tickets for their excursion on the Maine Steamship Company's new steamer *John Englis*, which carried passengers from New York to Portland, Maine, for $6. The vessel was fitted with the most modern and luxurious conveniences, catering to the comfort of its wealthy passengers.

The Alling family was fortunate to have traveled on the *John Englis* that summer because by the spring of 1898, the steamer was no longer available as a tourist vessel. It had been purchased by the U.S. government for $450,000 to be used as a transport and ambulance for American soldiers serving in Cuba. An additional $50,000 had been invested in refitting the ship to accommodate military needs. The newly fitted ship was a marvel—with its marble bathrooms, steam laundry, baking room and kitchen, water-carbonating machine producing 100 bottles an hour, and giant ice chest holding enough meat to serve 500 for at least thirty days. The operating room contained two operating tables with high-pressure steam sterilizers, electrical fans, and interlocking rubber tiles on the floor. Folding iron cots had been installed in anticipation of cradling as many as 500 injured soldiers. Painted a bright white with large red crosses on its sides to indicate its status as a medical facility, the ship was immune from enemy attack. Also, in deference to the status as a medical ship, it would never carry guns, ammunition, or any article of war, including dispatches. Some questioned the need for a photographic darkroom, but it made sense considering the military's plan to use the latest "photo-micrographic appliances," which would allow military doctors to take photos of injured and diseased tissues. Also, considering the modern Mauser rifles the Spanish soldiers were equipped with, doctors believed the X-ray capabilities of their new equipment would give them better insight into the specific character and extent of the injuries caused by the Mausers, which were known to be especially adept at splintering bones. The *John Englis* was renamed the *Relief*, a fitting name for a floating hospital.

In May, the military announced the makeup of the medical crew. The chief surgeon, Major George Torney, would be aided by twelve

Esther Voorhees Hasson NAVAL HISTORY AND HERITAGE COMMAND, WASHINGTON NAVY YARD, WASHINGTON, D.C., 80-G-1037199.

nurses—six males and six females. Esther Voorhees Hasson, a graduate of the Connecticut Training School for Nurses, was selected from a field of 700 applicants. On July 2, the *Relief* sailed from the Brooklyn navy yard for Cuba. It had taken an amazingly short amount of time to convert the mighty ship from a luxury liner to a floating hospital, but 650 men working around the clock had accomplished the gargantuan task. The *Arizona Republic* newspaper, reporting on the selection of female nurses for service on the *Relief*, labeled the women "the Bravest of Brave."

"We had a pleasant trip down, although it was quite rough, and the women nurses covered themselves with glory by not being seasick," Esther wrote back to friends in Connecticut. "Most of the men nurses were, and a good many of the doctors."

Anchored near the tiny village of Siboney, Cuba, the medical staff could hear the guns from the battles at Santiago, where American and Spanish forces fought for control of the city. Esther expected the numbers of wounded on the *Relief* to increase significantly in the aftermath. "We rise at 4 to-morrow morning and begin a hard day's work," Esther wrote. "We expect to take a large number of sick and wounded on board, and have to do so early as the water becomes very rough after 9 or 10 o'clock." As Esther predicted, the *Relief* took on more men because of the fighting in and around Santiago. And by August, the medical crew had treated almost 300 cases and transported 125 men back to hospitals in the United States.

"For three or four days they came so thick and fast that we hardly had time to eat and sleep," Esther wrote in early August. Six nurses were in charge of the seventy-two-bed surgical ward, and at one point, all but two beds were in use. One nurse was always in the operating room. "We were kept more than busy but were repaid by the gratitude of our patients."

In September, Esther wrote about her experiences in Puerto Rico. Over half her cases were extremely ill men suffering with typhoid fever with temperatures as high as 107. They begged for food and became distraught when the nurses explained that food would not hasten their recovery. Esther wrote that her second trip to Puerto Rico had been somewhat less hectic with only four deaths compared to fifteen in the previous trip.

As head nurse in one of the three wards on the ship, Esther was assisted by two male nurses and two army hospital corpsmen. "I have entire charge of the nursing, and as there are sixty beds in the ward it is not an easy position to fill to the satisfaction of everyone," she wrote. "At first the army physicians were much opposed to having women on board, but now I am happy to say they would take twice as many if they could only find quarters for them." In closing the letter, Esther asked for reading material—magazines and papers for the men.

In January 1899, Esther learned that she would soon be leaving for service in the Philippines, where American forces continued to serve. The *Relief* would travel by way of the Atlantic Ocean, the Mediterranean Sea, the Red Sea, and the Indian Ocean to its destination in Manila, where the medical staff would treat men on the anchored ship and transport them to hospitals in San Francisco. In February, Filipino freedom fighters and American forces had turned to fighting each other when the Filipinos realized the Americans had no intention of leaving the island after ending the war with Spain. The need for the services of the hospital ship was imminent; on March 4, Esther and a team of nurses, doctors, and army hospital corpsmen left New York on their way to Manila, Philippines, by way of an eastern route taking them to Gibraltar, through the Suez Canal, Ceylon, and Singapore. "When I entered the army, I did not dream that I would wander quite so far away from home," Esther wrote as she looked forward to new experiences in the Pacific.

"*Oh, say can you see, by the dawn's early light . . .*"
"*Goodbye, Mother dear, it is hard to leave you now . . .*"

Shortly before three in the afternoon on March 4, 1899, Esther stood on the deck of the *Relief* in a cold, drizzling rain as the ship glided away from pier 22 at Brooklyn, New York, to the sounds of the *Star Spangled Banner* and *Goodbye Mother Dear* sung by the hospital corpsmen. The ship carried a handful of nurses, thirteen doctors, about 200 army hospital corpsmen in addition to the crew. When they reached the Philippines, some of them would report to hospitals on the island; others would remain on the hospital ship. But it would be more than a month before the medical team would arrive at their new posts, and for those who weren't miserable with seasickness, the next few weeks would prove to be pleasant

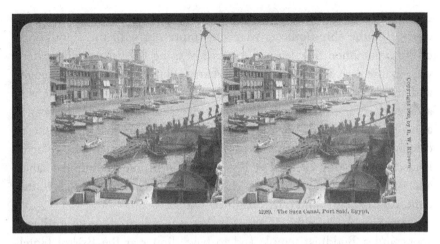

Suez Canal, 1899 LIBRARY OF CONGRESS PRINTS AND PHOTOGRAPHS DIVISION, WASHING-
TON, D.C., LC-DIG-STEREO-1S21801 (DIGITAL FILE FROM ORIGINAL), LC-USZ62-103003 (BLACK-
AND-WHITE FILM COPY NEGATIVE).

as the ship made its way across the globe stopping for fuel at strategic
coaling stations and giving passengers the opportunity to sightsee at foreign ports. Esther took full advantage of the sea voyage. The first stop was
Gibraltar, where she and her fellow nurses went ashore to shop, tour the
local hospital, and visit with the American ambassador enjoying a lovely
lunch of lamb chops, cauliflower, potatoes, buttered bread, lettuce salad,
asparagus omelet, oranges, tangerines, dates, and coffee at a local hotel.

On March 19, the *Relief* reached Port Said, Egypt, where it stopped
for coaling, and entered the Suez Canal. Esther was impressed by the
fueling process—Egyptian men bringing coal on board to the engine
room in baskets from large barges positioned alongside the ship. It was an
arduous job, resulting in a fine layer of coal dust covering the men and the
ship from one end to the other. And Esther complained that the loading
continued into the night and early morning, making it nearly impossible
to sleep. However, she was refreshed enough to venture onshore for a few
hours to shop and visit a mosque. She was disappointed with her lunch at
a local café where the "coffee was bad, the bread sour, and the butter too
awful for words."

Esther was fascinated with the journey through the canal, a nearly
100-mile trip moving at only five miles per hour, and according to the

canal officials, the *Relief* was the first hospital ship to pass through the canal. But the ship's officers were not impressed with the significance of the event when they learned the cost of using the time-saving water-way—more than $5,000 for tonnage charges plus ten francs per passenger and an additional $50 charge to hire a searchlight to illuminate the way after dark. None of this dampened Esther's enthusiasm for the scenes along the way—a little boy running alongside the ship making a game of catching oranges tossed by the passengers, men on camels, the colorful landscapes and tiny villages, an Egyptian train running beside the canal, and the "glorious moonlight" as she sat on the deck of the *Relief* after dark. The sixteen-hour cruise delighted Esther.

Arriving at Colombo, Ceylon, Esther was able to go ashore to visit shops and a Buddhist temple and to have dinner at the Bristol Hotel, where servers in spotless white jackets delivered smoked fish and olives, soup, mutton cutlets, and roast duck with green peas and string beans, fol-lowed by dates, raisins, almonds, and black coffee—all for only $1.50 each.

At 9:00 a.m. Wednesday, April 12, the *Relief* dropped anchor in Manila Bay thirty-nine days after leaving New York. Days passed as Esther and the other medical personnel waited for their orders. Esther had often been critical of the army hospital corpsmen throughout the voyage and expressed her disillusionment with the men: "They are the worst behaved lot of men I have ever seen in my life, and everyone will be glad when they leave the ship." According to Esther, they had been "absolutely malicious," throwing tables and chairs overboard and slashing the tires of a doctor's bicycle. The day after their arrival, Esther and the other nurses ventured onshore to visit friends and military wives and to do a little sightseeing. On April 22, with no patients or duties yet assigned to the nurses on the *Relief*, Esther was asked to go ashore to care for an officer's wife who was suffering from meningitis and required constant care. It became an exhausting responsibility for Esther, and she was not disappointed when she was recalled to the *Relief* on April 26 as seventy-five wounded men from the front had arrived on board. "After that we were never without plenty of work," Esther wrote.

Over the next two months, Esther tended the patients who entered her ward, writing about her experiences in a journal. Sometimes, she wrote about specific cases that touched her. James Kelley, a young man from Oregon, came to her ward suffering with smallpox, typhoid, and repeated attacks of dysentery. He was one of the men she could not save but stayed with beyond her required shift, offering comfort during his final hours of life. Some of her patients suffered ordinary medical conditions, such as hernias and appendicitis. Others were victims of battle, such as the young man who came to her with a "bullet floating around inside of him somewhere" and whom the doctors "seem rather afraid to meddle with." And there was the man from the engine room who came to her with a head cut he had obtained in a brawl with another crewman and the typhoid patient who in his delirious rantings called Esther "mama" and made her feel special—despite his habit of calling an especially unpleasant corpsman "papa." Overall, Esther spoke highly of the volunteer soldiers from the American West—"country boys" who were "used to work and roughing it." She complained about the young doctors just out of college with no hospital experience who were serving on the *Relief*: "The young and inexperienced doctors are certainly a trial to nurses." Esther was annoyed with the doctors who worked in the hospitals onshore and continually sent patients with fractures or bullet wounds over to the *Relief* for X-rays and then demanded they be sent back to shore for surgery. According to Esther, the onshore hospitals had X-ray machines, but they had never been installed.

Early in June, the *Relief*'s personnel learned that they would be leaving for San Francisco carrying 250 patients who were too sick to go by ordinary transport ships. Esther was overjoyed to hear the news but hoped to return for another tour. The *Relief* left Manila on June 22, 1899, stopping in Nagasaki and Tokyo, Japan, and Honolulu, where Esther took full advantage of sightseeing when the ship stopped for refueling. By the time the ship reached its destination in San Francisco, most of the injured men had improved and refused the use of stretchers as they walked ashore. But Esther was saddened by the deaths of three men over the course of the voyage. On arriving in California, Esther settled in for a little rest and recuperation while the *Relief* underwent repairs in anticipation of a return to Manila.

Esther continued her service in the Philippines, serving in hospitals in Manila and in Luzon. When she left the military in 1901, her commanding officer rated her service "worthy of the highest praise." In 1908, when the navy nurse corps was established, Esther was chosen as its first superintendent, becoming the highest-paid woman in the U.S. Navy at a salary of $1,800 a year. Officers who served with her in Cuba and the Philippines supported her appointment, one claiming that "many American soldiers owe their lives to her care and perseverance."

AMERICAN ORDER OF THE SISTERS: PROVING WHAT THEY CAN DO

"Four Redskin Sisters Who Have Done Good Work in a Southern Hospital"

The newspaper headline in December 1898 might have shocked some readers. After all, it hadn't been so very far in the past that most of the paper's readers perceived Native people as enemies and certainly not as workers in a southern hospital. If readers continued reading past the racist headline, they would learn that the Catholic nuns labeled "Redskin Sisters" were four Lakota Sioux women who had volunteered to serve as nurses in April soon after the U.S. government announced the nation was going to war with Spain. Mother Mary Anthony (Susie Bordeaux), Sister Mary Joseph (Josephine Two Bears), Sister Mary Gregory or Gertrude (Ellen Clark), and Sister Mary Bridget (Annie Pleets) made up the order of nuns known as the American Order of the Sisters.[4]

The order had been formed in 1892 by Josephine Crowfeather, who took the name Mother Catherine, and Father Francis M. J. Craft, who had formal medical training. Mother Catherine died in 1893; Father Craft continued to work with the nuns after her death, guiding them in their nursing education and in 1898 volunteering with the four nursing sisters to serve the needs of the soldiers of the Spanish-American War.

Although the nuns had volunteered early in the war, it wasn't until fall that they finally received their first appointment—to Camp Cuba

---

4. Also referred to as Convent of Indian Sisters/Sacred Heart Mission and Order of the Red Sisters of St. Benedict, according to the U.S. Department of Veterans Affairs, Office of Tribal Government Relations.

Libre, an army training camp in Jacksonville, Florida. Rumors had been swirling for weeks about conditions at the camp. When Secretary of War Russell Alger visited shortly before the nuns arrived, he was greeted with a seventeen-gun salute and a banquet at a local hotel and spent the day inspecting the camp, including stops at the camp hospitals, which he said were "in good condition" and where the "men looked well and healthy." But this conflicted with reports that were coming from other sources who claimed that malaria was prevalent and that "the troops as a whole were in poor health." Complaints had been issued about the quality of the food at the camp—meat that was spoiled, decaying fruit, inadequate amounts of bread, and canteen beer that had made men sick. A soldier serving with a Nevada unit wrote home, "The very air we breathe is laden with poison in the form of typhoid malaria and other death dealing microbes and corruption." He described experiences of sick soldiers: "They are not taken to the hospitals until it is often to [sic] late to keep the slight spark of life burning and they often lay in the receiving wards without medicine for so long before being assigned to their proper wards, that they end their earthly journeys in the dead tent." And a nurse at Camp Cuba Libre wrote, "Our work is not decreasing . . . I only hope we will have strength given to us to hold out."

At Camp Cuba Libre and other stateside camp hospitals, doctors and nurses treated a variety of conditions, including gun and stab wounds, cuts, bone fractures (often caused by horses falling on riders), and dysentery, which was treated with an enema of hot water mixed with boric acid. And of growing seriousness were contagious diseases, such as typhoid, malaria, and yellow fever—treated with cold sponge baths and special diets consisting of soups, broths, eggs, hot milk, and sometimes whiskey. Fresh milk was imported from New York in ten-gallon cans packed in ice. A special diet kitchen prepared food for the hospital patients.

This was the situation the four sisters—believed to be immune either simply because of their race or because they had survived yellow fever—encountered when they arrived at the 2nd Division hospital at Camp Cuba Libre on October 21, 1898, to care for the contagious soldiers. The hospital compound was located a distance from the main camp. On entering the hospital grounds, sick men were taken to a large circular receiving

American Sisters in Cuba with Reverend Francis Craft MARQUETTE UNIVERSITY ARCHIVES, BUREAU OF CATHOLIC INDIAN MISSIONS RECORDS, MILWAUKEE, WISCONSIN, ID 07436.

tent where a doctor diagnosed their illness and referred them to one of five wards—A, B, C, D, or E. Separate from these tents were wards G and H—set aside for measles and mumps patients. The nuns were assigned to these two wards. Each tent measured twelve by fourteen feet and contained six or seven iron-spring cots with mattresses. All the tents had wooden floors. Sister Mary Bridget oversaw the work of the other nuns, who in early November cared for fifty sick soldiers. Working in shifts, Sister Mary Bridget and Mother Mary Anthony covered the daytime hours, while Sister Mary Joseph and Sister Mary Gertrude tended during the night watches. In an interview with a reporter from the *Sioux City (IA) Journal*, Sister Mary Bridget said she was pleased with conditions at the hospital. Described by the reporter as "quite young," Sister Mary Bridget had "an ever ready and happy smile" that to the sick "must act as a means of forgetting the surroundings of a hospital." Sister Bridget was also "very sturdy, rugged, as if no amount of fatigue could be too much for her," according to the reporter. But he explained this away, stating that because the nuns were "of Indian blood," they were "accustomed to lives of hardship and privation" and therefore could better withstand the conditions in the army camps. Additionally, because the sisters were the only American Indian women serving as nurses in the war, the "work of the sisters here will be watched and followed with great interest."

When the nuns arrived, soldiers were already being shipped out of Camp Cuba Libre in hospital trains to other camps where officials promised conditions were better. But the sisters remained in Jacksonville until December 13, when they were sent to Camp Onward in Savannah, Georgia. Meanwhile, a peace treaty had been signed between Spain and the United States. However, it became clear that the American military would remain in Cuba and the Philippines indefinitely, and the need for medical personnel would continue. When the nuns arrived in Georgia, the entire camp was in flux. The military units were waiting for word about their next assignments; many had already left for Cuba. As the troops waited for their orders, they drilled, marched on muddy parade grounds, stood guard duty, and endured cold weather and boredom. They lived in brown canvas tents arranged in neat rows. At night, the soldiers gathered around bonfires, engaging in boxing matches or listening to military bands that had accompanied some of the regiments. The band from Nebraska was especially pleasing. When the cold became too much, some fellows used hot potatoes from the mess to warm their hands. The entire camp was abuzz when they were issued new weapons—Krag-Jorgensens—to replace the old Springfield rifles. Excitement surged throughout the camp when President William McKinley arrived in Savannah to review the troops on December 18. But one soldier was harsh in his assessment of the commander in chief: "Poor old McKinley! He looked tired and old, and his hair was perceptibly tinged with gray. When he put on his high silk hat he looked like an overworked actor." It's unclear if the nuns saw the president, as his visit happened to be the same day they left Camp Onward for their next assignment. On December 22, they arrived at Camp Columbia, in Havana, Cuba, serving at the 2nd Division hospital of the 7th Army Corps.

The nuns arrived just before the departure of the Spaniards and the beginning of American military occupation in Cuba, which would take place officially on December 31. It was a precarious time in Cuba, as the defeated Spaniards had not yet relinquished control of all facilities to the Cubans or the Americans. And the Cubans were not uniform in their acceptance of an occupying American force. "We have not fought for a change of masters. We have fought for liberty, and not for a new ownership. If we must fight again, then we are ready. No nation is strong enough to bully us," a former Cuban freedom fighter said. The nurses and doctors at the various hospitals found themselves treating Americans, Cubans, and Spaniards for sickness as well as wounds from the occasional confrontation or street brawl.

Camp Columbia, located on a section of high ground with a view of the sea to the west and mountains to the east and south, lacked water lines, and the Americans complained about the half-mile trek to fetch water for a cool drink or to bathe. Soldiers complained about food prices—turkeys sold for as much as $8, chickens for $5, and pork for fifty cents per pound. Only oranges and cigars were cheap—six oranges for five cents and a good cigar for two cents. And although there were complaints about inconveniences due to the change of government, a reporter who arrived in Cuba to write about the transition had become sick with measles and was taken directly by ambulance from his ship in Havana harbor to the division hospital, where he was impressed: "This is a beautiful spot for a hospital. . . . I received the kindest treatment."

The four nuns worked in Havana until the end of February 1899, when they were informed that their nursing contracts had been annulled. Ongoing troubles related to some officials of the Catholic Church and Father Craft, who had accompanied them to Cuba, had caught up with the priest. He blamed the problems on conservative churchmen who opposed the more progressive ideas that he supported. Foremost was Archbishop Placide Chapelle, a representative of the church in Cuba, who announced the expulsion of the nuns and Father Craft from the island. Father Craft blamed the archbishop for "the old hatred against the Indian sisters" whose mission "was to promote Indian civilization and to work also for all races." Father Craft believed the nuns were being targeted because of their race. "They wanted to send the sisters back to the Indian camps," he said of the officials' earlier attempts to impede the sisters' vocations.

No longer under contract with the U.S. Army as nurses, the nuns moved with Father Craft to Pinar del Rio province about 100 miles southwest of Havana, where they volunteered in a facility described by the priest as being "established for the purpose of carrying out, not only work for the sick soldiers and civilians here, but also the reforms which the military authorities may find necessary among the people of the country, especially those who are ignorant and degraded." (Father Craft's words were in line with imperialistic beliefs that White Americans were superior to Cubans, yet at the time, the Indian nuns would have also been viewed as inferior.) According to Father Craft, "Everything went well. Cubans and Spaniards were as well pleased as Americans with the American sisters and their work as nurses and physicians among the poor." Even the local parish priest was pleased with the nuns' musical talents in the church choir. "We will remain here with the army unless other means are found to drive us away," Father Craft said in April 1899.

But by the fall, circumstances had changed. Mother Mary Anthony had become ill and died, buried in the local cemetery with military honors. "She was much beloved by the soldiers whom she had nursed back to health at the sacrifice of her own life and American soldiers mingled their tears and prayers with those of Cubans and Spaniards who loved her for her care of their orphans and sick," Father Craft wrote. Early in December, Sister Mary Bridget and Sister Mary Gertrude wanted to leave. On December 7, Sister Bridget wrote a letter to a priest back in the United States asking him to help the nuns travel home, "Sister Gregory and myself left him [Father Craft] . . . he has sent us out without a cent among Cuban families in this wild strange country." She continued, "I want to come home because I am getting sick and very unhappy."

By January 1900, both Sister Gregory and Sister Bridget had returned to Standing Rock in North Dakota. Sister Joseph stayed with Father Craft for a time but eventually returned to the United States too. All three nuns ultimately left the convent and married. Father Craft became a parish priest in Pennsylvania.

The four American Indian nuns' contributions to the war effort were recognized by the U.S. House of Representatives in February 1899, when a congressman from Massachusetts introduced a resolution tendering the "thanks of the Congress to the . . . Sisters of American Congregation for ministering to the wants of soldiers in the Spanish-American war." And Father Craft wrote that the nuns "have proved what they could do, with the same care white Sisters get." But most telling was the comment from a patient they had cared for in Cuba: "We should give our attention to the lady nurses who are in the service. They are the kindest, gentlest and most patient of creatures and deserve a world of credit from the wives and the mothers of the boys in blue, and their names and heroic deeds should be chronicled on the pages of our great, grand and glorious nation's history."

3

Fighters

"Wielding Her Machete Like the Devil"

"THESE WOMEN SOLDIERS ARE FIERCER THAN MEN, THEY RIDE AND fight like furies. We captured a woman yesterday. She was white and good looking. Most of these 'Amazons' are colored. This one was dressed in men's clothes, astride a powerful horse, and wielding her machete like the devil." The Spanish general overseeing operations in Cuba admitted to a reporter that both male and female fighters made up the bands of Cuban fighters who resisted Spanish rule in 1898. While he dealt with these fearless troublemakers in Cuba, thousands of miles away in the Philippines, his Spanish comrades also grappled with freedom fighters of both genders.

Fierce warrior women known as Amazons had been enchanting mythical characters in various cultures across the ages when the Spaniard used the term to describe very real female fighters he encountered in the Cuban War of Independence. Women warriors played key roles in the struggles of the Spanish-American War and the Philippine-American War. For as long as Cubans and Filipinos had resisted Spanish rule, women had been part of the resistance. Known as Mambisas in Cuba, brave women courageously served in armed conflict against their Spanish rulers during the Ten Years' War (1868–1878) and again in the War for Independence (1896–1898). In some cases, detailed accounts of heroic deeds survived, while the names of the heroines did not. There was the young woman remembered by a revolutionary soldier for her actions during a battle in which Spanish soldiers began to gun down freedom fighters trapped in a lagoon. The woman, dressed as a man, urged her comrades to follow as she charged at the Spaniards with her machete. And people talked about "eleven women, colored" who had left their farms in Santiago de Cuba armed with machetes and revolvers to join the forces of Calixto Alvarez. American newspapers carried a story about an entire town of courageous women who burned their city rather than allow the approaching Spaniards access to their homes and businesses. When a regiment under the command of Colonel Antonio Nunez stopped a train, passengers were surprised to see two well-armed young women with the soldiers. One of the women explained, "The country needs arms which can carry those arms that she needs for her defense and does not make any distinction whether they be those of men or women." It was most important that the carrier of the arms "be courageous and have determination," the young fighter added.

Others earned headlines such as "Fair Cuban Patriots" and titles such as "Cuban Joan of Arc." Louisa Hernandez's story was repeated in various news outlets. When her husband, Damian Peresoto, was exiled to the Isle of Pines by the Spaniards for illegal political activity, she was permitted to go with him. One day as her husband and a group of prisoners were chopping wood, Louisa distracted the guard, asking to inspect his gun. As he handed it to her, Louisa turned the weapon on the unsuspecting fellow, grabbed his machete, and tied him up. The prisoners escaped to the coast and convinced a boat captain to take them to Cienega de Zapata, where they joined the revolutionary army.

Matilde Agramonte was a favorite subject of newspapers when she was "riddled with Spanish bullets" as she defended a shipment of arms being unloaded. She had joined the army when her family's ranch had been burned to the ground by Spanish soldiers who killed the servants and left the land covered in ash. According to news reports, Matilde volunteered to join a small cadre of fighters to draw fire while the others unloaded the shipment. Another woman who had witnessed the battle from her nearby home had rushed to help Matilde but had been wounded and taken prisoner. And although Matilde died in the battle, her fellow fighters said she never flinched as the Spanish bullets flew.

The Filipinas were no less courageous in their battles first against their Spanish occupiers and later against the Americans. Gregoria de Jesus, wife of independence leader Andres Bonifacio and one of the first women to join the secret revolutionary society the Katipunan, fled to the mountains when the group was exposed. As an independence fighter, she learned to handle a gun on horseback and to live life on the run from the Spanish authorities. "I had no fear of facing danger, not even death, whenever I accompanied the soldiers in battle, impelled as I was then by no other desire than to see unfurled the flag of an independent Philippines. I was considered a soldier, a true one," she wrote in her autobiography. "I learned how to ride, to shoot a rifle, to manipulate other weapons which I had occasion actually to use."

Accounts of legendary Filipino fighter Josephine Bracken Rizal filled American newspapers in 1897. Widow of independence leader José Rizal, Josephine had reportedly married her husband only hours before his execution by the Spanish. She promised to avenge her husband's death and to "raise her hand and voice whenever they would injure Spain." True to her word, Josephine joined the freedom fighters "armed with a revolver, dagger and rifle," fighting "with reckless dash and courage."

Josephine Bracken Rizal WIKIMEDIA COMMONS, FROM THE BOOK *LINEAGE, LIFE, AND LABORS OF JOSÉ RIZAL, PHILIPPINE PATRIOT* BY AUSTIN CRAIG, PUBLISHED IN 1913.

Agueda Kahabagan, also a member of the Katipunan, fought as a revolutionary soldier beginning in 1897 and became known as Henerala (general). Another general described her: "Astride a horse, she held a revolver in her right hand and the reins and dagger in the left." She also at times used a rifle or a bolo as she rode into battle. She fought against the Americans in 1900 and 1901. In January 1902, American newspapers reported that Agueda, commanding a force of 800 freedom fighters carrying 300 rifles and 500 bolos, was captured by the men of the 8th Infantry at Laguna province.

Trinidad Perez Tecson, admired for her nursing skills, became renowned for her prowess in securing much-needed guns, and her bravery on the battlefield became legendary. She and her accomplices stole arms from a courthouse and a jail under the jurisdiction of the Spaniards. In addition to getting the arms to freedom fighters, she was responsible for finding and delivering food to the soldiers' hideouts. And when she wasn't busy with those tasks, she joined in the battles—first against the Spaniards and later engaging in guerilla warfare against the Americans. A wound to her thigh sidelined her for a short time, but she soon returned to the battlefield.

American women were also eager to take up arms against the Spaniards when the United States declared war on Spain in 1898. Emma Whittington was commissioned a colonel in the Arkansas State Guard in Company A, 3rd Infantry, and reported for duty at the army camp at Chickamauga, Georgia. In Reading, Pennsylvania, an all-female military regiment of "patriotic amazons" formed and had packed their leather knapsacks in preparation for a call to arms in May 1898. Dressed in uniforms of white shirtwaists, blue jackets, and red skirts, the "soldier maids" drilled with rifles and promised they "could do severe execution" against regiments of Spaniards, whom they professed to hate as much as "a snake, a toad, a cow, or a mouse." In Chadron, Nebraska, a female cavalry company had organized and was prepared to serve as sharpshooters in the army should they be called. According to the reports, they were said to be "daring horsewomen and dead shots," and had all sworn to "shoot a Spaniard on sight." Marguerite Raymond, a voice teacher from Chicago, enlisted as a bugler with Company H of the 2nd Regiment, Nebraska National Guard. In addition to her musical talents, it was said she was "quite as expert with the revolver as with the bugle." Martha A. Shute, a Colorado horticulturist, promised to organize a troop of cavalry composed entirely of women in March 1898. It was reported that she was a fearless horsewoman and uncommonly capable with a rifle. May

Stevens-Boysen had followed her son to the Philippines in 1899, when he volunteered for military service. Although she served as a nurse, she didn't limit her activities to medicine. As she tended wounded soldiers in battle "with bullets flying around her," May was known to pick up her rifle and direct it at the enemy. A general who had witnessed May in action said, "For the first time in my life I have seen a woman on the firing line."

Although American women expressed interest in volunteering to serve as soldiers in the conflict against Spain, Cuban and Filipina women often found themselves in positions allowing them little choice. They were thrust into situations that required them to fight for their families, country, and ideals and for justice.

EVANGELINA CISNEROS: HEROIC MAMBISA OR FAIRY-TALE HEROINE

"I had many fantastic dreams in my prison, but I never dreamed of liberty coming to me from an American newspaper."

The story of Evangelina Cisneros, a tale of a damsel in distress, an evil villain, and a heroic savior as well as spies, international intrigue, and a fairy-tale ending, captivated Americans in the days before America went to war with Spain. Evangelina, a nineteen-year-old Cuban woman, was introduced to the American public beginning in the summer of 1897, when William Randolph Hearst's *New York Journal* ran sensational news stories about her plight after being arrested by Spanish authorities and charged with attempted assassination.

As a young girl, Evangelina had lived with her widowed father, Jose Augustine Cossio y Serrano, and younger sister, Carmen, in a rural village where she enjoyed a peaceful childhood. As she grew older, her father began to share stories of his experiences fighting in the Ten Years' War (1868–1878) as a resister of Spanish rule. "Every drop of blood in my veins was afire with the love of my brave country," Evangelina wrote in her memoir years later as she recalled her father's inspiring words. In May 1895, Jose confided that he was joining the freedom fighters to once again fight the Spaniards who continued to occupy the Cuban island. "Father, I am going with you, and from that moment my father knew that my mind was made up," Evangelina wrote about her intention to join the army. For weeks, her father and fellow freedom fighters had hidden arms and ammunition in the nearby countryside. June 22 was the day chosen for Evangelina and her father to join the army, but someone had betrayed Jose, and he was arrested on June 21, 1895. Initially, he was sentenced to death, but Evangelina petitioned Spanish Captain-General Valeriano Weyler (also known as "The Butcher") on his behalf, and Jose's sentence was reduced to exile on the Isle of Pines. Evangelina and Carmen were permitted to go with him, and the family lived in relative comfort in a two-room cottage on the island until the arrival of a new Spanish colonel on the Isle of Pines in July 1896. Colonel Jose Berriz, a "short, ugly, dark little man with bushy hair and black whiskers on his cheeks," very quickly noticed Evangelina and began his quest for her affections. Suddenly, for no reason, Evangelina's father was arrested and taken to the island jail. Late one night, Berriz arrived at Evangelina's cottage and impressed on her that he was interested in her romantically, and he reminded her that he had power over her father's fate. She spurned his advances, but he became increasingly aggressive, causing neighbors to become involved. As the situation escalated, other Cuban exiles living on the island arrived to defend Evangelina. When armed Spanish soldiers arrived, the Cuban revolutionaries ran, escaping capture. Evangelina and Carmen were arrested and sent to a Havana prison called Las Recogidas, a notoriously offensive facility for women noted for its squalor and filthy conditions. She was charged with attempted assassination, as the Spanish claimed she had enticed Berriz to her house so that the Cubans could kill him.

After Evangelina had been in the prison for more than a year, in the summer of 1897, the warden showed her a copy of an American newspaper, the *New York Journal*, which included her picture. She was surprised and puzzled by the attention she was getting in the United States. "I did not know how my picture could be in the paper from far-off America," Evangelina wrote while recalling the warden's chilling words: "You have some fine friends; they will cry when you stand up before the soldiers with a bandage over your eyes and the word is given to shoot." Shortly after, Evangelina was visited by George Bryson, a correspondent from the *New York Journal*, who told her the newspaper had an interest in her situation and was working to free her. And soon after that, the wife and daughter of American Consul General Fitzhugh Lee came to the prison to speak with her, after which she was moved to a more pleasant area of the prison where she shared space with a small group of women who were permitted limited freedoms. Bryson returned for a visit and informed Evangelina that some influential American women had learned of her situation and were taking steps to help. Julia Ward Howe, author of the "Battle Hymn of the Republic," had written the pope asking for his intervention. The widow of President Ulysses S. Grant, the widow of the former president of the Confederate states Jefferson Davis, and even President McKinley's mother had signed a petition sent to the queen of Spain, Maria Cristina, asking for her intercession. When the queen asked General Weyler to show leniency for Evangelina, he chose instead to keep her imprisoned and eventually ordered her incommunicado—no visitors, no messages in or out. At one point, she was visited by a Spanish official pressuring her to withdraw her accusations against Berriz, and she replied, "I would die in Recogidas first." It was soon after that, in July 1897, that Evangelina learned that *New York Journal* correspondent Bryson had been banished from Cuba. "Then everything was dark to me and there no longer seemed any hope. How little we know what the future has in store for us," Evangelina wrote. But before Bryson left, he managed to get a message to Evangelina—another *New York Journal* correspondent would arrive to replace him. His name was Karl Decker, and he arrived in Cuba the last week of August.

Decker immediately began plotting the escape. He managed to meet with Evangelina once before she became incommunicado, but soon, it became impossible to openly communicate with her, and he realized detectives were on his trail. Still, Decker lined up men who would help in his rescue mission. He furtively surveyed the neighborhood around the prison, looking for possible access points.

Throughout September, Evangelina's plight was the subject of news stories in the *New York Journal* and its rival publication the *New York World* owned by James Pulitzer. The two newspapers offered conflicting versions of the young Cuban's travails—the *Journal* portraying her as a helpless young girl at the mercy of a brutal Spanish regime and the *World* offering its version of Evangelina as a wicked temptress. Quoting Consul

General Lee, the *World* reported that Evangelina "was implicated in the insurrection on the Isle of Pines" and that "she herself in a note to me acknowledged that fact and stated she was betrayed by an accomplice."

One day, Evangelina received a secret message asking if she could think of a way to escape if she had help. She sent a secret reply to the mysterious writer. "My plan is the following: To escape by the roof with the aid of a rope, descending by the front of the house at a given hour and signal." She included a sketch of the interior of the prison wing where she was housed, including the location of a second-story, bar-covered window that faced the outside and opened onto a flat-roofed section of the prison. A high parapet running along the front of the prison hid the window from sight from the street. It was sheer luck that a house adjacent to that side of the prison happened to be available as a rental property, and Decker lost no time in signing a lease. A modified version of Evangelina's idea was ultimately implemented. The plan was to create a sort of walkway between the roof of the house and the roof of the prison by extending a ladder over the twelve-foot space that separated the two buildings.

On October 5, Evangelina received a message to appear at the window at midnight. Drugging the other women in her cell area with laudanum she had obtained from the prison doctor for an imaginary toothache, she made her way to the window and spotted a shadowy figure on the roof of the house next to the prison building. She watched as the figure made his way gingerly over the ladder. When he reached the prison window, he grasped her hand through the bars and said, "We will soon have you out of here." The man proceeded to saw at the iron bars, but the noise woke one of the other prisoners, who asked Evangelina what she was doing, just as the man escaped across the ladder to the safety of the neighboring house. Evangelina told her cell mate she was feeling sick and had gone to the window for air. The escape plan had been delayed, Evangelina could only guess, until the next night.

The following night, Evangelina again drugged her companions and stood by the window. In time, the man returned and continued his work of the previous night—sawing to loosen the already compromised bar. After twisting and turning and sawing for some time, at last, the bar broke loose, and the man worked for some time with all his might to pry the bar up, creating a space large enough for Evangelina to squirm through. The man lifted Evangelina onto the roof, where two accomplices waited. One offered to carry her over the ladder spanning the two roofs. "As if I needed that!" Evangelina later recalled. "I was so light I could have flown across. I ran over the ladder as surely as if it had been solid ground; the men crawled over slowly and carefully, and I almost laughed at their awkwardness."

A carriage whisked Evangelina through the streets of Havana to a house where she lived in secret for three days. On Saturday, October 9, she

Evangelina Cisneros LIBRARY OF CONGRESS PRINTS AND PHOTOGRAPHS DIVISION, WASHINGTON, D.C., LC-DIG-DS-04264 (DIGITAL FILE FROM ORIGINAL ITEM).

was given a set of boy's clothes and a cigar in preparation for her walk from her secret hiding place to the wharf, where she would board a ship. Tucking her long, thick hair under a hat and positioning the cigar in her mouth, she made her way through the streets, strutting like a brash youth on his way to an imaginary social engagement. All the while, she noticed the three men who had rescued her—walking on the opposite side of the street or a few steps behind her—as she made her way to the wharf, where she showed her passport bearing the name Juan Sola before boarding the *Seneca*. As she passed a man she knew to be the chief of police, she exhaled a mouthful of cigar smoke, obscuring the man's view. "I might have been his grandmother for all he could see through the smoke," Evangelina recalled. She was taken to a cabin where she stayed until a man entered and said, "We are from Havana one hour out and nobody can harm you now."

When Evangelina arrived in New York City on October 13, she was overwhelmed with the reception she received from the Americans who had followed her saga in the pages of the *New York Journal*. She and Karl Decker were treated as celebrities at a reception at Madison Square and even at the White House. The *Journal* published a book, *The Story of Evangelina Cisneros Told by Herself*, in which she and Karl Decker presented firsthand accounts of their experiences with all proceeds from sales going to Evangelina. "I never could get used to being of so much consequence," she wrote. Celia Whipple, a wealthy Chicago widow, expressed interest in adopting Evangelina, making her heir to a fortune. Eventually, Evangelina married a Cuban American who had been involved in her rescue, and after the Spanish-American War ended in late 1898, they returned to Cuba. When she wrote her memoir in October 1897, her father was still in prison, and her little sister, who had been released from prison after only three weeks, was living with family friends. Her father was released eventually but suffered from poor health.

The remarkable events surrounding Evangelina's imprisonment and rescue seemed simple enough to many newspaper readers at the time; however, there were those who viewed the story with more than a little skepticism. Newspapers in addition to the *New York World* questioned the veracity of the entire affair. Some called it a hoax perpetrated to increase readership of the *Journal* and to turn public opinion in favor of war with Spain. Up to this point, most Americans hadn't paid much attention to the activities of Cuban fighters who were attempting to overthrow their Spanish rulers. The captivating drama of Evangelina caught the attention of thousands of ordinary Americans.

Some of the skepticism sprouted from statements made by Consul General Lee, who said that Spanish authorities "must have winked" at Evangelina's courageous escape for it to have succeeded. Then, soon after making those remarks, Lee backtracked, saying the idea of the Spanish being willing accomplices was "absurd." Others speculated that Evangelina was not the innocent victim the *Journal* had claimed, pointing to a novel written after the rescue in 1897 and supposedly based on factual events. In the preface of *A Cuban Amazon*, author Virginia Lyndall Dunbar claimed, "The statements have all been sworn to, and their truthfulness is not to be doubted." Dunbar wrote that Evangelina had indeed fought with the freedom fighters as a captain before being arrested. According to other reports, the rescue was easily executed simply because the prison guards were bribed and the bars on the window were already loose when Decker lifted them to release Evangelina. And while some turned to Evangelina's autobiography, *The Story of Evangelina Cisneros Told by Herself*, to get the definitive account, others noted that the book was published by William Randolph Hearst. Later in 1933, a former *Journal* editor, Willis J. Abbot, wrote in a book about the "magnificent farce of the rescue of Evangelina Cisneros." According to Abbot, Hearst's employees at the *Journal* "cursed the whole thing for a false bit of cheap sensationalism." And much later in an interview with *Granma*, a Cuban Communist Party newspaper, Evangelina admitted to a reporter that she had intended to capture Colonel Berriz and possibly aid in his assassination. In that interview, she said that she had not initiated the plot and that others had convinced her to participate. She added that she considered it a foolish idea.

Historians continued to write about Evangelina Cisneros long after she was gone. Wilbur Cross, in an article titled "The Perils of Evangelina" in *American Heritage* magazine in 1968, let readers decide what to believe—"No matter which story is true," and "again the facts are thin, the evidence discolored by propaganda." *American Journalism* magazine published an article by W. Joseph Campbell in 2002 titled "Not a Hoax: New Evidence in the *New York Journal*'s Rescue of Evangelina Cisneros." In 2005, historian Teresa Prados-Torreira, in her book *Mambisas: Rebel Women in Nineteenth-Century Cuba*, explained the encounter between Evangelina and Col. Berriz this way: "A group of exiled rebels conspired with Evangelina to trap the officer." And she included Evangelina's comments: "The truth is that I took part in this plot without thinking it through, but with knowledge of what it was." Prados-Torreira referred to *The Story of Evangelina Cisneros Told by Herself* as a "so-called autobiography."

Despite uncertainty surrounding the role Evangelina played in the late 1890s in the Cuban War of Independence against Spain, Evangelina, in her nineties, was asked if she would have fought in the Cuban Revolution of the 1950s with Fidel Castro had she been able. She replied that she would have welcomed the opportunity—if he had allowed her to be in command. And when Evangelina died in 1970, she was buried with full military honors as a *capitana*, remembered for her role as a revolutionary, and praised for her courage as a "heroic mambisa to the freedom of Cuba."

PAULINA RUIZ GONZALES: "A CUBAN TIGRESS"

"Were you ever afraid?"

"Gracious! No Senor."

"Did you not feel a little strange when you heard the first volley and saw men falling about you?"

"No, Senor, I never felt afraid in my life, but in my first action I was impatient. My horse could not go to the enemy quick enough. I rode my first charge without giving the machete to any one. I saw the machetes flash near me, and heard the rattle and clash, but I found no one in front of me. Then it was all dust and the enemy had gone."

The exchange between writer Grover Flint and Cuban revolutionary fighter Paulina Gonzales took place in the summer of 1896 a couple of years before America went to war with Spain and before American soldiers had shed any blood on the island. Cuban freedom fighters were intent on defeating the occupying Spanish, and Paulina, the wife of Captain Rafael Gonzales, had left her village to join a brigade on the hunt for Spanish guerrilla fighters spread throughout the countryside. Flint came on the female fighter in a secret settlement carved out of the thick brush and trees in the province of Cienfuegos, where a few fighters and their families lived safe from Spanish soldiers, who had been known to commit unspeakable atrocities on the Cuban populace. Flint had gained access to the clandestine camp after becoming embedded with revolutionaries in March. His encounter with the female fighter was recounted in detail in his book *Marching with Gomez: A War Correspondent's Field Note-Book Kept during Four Months with the Cuban Army* published in 1898.

Described as a twenty-one-year-old woman with "soft dark eyes and glossy black hair," Paulina wore a linen coat and short skirt revealing a pair of striped trousers beneath. This "slim as a poplar" and "very graceful" woman had ridden with the notorious leaders Pancho Perez and Manolo Menendez. Meeting up with Perez's band of soldiers in January, she begged the leader to allow her to carry the revolutionary flag, a position of honor usually filled by one of the men, and after successfully keeping the flag aloft through "a shower of Mauser bullets," Paulina was commissioned a lieutenant. Paulina proved her prowess in battle, draping the flag over her arm while brandishing her machete and riding alongside Perez as he led troops in brutal skirmishes and deadly ambushes. At Corral Falso, she struck down two Spanish guerilla fighters with her machete, shouting "Viva Cuba Libre" as her victims lay dead on the battlefield. Flint reported that when he met Paulina, she had had two horses shot from beneath her through ten battles, but she had never been wounded herself. He interviewed the female fighter as she awaited the return of Perez, who lay wounded in a hospital at Zapata.

The "flag captain" and her autograph.

Paulina Ruiz Gonzales FROM *MARCHING WITH GOMEZ* BY GROVER FLINT, P. 86.

Paulina offered her perspective of the fight for her country's freedom: "I would not for the world kill any one, but when you ride against an enemy, that is a different thing. You strike for Cuba and you think only of Cuba. I have struck with the machete, but it was not as if I had hurt any one. They fell, but you know it was for Cuba and I would not hurt any one."

Newspapers across the country ran versions of Flint's encounter with Paulina—all based on his description in his book. Most used word-for-word excerpts, such as the *San Francisco Examiner* under the headline "A Woman Bravely Fighting for Cuba," while others, such as Montana's

Great Falls Tribune, published an embellished version provided by the *New York World* under the headline "The Cuban Joan of Arc." Describing Paulina as a "Cuban tigress" who "will fight until the last drop of blood flows out of her patriotic heart" and going to war "ready to avenge the fallen," the *World* reported she nursed Perez back to health when he was wounded. Her reputation as a "dead shot with the rifle or revolver" and her skill with the machete "envied by many seasoned troopers" had made Paulina an object of veneration among the Cuban people, as the mere mention of her name was "greeted with the raising of the sombrero." And according to the *World*, Paulina's mere presence by her soldier husband's side had inspired daring actions that ultimately earned him the rank of colonel in the revolutionary army.

Joseph Pulitzer's *New York World* and William Randolph Hearst's *New York Journal*, well known for yellow journalism—a "style of newspaper reporting that emphasized sensationalism over facts"—couldn't get enough of Paulina's story. Grover Flint, a Harvard graduate who had inherited a vast fortune and had been hired by the *New York Journal* as a war correspondent in 1896, found himself in an extraordinary position as he traveled with the Cuban freedom fighters in the days of the independence movement. Having firsthand access to the fighters provided invaluable sources of prized information unavailable to other journalists. His father-in-law, John Fiske, a respected historian of the time, wrote the introduction to Flint's book in which he claimed his son-in-law's primary purpose was to tell the "plain unvarnished tale" of what he saw and heard during his stint in Cuba.

Fact or fiction? Was Paulina Ruiz Gonzales a romantic configuration of Flint's imagination, invented to help sell newspapers and his book? Or was she a courageous daughter of Cuba who "heads the spirit of war" that had "risen among the women of Cuba" in the days of the island's fight for freedom? In a footnote in his book, Flint admits other "interesting stories" had been published about Cuban women who followed their husbands, "sharing the hardship of the always moving camp and the chances of a stray bullet," carrying machetes, sleeping in hammocks, and wearing trousers. But Paulina Ruiz Gonzales was the "only one it was my fortune to meet," Flint wrote.

The idea of a daring young female fighter captured the attention of playwright Livingston Russell, known for producing plays "full of intense interest . . . suitable for the drawing room and the stage." The story of Paulina Ruiz Gonzales, true or otherwise, presented the creative writer an opportunity he couldn't resist. Paulina offered audiences a lively, engaging heroine set in a dangerous, life-threatening situation—a love story set in the uncertainty of war—and Russell sprang into action, creating a monologue titled "Viva Cuba Libre!" centered around Paulina as she stumbled into an army camp in Santa Clara, Cuba, carrying the flag and demanding to know details of her dear husband Rafael, whom she believed was killed by the Spaniards. Learning that he was only slightly wounded and recovering in a camp hospital, Paulina described the scenes she had witnessed in Havana: "Our kinfolk dead and dying by the thousands—torturously murdered by the demon Spaniards! They die in dreadful agony and lie unburied by the hundreds, poor prey for the grim, watchful buzzards. Humanity cries aloud for revenge!" Captured by Spanish guards and taken to their captain, Paulina confronted her enemy, who angrily cried, "What, another snarling wench!"

Russell's Paulina replied, "No snarling wench but one of Cuba's native daughters, come to tell you, to your very face, that as there is a just God, you and your bands of murderers shall perish! Cuba has brave women—women of will—as well as men! For wherever good women are, there is goodness, and there is truth held high, and mercy and tenderness working for the right! We shall fight for freedom, and we shall win!"

Released by the Spaniards, who predicted she would soon be a prisoner of the grave, the stalwart Paulina made her way to the camp happy in the knowledge that a secret agent had infiltrated the Spanish army and learned valuable, safely guarded secrets that led to the fall of Santiago and defeat of the Spanish. As the brave heroine hoisted the flag and brandished her machete high over her head, she looked heavenward and cried, "Out, machete, and to heaven pledge your loyalty to Cuba Libre!"

Gazing off to a shape in the distance, Paulina cried, "Ah! Here comes my husband, my Rafael! I am coming to you, my love, my life! We shall live—live for each other and our own Cuba Libre! Viva Cuba Libre!"

Russell's play inspired others—even school performances. When Miss Rodeffer's music class in Salida, Colorado, presented a class recital complete with chorus numbers and orchestra selections at the opera house on June 8, 1899, they included Livingston Russell's monologue "Viva Cuba Libre," described as "a dramatic setting of incidents connected with the patriotic daring of Paulina de Ruiz Gonzales—the Joan of Arc of Cuba; together with the introduction of historical matter regarding the sufferings of the Cubans during their struggle for liberty." Miss Beatrice Brown delivered a memorable performance as the Cuban heroine; Miss Irene Parks provided the piano accompaniment. And according to the *Salida Mail* newspaper, the "appropriate stage setting and accessories rendered the effect as a whole quite thrilling and realistic."

The crowd was smaller than expected that evening at the Salida opera house—only the ground-floor seats were occupied, but those who attended were "thoroughly appreciative" of the pleasing event. By June 1899, when the class presented their recital, America and Spain had signed a peace treaty, and many Americans were eager to put thoughts of war behind them. Although fighting continued in the Philippines between Americans and Filipinos, Paulina Ruiz Gonzales and her fellow soldiers no longer fought the Spaniards in Cuba. But the war was still fresh in the minds of many Americans, including the citizens of Salida, and they may not have questioned the authenticity of Paulina Ruiz Gonzales. They may simply have desired a pleasurable hour of music and elocution featuring the exploits of a daring young woman who may or may not have donned a pair of trousers, flung a flag over her arm, raised a machete against a brutal enemy, and reunited with a lost lover.

TERESA MAGBANUA: TEACHER AND REVOLUTIONARY FIGHTER

"The insurgents will have 1,000 men and 3,000 or 4,000 rifles there. General Magbanua . . . plans to attack the suburbs of Iloilo with this force, carry the city and slaughter the Americans."

The disturbing statement carried in American newspapers in October 1899 certainly caused some readers to cringe at the reference to slaughtering Americans. After all, many American families had sons, brothers, and husbands fighting in the area around Iloilo City on Panay Island in the Philippines. If readers gave any thought to the general named in the article, they may have assumed that General Magbanua was a man, and they may have been correct. However, three Magbanua siblings were officers in the Filipino army, and one of them was Teresa, a feisty, determined woman who was intent on doing her part in the war for independence. By this time, Americans were well aware that the Filipinos, who along with the Americans had defeated the occupying Spaniards months before, were not about to let the Americans

Bust of Teresa Magbanua by Frederic L. Caedo COURTESY OF FREDERIC L. CAEDO.

replace Spain as foreign occupiers. Filipinos were eager for independence, and their armies had turned from fighting Spaniards to fighting Americans in their quest for freedom.

Teresa Magbanua had become a freedom fighter and leader in 1898, and by late 1899, she was a heroine fondly known as Nay Isa by her soldiers. Born in Iloilo province in 1863, she was an "energetic and robust" child. It may have been her early years wrestling with her brothers and climbing trees that prepared her for a life as a revolutionary fighter, but she also spent years as a student and teacher, honing skills that would become valuable as a leader and military strategist. She attended schools in Jaro and Manila, earning a degree from the College of Santa Cecilia and working as a teacher before marrying Alejandro Balderas, a wealthy landowner in 1894. As a farmer, she learned to ride horses and handle a weapon, two skills that served her well as a soldier. Only two years after her marriage, events in her homeland changed the course of her life.

Uprisings against the Spanish had occurred many times over the 400-year occupation of the Philippines by Spain. In 1892, the secret "militant underground organization" known as the Katipunan began operation in the Philippines at the national level and at local levels. Headed by Emilio Aguinaldo, the group consisted of a variety of individuals in small villages across the Philippines who supported a free and independent Philippine nation. In 1898, two of Teresa's brothers, Pascual and Elias, joined the Filipino Liberating Army in Iloilo province, engaging in confrontations with Spanish soldiers in the countryside, and Teresa wanted to join too. Her uncle, General Perfecto Poblador, was a commander, and she convinced him to consider her skills as a fighter. "You know very well that I can ride and shoot better than you," Teresa said. "Give me men to command and I will show you how a woman can fight for our beloved Philippines." In time, Teresa found herself heading up a battalion of fighters eager to do her part in driving the Spaniards out of her homeland. At the time, she couldn't have known that before long, she would turn her attention to another enemy—one that would in the end defeat her cause.

On May 1, 1898, the Americans, under the command of Admiral George Dewey, had essentially destroyed the Spanish navy in Manila Bay, which would have been a cause for celebration for the Filipinos, but it wasn't long before the Americans began to show signs of staying in the Philippines themselves. Although Manila Bay was in the hands of the Americans, the city of Manila was controlled by the Spanish, with the surrounding suburbs infiltrated by the Filipino freedom fighters. The situation was described as "wolves surrounding a wounded stag. They all wanted a morsel." Over the next few months, things were at a stalemate, but by August, the Americans had control of Manila, and the Filipinos were aware that the 15,000 American troops on the island just might become their new enemy.

Meanwhile, 300 miles away from Manila, Spanish General Diego de los Rios controlled Iloilo City in Iloilo province, where Teresa and her family were actively involved in independence activities. The Filipinos had taken control of the towns of Jaro and Santa Barbara, where General Martin Delgado set up headquarters and a provisional government. In November and December, Teresa commanded a battalion of perhaps a thousand bolomen[5] horsemen traveling to the neighboring province of Capiz, where they engaged Spanish soldiers in the Battle of Barrio Yating in the city of Pilar and at Sapong Hill in the town of Sara, where Teresa had once taught. On December 24, the freedom fighters, including Teresa under the leadership of General Martin Delgado, entered the city of Iloilo, one of the last strongholds of the Spanish, and claimed the city for the Filipinos.

When reports of the evacuation of General Rios and his forces from Iloilo and the success of the Filipino soldiers in securing the city reached American officials in Washington, there was confusion. In fact, the Americans were "somewhat disturbed" by the news. A peace treaty between the Americans and the Spanish had been signed on December 10, handing over the Philippines to the United States. Hadn't the Filipinos gotten the message? Apparently, there was a misunderstanding because news had reached Washington that the freedom fighters had hoisted *their* flag over the city. "It appears that the American forces had arrived too late on the scene," newspapers reported.

But the Filipinos were not in the least confused. They had been intentionally excluded from the peace negotiations, and they were not happy. Teresa Magbanua and her fellow Filipinos were not about to allow their homeland to be occupied again—this time by the Americans. The U.S. Congress was scheduled to take the official vote to approve the treaty ending the war in early February. Even before the vote had been concluded, fighting had erupted between the Filipinos and the Americans in Manila. On February 6, 1899, Congress voted to approve the treaty between Spain and the United States, allowing the United States to annex the Philippines. For the Filipinos, the struggle for independence continued with a new impediment, and the fighting continued—with the Americans instead of the Spanish.

It didn't take long for things to heat up. On February 11, American soldiers who had been waiting for a chance to fight the Filipinos went ashore into the town of Iloilo, where General Delgado and other fighters,

---

5. Bolomen were Filipino fighters whose principal weapon was a long, broad-bladed knife called a bolo.

including Teresa, fought to defend their city. An American soldier from the 18th U.S. Infantry described his entry into Iloilo: "It was a sight to see the shells burst. They fired the city and set many buildings on fire." When the Americans went ashore, they were hindered by thick smoke from fires set by the Filipinos and greeted by shots fired from inside houses and from treetops. "It is no fun I must say for the bullets to be flying over our heads and all around us. It was a hot place indeed but soon the shots were few and far away and by night all was quiet," the American soldier wrote. At the end of the weeks-long confrontation, "much of the city was a blackened ruin." And Teresa and her fellow freedom fighters retreated into the surrounding areas. They may have been invisible to the Americans, but they were decidedly active.

In March 1899, Delgado, Teresa, and the other Filipino soldiers, including her brother Pascual, fought the Americans in the Battle of Balantang, Jaro, where, according to some reports, 400 Americans were killed. Although the American artillery poured "shell and shrapnel upon the insurgents"—almost 63,000 rounds—the Filipino fighters' "persistent attacks" took a toll. The Americans suffered greatly from heat and exhaustion and from wading through the rice and sugarcane fields. By the end of the fierce battle, the Filipinos had retaken Jaro from the Americans. Teresa, perched on her white horse, led her troops into the city, relishing the cheers of the town's citizens.

By late spring of 1899, when a new commander of U.S. forces arrived on Panay Island, he found "much of the countryside controlled by" Teresa and the freedom fighters. Throughout the summer, Brigadier General Robert P. Hughes used a variety of tactics to conquer them—raiding refugee camps for suspected fighters and banning trade from Iloilo City to starve the enemy soldiers. But Teresa and the others continued their guerilla attacks throughout 1899. She was bolstered by the loyalty of her men, who were known to "attack any position upon her orders." Freedom fighters seemed to be firmly entrenched in the countryside between Jaro and Santa Barbara. It was in October 1899 that American newspapers reported that General Magbanua was prepared to attack the suburbs of Iloilo City with a force of 1,000 men carrying 3,000 to 4,000 rifles intent on slaughtering the Americans. It was reported that bolomen around Jaro and Iloilo City hid in the tall grasses, firing volleys throughout the night. In late October, an American soldier wrote to his family about Santa Barbara, "It has never been conquered by the Spaniards, and is probably a strong position. I expect something will happen there shortly." The soldier was correct in his prediction. Late in November, the Americans engaged in fierce fighting with the Filipinos in the countryside between Jaro and Santa Barbara as the freedom fighters stubbornly held their ground. Finally, the regional headquarters under the command of Delgado fell to the Americans late in 1899. With their base of operations in the hands of the Americans, the Filipinos intensified their guerilla warfare against the Americans. It was in December 1899 that Teresa was dealt a personal blow when both her brothers were killed under mysterious circumstances—possibly murdered by assassins.

In the summer of 1900, thirty American infantry companies with 6,000 men were stationed on Panay Island. But "the pervasive reach of the Filipino resistance" continued to cause trouble for the Americans. Teresa and the freedom fighters continued their guerilla tactics, and with each attack, the Americans retaliated with severe retribution. "The situation of the island of Panay is simply hell," the American commander reported. Throughout 1900, the Americans intensified their efforts to quash the freedom fighters. Brutal interrogation techniques were used to obtain information on General Delgado, one of the last revolutionary leaders operating in late December. Finally, in February 1901, he surrendered to the Americans. Teresa had surrendered late in 1900 and returned to her husband and her farm.

4

Activists

"A Trumpet Call to Us to Be Up and Doing"

"WE CONSIDERED THE DECLARATION OF WAR A TRUMPET CALL TO US TO be up and doing." May Wright Sewall, president of the International Council of Women, addressed a gathering of women from across the globe in London in 1899. Her remarks came after the women had heard a speaker describe war as a "massing together of engines to kill men" and "men dealing death blows while the ground drinks blood and corpses lie thick as autumn leaves." May was referring to America's recent war with Spain—a call for the nation's women to take action. And plenty of women answered the call.

While some sprang to action as nurses, volunteers, and magazine and newspaper correspondents, others directed their wartime furor to a cause. And, as is often the case with causes, fierce emotions shaped events, spokespeople didn't shy away from expressing opinions, and proponents versus opponents provided entertaining clashes.

When Ellen M. Henrotin, national president of the General Federation of Women's Clubs, sent an open letter to President McKinley in early April asking him to avoid conflict with Spain because "on us war will fall the heaviest, for we must give our sons, and must during and after the war help to repair the ravages and losses," she may have been surprised at the response her words provoked. The USS *Maine* had sunk a few months earlier carrying more than 200 American sailors to watery graves, but the United States had not yet declared war. Newspaper publishers pounced. An Iowa paper editorialized that Mrs. Henrotin did not speak for all women and simply suffered from a "case of a big head" from her position as president of a prestigious women's organization. And within days, papers across the country carried reaction from Harry Shillington's mother, still grieving the loss of Harry on the *Maine*, after seeing Mrs. Henrotin's letter. "I've already given one of mine. My Harry . . . buried in the mud of Havana Harbor. . . . I have no appeals to make to the president for peace, I'm a mother, and have suffered as perhaps not many mothers who have joined in Mrs. Henrotin's appeal have suffered, but I do not shrink at the notion of war." As one newspaper pointed out, Mrs. Shillington's second son, seventeen-year-old Charlie stationed on the battleship *Alliance*, currently served his country while avenging his brother's death. And Katharine D. Fletcher, vice president of the Utah Federation of Women's Clubs, issued a statement of sympathy for Mrs. Shillington and repudiation of Ellen Henrotin's words. Speaking on behalf of the Utah group, Mrs. Fletcher indicated they had not been consulted about the letter and did not agree with the sentiments expressed in it.

After the United States declared war in late April, it took a fair amount of courage for anyone to suggest that the nation's commitment to fighting the Spanish in Cuba and the Philippines was anything but honorable. In Grand Rapids, Michigan, every business in town shut down, flags decorated homes, and leading citizens belted out patriotic speeches as the local boys set out for camp in anticipation of active service in Cuba. At Owosso, Saginaw, Bay City, and Lansing, Michiganders marched in a body to train stations to see their boys depart for war. More than 4,000 fighting men marched out of Chicago bound for war, and in Buffalo, New York, nearly 200 recruits enlisted in one night. The Women's Patriotic League was formed in Washington, D.C., members pledging to boycott French imports including wine and clothing simply because the French had failed to come out in support of America in the war. "I will most willingly deny myself all such indulgences as French importations so long as the necessities of the case may require," a West Virginia woman said.

Still, Anna Garlin Spencer, president of the Council of the Women of Rhode Island, sent a letter to the state's congressmen, writing, "We plead that all possible means for a peaceable ending of such cruelty and wrong be exhausted before recourse is had to the sword . . . which when wielded in any cause, even the most righteous, brings moral confusion, social degradation, family bereavement and financial loss to both the avenger and the evil-doer." And May Wright Sewall, with seventeen officers from women's clubs around the country, penned a letter to President McKinley, writing, "We think it impossible that the death of 260 brave and innocent men who found death in the disaster of the *Maine* can be atoned for by the death of any number of Spaniards."

At the end of the war, as government leaders looked ahead to a new era in which the United States assumed its role as a major world power, the nation found itself awash with patriotic fervor. Groups like the Anti-Imperialist League, advocating restraint in foreign affairs, were labeled fanatics, disloyal Americans, and national enemies. When a Massachusetts woman, Mary L. Abbott, submitted a petition to the *New York Sun* stating her opposition to the ongoing fighting in the Philippines in 1899, the paper refused to publish it, accusing her of "giving aid and comfort to the barbarous creatures who are killing our soldiers in the Philippines." Addressing the National Council of Women (the American branch of the International Council of Women), May Wright Sewall cautioned that America should enter relations with other nations of the world "not by becoming a terror because of its invincible navy, invulnerable ships and unmatched soldiery, but rather because of its sense of human equality, which is the inevitable outcome of a true sense of human kinship."

Women viewed the war in 1898 as a trumpet call that couldn't be ignored. In opposition or as proponents, they responded. Some marched in step with the crowd; others marched to a different drummer.

CHARLOTTE SMITH: COMING TO MAKE TROUBLE

"A Yankee battleship!

Prepare to fight!

As the Spanish sailors began to engage, they noticed something peculiar about the approaching warship. Lace curtains over the portholes, colorful rugs hanging over the rails, doilies decorating the big guns, bright fabrics over the cross trees, and women swarming over the decks. Within an hour the Spanish flagship was 'fading to a dim speck on the horizon' with the battleship 'Charlotte Smith' in 'close pursuit.'"

Of course, there was not a battleship named *Charlotte Smith* with lace curtains, colorful rugs, or doilies. The article published in American newspapers across the nation was simply a humorous spoof of the notorious Charlotte Smith, a well-known reformer and activist for working women.

Charlotte Odlum Smith was never one to walk away from a cause. For years, her name appeared in countless newspapers, more times than not poking fun at the outspoken reformer. The all-female staff at her *Inland Magazine* produced scientific, historical, and philosophical themed articles as well as love stories and society personals in St. Louis and Chicago in the 1870s. She moved to Washington, D.C., in the early 1880s, believing it was a reasonable location from which to pursue her advocacy for wage-earning women. It didn't take long for Charlotte to become a familiar figure in government facilities and at politicians' offices. In 1882, she was indignant to find that hundreds of new government clerks had been hired and that although females had applied, none were offered positions. When she demanded an answer for the discrepancies, she was told that the hiring official believed that women were not as efficient as men and that the presence of women in the departments was "corrupting." In 1885, Charlotte published an open letter to the press, highlighting many of the wrongs she had witnessed in the nation's capital. She chose the press because, as she stated, newspapers were the "great lever which moves public opinion." In her letter, Charlotte called attention to the inequalities she found: "I found here women employed in government positions, say for the last twenty-four years, who receive on an average one-half the compensation paid to men." She encouraged the collection and dissemination of data about working women by the newly established Bureau of Labor. On one occasion when Charlotte attempted to enter the Senate chambers and was stopped by a Capitol policeman, she brought charges against him for behaving in a rude manner. In 1888, when President Grover Cleveland vetoed Congress's awarding of a pension to a woman who he said was "a bad character," Charlotte asked Congress to allow her to sue the president for libel. When she and other women in the congressional galleries became outraged by the salty language used by congressmen on the floor of the Senate and the House, she asked for the formation of a standing committee on "morals, restraint of vituperative language and reflection on ancestry." In 1891, she took aim at the U.S. Patent Office, advocating for more just laws for women inventors. Her publication *The Woman Inventor* highlighted the stories of overlooked female inventors, including Nancy M. Johnson, the inventor of an ice cream refrigerator in 1843. And calling attention to the special challenges Black female inventors faced, Charlotte wrote about Eden Eglin, who had invented a washing machine clothes wringer and had sold the rights to her patent in 1888 for only $18, allowing the buyer to make a small fortune on her invention. When asked why she had sold it for the paltry sum, Eden said, "I was afraid to be known because of my color—in having it introduced in the market, that is the only reason."

Plenty of people found Charlotte to be nothing more than a crackpot, her peculiar ideas simply laughable. There was her crusade against bicycle riding by women. She wasn't the first person to question the perceived threat to the health and morality of women participating in this increasingly popular sport, but she was one of the more vocal. In the late nineteenth century, the bicycle and bloomers had become a symbol of controversy related to women's independence and the suffrage movement. Although both gave women freedom to travel and exercise, the bicycle also was attacked for causing health problems and promiscuity in female cyclists. While the wearing of bloomers made bicycling easier according to some women cyclists, critics labeled the trousers immodest for bringing "certain portions of the anatomy closer to the surface." After completing investigation into the subject, Charlotte had concluded that "women who wheel will be physical wrecks." Warning that bicycling by young women could lead to "evil associations" resulting in "opportunities for imprudent action," Charlotte claimed bicycles had done "more to swell the ranks of reckless girls" than any other vice. The bicycle was nothing less than "the devil's agent." Bicycles, coupled with the very improper wearing of bloomers by young female riders, could lead only to ruin, according to Charlotte and others at the time—including medical doctors and politicians.

The New Woman and Her Bicycle LIBRARY OF CONGRESS PRINTS AND PHOTOGRAPHS DIVISION, WASHINGTON, D.C., LC-USZC2-1227, ILLUSTRATION FROM *PUCK*, JUNE 19, 1895.

Charlotte's efforts to tax bachelors and make marriage mandatory may have contributed to the crackpot label. Often citing statistics to back her radical ideas, she made a connection between labor issues of the day and her ideas about mandatory marriage. According to Charlotte, 60 percent of men refused to marry; consequently, 60 percent of women were forced to work—resulting in women and men competing for jobs. Her mandatory marriage law would allow women to become housewives, taking them out of the job market. She managed to convince a New Jersey legislator to introduce a bill to tax bachelors with the revenues going to the support of "old maids." A second legislator added an amendment providing for a tax on old maids for the support of dependent old bachelors. The bill failed to pass. Taking it one step further, Charlotte pressured Congress to appropriate $100,000 to transport women who were not married to the Klondike, where they were presented with the opportunity to make their fortunes as miners.

When war broke out between the United States and Spain in the spring of 1898, it was only natural that Charlotte would have opinions and an assortment of creative ideas related to war. From the start, she opposed the war: "Why our men are again to be killed off I can't understand." In her opinion, Spain was not worth the loss of American lives. "The idea of this noble country licking a bankrupt country of cowards is ridiculous," Charlotte said. As it looked more and more like the nation would go to war with Spain and talk of raising a volunteer military broke out, Charlotte had an idea, and she began to seek out powerful men who could help develop it. First, she visited Assistant Secretary of War George Meiklejohn, assuring him she had enough women to make up several regiments; as soon as they were outfitted with uniforms and arms, they would be ready to face battle. Moving on to the Navy Department, she encountered Assistant Secretary of the Navy Theodore Roosevelt, offering him at least 2,000 female sailors. Newspapers had fun with this—claiming that Roosevelt, well known for his fighting spirit and a man who had stood up to powerful politicians in Washington and buffalo bulls on the prairies of the Wild West, had shown himself to be "a poor, weak, miserable coward" when confronted by Charlotte Smith. According to some reports, this supposedly courageous official "fled in terror" when pinned down by the "the working girls' friend."

When the *Evening Star* (Washington, D.C.) reported that Charlotte proposed military enlistment for women as well as men because "there are so many women to spare," the paper quoted her as saying, "There are ten women to one man now. . . . If the President will see that thousands of the new women and the bicycle women in bloomers are sent to be killed, the country will be benefited, for then the maiden ladies will have a show." It's unclear how seriously she was taken—assuming the story was accurate. But the *Times* (Shreveport, La.) printed an editorial from a Dallas newspaper pushing back: "Mrs. Smith has startled and stirred conventional ideas deeply. It is a difficult matter to start in on anything like a steady view of her proposition. She would have it that women might as well die for their country as men, just as well do this as to stay behind and pile up to even greater proportions the now heavy excess of unmarried women over the supply of marriageable men. Mrs. Smith, you have spread a new terror over the land when it was in no shape to meet it."

Always the champion of women wage earners, Charlotte proposed a novel way to supply uniforms to the fighting men while at the same time helping women back home. Why not convince the government to hire women whose male relatives had enlisted to make the thousands of uniforms needed to clothe the soldiers, sailors, and marines? Many families had been left without their major breadwinner when a husband and father enlisted; this would alleviate some of the financial burdens thrust on them by the soldier's absence.

When Charlotte heard that the widow and children of one of the men killed on the USS *Maine* in Cuba were struggling, she spun into action. Drawing a group together at the Arlington Hotel in Washington, she commenced plans to locate and assist families of service members in the area. Pointing out that hundreds of thousands of dollars had been raised to erect a monument to the men killed on the *Maine* and that tons of provisions had been sent to aid the Cuban people, Charlotte argued nothing was being done to alleviate the needs of the American families affected by the war. She directed a group to identify military families in need of help, consulting with the War Department to obtain additional names. She planned to establish workshops where family members could find employment if needed.

Charlotte insisted there was no reason each regiment shouldn't have a resident mother with them wherever they were stationed. The camp mothers, from the state where the regiment originated, would mend uniforms and tend to the general welfare of the boys, who were far from their real mothers. She immediately sent an older woman to Camp Alger, Virginia, with a group of soldiers from the Washington, D.C., area. She ran up against some resistance from army headquarters, which issued a statement that the men should do their own mending and that the army was "not the place for any woman, even though of mature years." It didn't seem to faze Charlotte, who went ahead making plans to line up women from each state.

In the spring of 1898 as the nation geared up for war and families began to plan for the possibility of men leaving for battle, many had to face the reality that some would never return home. Adding to the stress of separation was the knowledge that, if a husband died in war, his life insurance policy may not be valid. At the time, insurance companies differed in their handling of life insurance policies for soldiers—ranging from terminating coverage of men who entered the military during wartime to increasing premiums on existing policies for servicemen. And while some policies were free of any wartime restrictions, others required men who volunteered for wartime duty to forfeit their life insurance policies. Others differentiated between men who volunteered and those who were called up for compulsory service. Some companies increased soldiers' premiums by as much as 3 percent while serving—with the option for the additional costs to be deducted from the beneficiary's payout should the soldier die in service. Others refunded the increased premium costs at the end of service if the soldier survived. And during the Spanish-American War, Cuba and the Philippines presented an especially troubling situation for some soldiers whose policies became invalid during travel to places where tropical diseases were a threat.

There were calls from politicians and others for insurance companies to step up and treat soldiers equitably and not to penalize men who volunteered for service. They were reminded that brave soldiers, sailors, and marines were taking risks by joining the fight, and it was only right that insurance companies assume some risk too. Many did strive to be fair. A Pennsylvania company advertised "A War Declaration for Our Noble Soldiers," promising to "treat with liberality the brave men who have or may enlist in the service of their country." Some local service organizations and church groups volunteered to pay for a soldier's life insurance policy while he was serving.

It didn't seem like an insurmountable barrier to Charlotte. After all, she had devoted years to pressuring local legislators and congressmen to introduce bills and pass laws that she believed were practical resolutions to some of the country's pressing predicaments. And foremost were issues related to women who were concerned with the welfare of their families. Charlotte proposed a national insurance program for soldiers, sailors, and marines. Once again relying on statistics she had gathered, she cited data related to the loss of life during the Civil War and the suffering endured by dependent families of servicemen killed in that conflict in the 1860s. She wanted Congress to establish a "national military-naval industrial insurance bureau." While she left the details to Congress, Charlotte insisted that the government adopt a system of insurance by which soldiers could be insured for a "nominal fee" and that the program be compulsory. In her opinion, such a program would go a long way in relieving stress for women and their families in wartime. A New Jersey congressman introduced a bill authorizing the president to appoint a board of commissioners to adopt rules and regulations for a military life and accident insurance to be paid on loss of life or injury in the service.

After the war in Cuba ended, a controversy arose involving two of the navy's war heroes—William T. Sampson and Winfield Scott Schley. During the decisive Battle of Santiago in July 1898, in which the American navy destroyed the Spanish navy and essentially sealed the fate of the Spaniards in Cuba, Schley had assumed command of the American fleet of ships blockading the Cuban harbor while his superior officer Sampson was temporarily away. Both men wanted to claim credit for the colossally significant American victory. Although Sampson had not actually participated in the battle, he had devised the battle plan. And some were critical of questionable actions taken by Schley in earlier military encounters. Americans were divided into two camps, siding with one or the other of the two naval heroes. Newspapers covered aspects of the dispute as it unfolded over several years. Ultimately, a military court issued a somewhat conflicting decision—praising some of Schley's actions while criticizing others.

It came as a surprise to no one when Charlotte Smith waded into the newsworthy affair. As president of the Washington branch of the Woman's Industrial and Patriotic League, Charlotte proposed that the group start a fund to purchase a house for Schley in Washington, D.C., "in order that the women of the country might take the lead in honoring him." With a pledge of $1 per member, the women's $300 gift jump-started the campaign, which Charlotte imagined spreading across the country. An advisory board of 100 men was formed at the invitation of the women, and similar committees were planned in each state. By November 1899, committee members had contributed more than $700 with another $500 in pledges from around the country. It was believed the group would have little trouble raising the $25,000 goal. A woman from Mississippi enclosed $5 in her letter to the committee, stating that Schley "deserved a home on account of the persecution to which he had been subjected."

Charlotte's campaign ran into a glitch when a quandary erupted over a house that had been purchased for another Spanish-American War hero, George Dewey. Thinking the house he had been given in appreciation for his wartime contributions carried no stipulations, Dewey had deeded the house to his wife, who in turn deeded to it to Dewey's son and her stepson, George Goodwin Dewey. Americans were outraged. In response to this, Charlotte suggested adding a clause in the deed of the proposed house for Schley to specify that the house could not be transferred during Schley's lifetime and that after his death, it could go only to a descendant. She hoped to anticipate future problems should Schley at some point become a widower and a victim of "any possible wiles of wealthy widows" who might be attracted to his lovely home.

That wasn't the only problem encountered by the group. A Kentucky newspaper called for an end to "the gift house business" and advised Schley to decline the proposed gift in advance, claiming that such an act would make him "secure in the hearts of his countrymen." At the same time, reporting that more than $5,000 had been raised for the Schley house, another paper posed this: "We wonder where all this foolishness of giving houses and gifts galore to our heroes is going to end. Why not switch off now and then and give a house to some poor devil who needs it?"

As the campaign to purchase a house for Schley heated up, resistance took an ugly turn. At one point, Charlotte warned the public that Schley's enemies were spreading a lie that he had been drinking before the Battle of Santiago, to which Schley replied, "Why I never take a drop of anything." The *Charlotte (N.C.) News* reported that the movement to buy Schley a house had denigrated into a purely partisan contest—pro-Schley people versus pro-Sampson supporters, reaching into the ranks of officers at the Navy Department in Washington. According to the paper, Secretary of the Navy John Long was doing all he could to derail the gift house project, and officers under him would not risk their hopes for advancement by speaking out in support of the project. It's unclear if Schley was ever gifted a house, but in early 1902, President Theodore Roosevelt issued a statement about the Schley–Sampson affair: "There is no excuse whatever from either side for any further agitation of this unhappy controversy. To keep it alive would merely do damage to the navy and to the country." It appeared Charlotte may have put the house project aside too, but she had already earned a reputation as a woman who would not sit on the sidelines when she saw a wrong that needed righting.

Charlotte claimed to have initiated seventy-five bills in Congress that had become laws—all "in the interest of humanity." Yet that reputation came with its pitfalls. At least one U.S. senator seemed to want to hide from Charlotte when he spotted her in the halls one day. "Here comes that Smith woman to make trouble," the senator said as Charlotte approached, to which Charlotte responded, "Yes, and I'll make it hotter and hotter for you till we women get what we want."

LUCY PARSONS: "NOT A HELL-RAISER; MERELY RAISING OBVIOUS ISSUES"

"Ah, the shame of it all! You are told that the Filipinos are not capable of self-government. I ask you—you have in your veins the blood of the men which redden the snow at Valley Forge more than a hundred years ago—were not your forefathers accused of the same thing? Were they not called rebels and insurgents? Were they not fighting for exactly the same grand principle that is involved in the struggle being made now by the Filipinos?"

Lucy Parsons posed her questions to the crowd that had gathered at the corner of State and Quincy streets in Chicago on a July night in 1899 and urged them to consider their own history before volunteering to fight against the independence advocates in the Philippines. Who was this fiery speechmaker who vehemently opposed America's war in the Philippines and sympathized with the enemy?

Born into slavery in Virginia in 1851, she later lived in Texas, where she married Albert Parsons, a Confederate army veteran. A Black woman marrying a White man in 1872 was a head-turning event and against the law in some parts of the United States. The couple's move to Chicago in 1873 marked the beginning of their notoriety. As their activities began to garner attention in the city and ultimately across the country, Lucy constructed a myth surrounding her background. She credited fictitious Mexican and Indian parents for her dark skin. And a Mexican Indian ancestry classified her legally as a White citizen. It's difficult to know if this was a strategic move on her part to distinguish herself from foreign-born anarchists at the time.

By 1886, Albert and Lucy were well-known self-proclaimed anarchists. It would surprise no one that the two were involved in the Haymarket Square gathering of workers and activists on May 4, 1886, to protest police actions the day before at the McCormick

Lucy Parsons, 1886 LIBRARY OF CONGRESS PRINTS AND PHOTO-GRAPHS DIVISION, WASHINGTON, D.C., LC-DIG-DS-10459. PHOTOGRAPHER AUGUST BRAUNECK.

Reaper Plant, where strikers and police had clashed. At the Haymarket rally, someone threw a bomb, killing several police and protestors. Albert spoke at the event, but when the bomb was thrown, he and Lucy had already left. The bomb thrower was never positively identified, but Albert Parsons was convicted in what many believed was an unfair trial and hanged in November 1887. The Haymarket affair captured the attention of the nation and changed Lucy Parsons forever.

Lucy had been a zealous activist before her husband's death in 1887 defying capitalism and its captains of industry the likes of Philip Armour, "a slaughterer of children as well as hogs," for his liberal use of child labor in his meatpacking plant. She made her opinions about war crystal clear in the late 1870s, calling out the "parasitic capitalist class" of wealthy business owners who had "sent the working class to die" while they profited a decade before during the Civil War. Singling out a newspaper editor when he called homeless Civil War veterans "relics from the late carnage," Lucy reminded her audience that the editor had "stayed at home, fared sumptuously, and waxed fat on the spoils of a cruel, cruel war." An outspoken proponent of freedom of speech, she railed against police brutality, political parties, and voting. She invited Americans in 1886 to visit New York City and witness for themselves the plight of the poor: "Go through the byways and alleys of that great city. Count the myriads starving; count the multiplied thousands who are homeless; number those who work harder than slaves." As an ardent anarchist, she believed all forms of government were harmful and unnecessary. "Liberty" she said, "calls forth our best efforts; government restrains them." Lucy promoted her beliefs by writing for radical periodicals, speaking at rallies, persuading anyone who would listen, and getting arrested countless times. "I can't tell how many times I've had trouble with the police," she told a reporter.

Albert's conviction and death only bolstered Lucy's spirit. Arrested in June 1888 for distributing fliers; arrested in Newark, New Jersey, in November 1890 for inciting a riot; and threatened with arrest when she spoke at a rally in November 1895, saying of the judge who presided over Albert's trial, "I would rather be consigned to the bottomless pits of hell than walk the Golden streets of Heaven with Judge Gary," Lucy was a celebrity of sorts by the time she began speaking out against the war in the Philippines.

About the time the United States and Spain went to war in the spring of 1898, Lucy embarked on a speaking tour. War certainly was on the minds of many Americans, but so were other concerns that didn't disappear with the advent of the conflict with Spain. In her talk titled "Trades Unions: Their History, Development and Destiny" in Buffalo, New York, in March, she asserted that the only relief for workers was a shorter workday. In Philadelphia at the Friendship Liberal League in April, she offered two topics: "Religion and Humanity" and "The Cuban Question." In Boston, Wells Memorial Hall was filled for her lecture in which she reminded the audience of the suppressive rule of the Spanish in Cuba—proof that government of any ilk was the enemy of human progress and thereby making a case for anarchy. She visited New York City twice that month as well as New Haven, Connecticut. In Paterson, New Jersey, she delivered a fiery speech titled "What Is Anarchism, and What Is Not." By August, back home in Chicago, Lucy spoke at a gathering of nearly 2,000 unemployed workers. A Kansas newspaper reported it was an "anarchistic tirade" that was met with "loud howls at everything in the country" by the audience, consisting almost entirely of "foreigners" who couldn't speak English. The audience cheered at Lucy's demand for bread for the starving and her advice to the workers to "wade in gore rather than lose any of their rights." And, according to the news report, the unemployed workers then "spent enough money for beer to have kept a dozen families for a fortnight."

In July as Cuban, Filipino, Spanish, and American soldiers, marines, and sailors were killing one another in Cuba and the Philippines, the socialist newspaper *Industrial Freedom* quoted Lucy: "We know that we belong to one common brotherhood; and that it is only despots who believe because you happen to be born on another boundary line you should attack others. We have only one enemy to conquer, and that enemy is poverty, and it is known to all nations."

A year later in April 1899, after the peace treaty had been signed ending the Spanish-American War and with the Philippine-American War raging on with Washington politicians calling for all-out subjugation of the Filipinos, a group consisting of university professors, ministers, and others—individuals with the "tendency toward sensationalism in religion and toward mugwumpery in politics," according to a local newspaper—gathered at Central Music Hall to form the Anti-Imperialist League in Chicago. It turned into a raucous affair with a few imperialists infiltrating the event. "Treason!" "Traitors!" they interjected as anti-imperialist speakers lambasted President McKinley's policies in the Philippines as a "crusade in behalf of trade and religion" and labeled the American flag "the emblem of tyranny and butchery." And as a speaker characterized the war against the Filipinos as "criminal aggression" and American soldiers as "invaders," the protesting guests were led to the door. With the disruptors safely removed, the anti-imperialist speakers continued: "We deplore and resent the slaughter of the Filipinos as a needless horror, a deep dishonor to our nation. Our government should at once announce to the Filipinos its purpose to grant them . . . the independence for which they have so long fought."

Many of these sentiments were shared by Lucy. As she prepared for a speech she planned to give on July 16, the *Inter Ocean* newspaper speculated as to the tone and attendees at the upcoming event to be held in the open air at the corner of State and Quincy streets. Identifying their sources as friends of Lucy, the *Inter Ocean* reported that although the organizers of the newly formed Anti-Imperialist League would not attend the meeting, Mrs. Parsons would be echoing their words from the April meeting—support for the Filipino freedom fighters and a plea for removal of American troops. However, according to the newspaper, Lucy, always looking out for workers' rights, would address her concerns for American workers as they related to America's policies in the Philippines. According to the report, Lucy believed the American worker had nothing to gain by the acquisition of the Philippines and other Pacific islands. The wealthy capitalists would be the gainer, while the laborer would reap no benefit from the industrialization of the new possessions, as the natives of those new acquisitions would be hired for small wages while their manufactured products would be shipped into the United States in competition with the goods manufactured in America by skilled workers.

And on the sweltering evening of July 16, Lucy did not disappoint the crowd that gathered. "Cuba has been freed from Spanish tyranny at least, and the war which President McKinley said was not to be a war of conquest is over, so far as the people of that island are concerned. But lo! The scene of conflict has shifted to the far-off Philippines," Lucy said. She urged the young men in the crowd to stay home and "fight the trusts and monopolies instead of shooting at Filipinos."

"Suppose you do enlist and finally subjugate an innocent people; and suppose they are harnessed to the taskmaster's wheel to make more wealth for the American millionaires, what will it avail you? Don't you have to fight enough battles against the trusts here, without traveling across the Pacific?" she asked. "Every stripe of the American flag has become a whip for the monopolist to thrash your backs with. Every star in that flag represents the distilled tears of the children who work out their lives in the factories," she concluded.

People may or may not have been shocked only days later to see headlines claiming Lucy had committed her only son to a mental hospital to prevent his enlistment in the army. The events surrounding the situation were somewhat murky. On July 20 Albert Parsons Jr. appeared in the prisoner's dock at the Logan Square police court facing charges for drawing a knife on his mother. According to his story, Lucy and he were arguing over his desire to enlist in the army to fight in the Philippines. When he appeared in court on July 27, Lucy was there to testify that he was mentally unsound, having changed from a gentle, good-natured youth to a lazy, listless, and violent person. At the next court appearance, it was reported that Lucy made a strong plea for his confinement, saying he had been acting strangely for the past year and threatening to kill her more than once. Although several friends testified on his behalf, saying that he had never shown any signs of insanity in their presence, he was sentenced to the Illinois Northern Hospital for the Insane at Elgin, Illinois. On his arrival at the hospital, a doctor examined Albert and claimed he could find nothing abnormal about the young man. However, he spent the rest of his life in the facility. It's unknown if Lucy ever visited her son during his years in the hospital. He died in 1919.

In 1900, the *Inter Ocean* newspaper reported that Lucy denied having sent her son away merely because he wanted to join the army. "The story that I placed my son in an insane asylum because he did not agree with me is absurd. No person of intelligence will believe that the state of Illinois would help an anarchist in a scheme of that kind. I am sorry to say that my son is insane. It is preposterous to believe that an anarchist mother does not love her offspring. It is a painful subject and I do not like to talk about it," Lucy said, according to the paper.

Long after the wars in Cuba and the Philippines ended, Lucy remained a voice in the labor movement, drawing attention to workers' rights, the unemployed and poor, and the evils of capitalism through her writings and speeches. Chicago police watched her movements and repeatedly interrupted her speaking events, arresting her in what she and others believed violated her freedom of speech. In 1901, she spoke about her work: "We are getting young workmen into our ranks—men of brain and muscle, and women too—and I can safely now say that the cause is in safe hands."[6]

---

6. "Like most advocates of the White working class, she had little sympathy for either Chinese workers or African Americans," according to Jacqueline Jones, author of *Goddess of Anarchy*. "And her claim in 1901 that substantial numbers of young workmen and women were joining the ranks of anarchists is just plain wrong" (e-mail correspondence January 18, 2020).

When a reporter visited Lucy at her home in 1900, he was surprised by the apparent normalcy of the woman known by the world as a dangerous radical. He described her welcoming little cottage where she tended chickens and her flowers. With renters on the ground floor, Lucy lived on the top, where the rooms were tastefully decorated and furnished with plush furniture, brightly colored carpets, lace curtains, and pots of flowers in the windows. Lucy was in the process of cutting and sewing a new dress, and a copy of *Ladies' Home Journal* sat on a side table—all signs of a person who had benefited nicely from the effects of capitalism, in the reporter's opinion. The reporter promised Lucy he would not misrepresent her in his finished piece, to which she responded, "Oh, I don't care, I'm used to it." The title of the published article, "Lucy Parsons Is Mild," seemed to contradict the headline "Anarchist Queen" over a sketch of her being loaded into a police wagon as uniformed men threatened her with police clubs.

But Lucy was a complex individual. A minister who was once arrested with her said, "Lucy Parsons wasn't a hell-raiser; she was only trying to raise the obvious issues about human life."

CONSTANCIA POBLETE: "GUIDING ANGEL OF PEACE"

After four centuries of domination by Spain and years of fighting the Spanish and the Americans, the people of the Philippines must have been drawn to a woman known as "the guiding angel of peace" in 1901. Constancia Poblete earned the title when she established the Women's Peace League, an organization consisting of Filipino and American women who lived in the Philippines and who, "armed only with faith and good will," succeeded in accomplishing "what armed force could not do."

"It is the greatest hope of my heart that the women of America and these islands may stand with the men of these countries in putting down this bitter war which is cutting off fathers, sons and brothers," Constancia told a group of American women who had gathered to learn about the objectives of the women's group in May 1901. "Though great obstacles stand in the way, I have no fear of the results, because I have faith in our cause."

By the time the Women's Peace League was being organized, the Spaniards had been defeated by the Filipinos and Americans working together, but the Filipinos had turned their attention to the Americans, who refused to grant independence and continued to occupy the Philippines. Hundreds of Filipino freedom fighters continued armed resistance. However, Constancia and other Filipino women worked with the American women, resulting in the formation of the organization. They decided that as mothers, wives, and sisters, they had great influence over the men who fought. What son could resist the pleas of his mother and what husband the appeals of his loving companion?

Early in 1901, 200 Filipino women and fifty Americans gathered at the Libertad Theater in Manila and organized the Peace League. They adopted a resolution stating they had formed "for the purpose of aiding in bringing about peace." Within days, the executive committee of the group gathered at the home of William and Helen (Nellie) Taft (future president and First Lady of the United States) to iron out details. There would be a board of directors composed of four Americans and four Filipinos and an advisory board with twelve women from each country. There would be an accountant, a treasurer, and secretaries. Delegates elected from towns across the islands would join the league as well.

The Tafts offered their home as a meeting place for the women because, despite the ongoing and robust activities of the Filipino fighters, William, serving as civilian governor and at the request of President McKinley, was charged with organizing a civilian government. They had brought their three kids—including two-year-old son Charles nicknamed "The Tornado"—from Cincinnati, Ohio, to make their home temporarily in the Philippines. Nellie wasn't shy about taking an energetic role in the work expected by the president, and she became a member of the board of directors of the Women's Peace League. Although the Tafts were disappointed in their options for houses when they arrived in the Philippines, as they gathered at the Taft residence, the women of the Peace League were undoubtedly awed by the grand marble steps leading into the tiled veranda overlooking the spectacular view of the bay through the stunning windows embellished with translucent pearl shells.

Helen "Nellie" Herron Taft in Manila, 1901–1903 LIBRARY OF CONGRESS
PRINTS AND PHOTOGRAPHS DIVISION, WASHINGTON, D.C., LC-DIG-DS-04248.

Although they shared common goals, the Filipino and the American women of the Women's Peace League brought diverse perspectives to the table—likely at least partly influenced by their life experiences. The Americans had come from relatively safe, secure environments in a country where thirty-five years had passed since the last war. Nellie Herron Taft admitted that the Spanish-American War "did not touch us directly." Certainly, when she learned of her husband's new position in the turbulent Philippine islands, she understood that her tranquil life as wife of a federal judge in a midwestern American city would take an unsettling turn. And it did almost immediately as she hastily made plans to store the family's household goods and close the household for an indeterminate stay in the tropical islands. Most worrisome to Nellie was the uncertainty of who would take over her duties as patron of the Cincinnati Orchestra Association. And as the exceptionally popular Tafts began to receive an avalanche of farewell invitations to banquets, teas, and receptions, it fell to Nellie to juggle the functions the couple could realistically fit into their final days in Cincinnati. And while many of the Filipina members in the Peace League were well educated and wealthy, they had lived under Spanish rule for generations and by 1901 had seen firsthand the pain and insecurities inflicted in the fight for independence. Constancia surely was influenced by her writer/activist dad, Pascual Hicaro Poblete, a member of the Katipunan, the secret society that worked for the overthrow of the Spaniards. It would have been unlikely that the Filipino members of the Women's Peace League could say their lives had *not* been directly touched by war.

At one of the first meetings of the Peace League, Constancia introduced a resolution asking the American military forces to release Filipino citizens who had been rounded up and imprisoned. The Filipino women knew many to be innocent people who had never been charged with a crime and were unaware of any justification for their imprisonment. It is unclear what methods were used to authorize resolutions in the Peace League, but Constancia's resolution was never enacted due to opposition by the American members. However, a resolution introduced by the American members calling for the surrender of all Filipino fighters was adopted.

Undeterred, Constancia pulled together a group of several hundred women in Manila and marched through the streets, carrying their children and American flags to the American military headquarters to petition for the release of the prisoners. Military commanders refused the women's request but devised a plan that they thought might interest the Filipinos who were still fighting. The plan called for an even swap—for every rifle surrendered by a fighter, one prisoner would be released.

Despite the efforts of the women of the Peace League, freedom fighters continued to operate across the islands. The women's group persisted in spreading their message: "Enough of war, desolation, and bloodshed. Enough of ruin and death!" They pleaded with the fighters, "Join hands, Filipinos and Americans! . . . for you are brothers, as are all men!"

General Mariano Trias, leading an army of 200 freedom fighters from various mountain hideouts, had been especially troublesome for the Americans as they doggedly carried out uprisings against the American military. The U.S. 39th Infantry encountered Trias and his band of fighters several times, causing multiple deaths and injuries to the Filipinos while experiencing few losses themselves. In February 1901, U.S. forces had raided Trias's camp, destroying barracks and large quantities of supplies; except for three fighters, one of whom was killed and two wounded, the others, including Trias, escaped. Finally, in mid-March, the U.S. War Department reported that General Trias had surrendered to the Americans at San Francisco de Malabon and gave credit to the work of two American military leaders for the defeat of the Filipinos. No mention was made of the role the Women's Peace League may have played.

The women offered their version of General Trias's surrender. In late February, the women decided to do all they could to convince General Trias to give up his fight. They asked permission from American military personnel to intervene, and it was granted. Outlined in a letter to Trias, the women explained the terms of a peaceful and respectful option for surrender. The general would receive thirty pesos for every gun relinquished to the Americans, and he could name a prisoner to be released for every gun turned in. The women chose a man to deliver the letter and soon received the general's response: "If the women will come, I will possibly listen to them."

A small group of women set out for the mountain camp—a long and dangerous journey by boat and carriage. But before they reached their rendezvous point, Trias had decided to surrender. He sent messengers ahead to explain his plan to the Americans. Yes, he would surrender to them—but only after meeting with the women who were already traveling and unaware of his new plan. Armed with white flags, the Filipino freedom fighters led by Trias met the U.S. military personnel, who accepted the general's sword as a gesture of his surrender and allowed him to meet the women of the Peace League. According to the women's account, the occasion turned into a party in which the Americans and the Filipino fighters together entertained the women. The general told the women their letter had been a powerful influence on his decision to surrender. Although he had given his sword to the Americans, he handed over his most prized belt and gold and ivory daggers to the women of the "La Liga Femenina."

"We rejoiced, for we saw the sun through the clouds and the storm had passed its crisis," the women of the Peace League reported.

Within days of Trias's surrender, Filipino leader Emilio Aguinaldo was captured by the Americans. Early in April, Constancia had the great privilege to interview the revered leader and reported that he was greatly conflicted—desirous of peace yet reluctant to give up the dream of Filipino independence. Aguinaldo suggested a conference for the Filipino people to decide the matter. Constancia assured him that "90 percent of the population were in favor of peace."

"Even so, my lot is yet with those upholding the cause of the insurgents," Aguinaldo told Constancia. He asked to confer with General Trias, also held by the Americans, and Trias encouraged the leader to consider the terrible destruction and ruin that had already occurred through war with the Americans and to accept the American victory, which, in time, he did.

By the summer of 1901, with key leaders Trias and Aguinaldo in the hands of the Americans, it became more difficult for the dwindling freedom fighters to remain effective. But the resistance persisted. One by one, the Americans rooted out guerilla fighters and filled the prisons. Two elusive leaders, General Miguel Malvar and Brigadier General Vicente Lukban, fought on into the fall of 1901 and into 1902. And although the women of the Peace League sent letters to both Filipino leaders praising their tenacity in the fight while urging their surrender, the two remained active. Their determination and the Americans' relentless pursuit of the remaining fighters resulted in more destruction and bloodshed. In October, American forces from the 21st Infantry went in pursuit of Malvar and his men, who were entrenched in a mountain camp along a ravine near the village of Talisay. As the exchange of bullets unfolded, most of the Filipino fighters dispersed into a nearby forest, but an American lieutenant and a private were killed. Captain Jas. H. Aldrich, in his condolence letter to Robert Bean's family in Knoxville, Tennessee, wrote, "Your son was killed by the last volley just as he was in the act of climbing up the slope to the insurgents at the head of his company. He was shot through the head by a Mauser bullet which entered just below the right eye." And, maybe to soften the blow for the family, Captain Aldrich ended with "He sank slowly to the ground, murmuring the words, 'Father, Mother,' and expired."

American newspapers reported late in 1901 that the Women's Peace League had received a cablegram from Lukban in Samar in which he indicated he might be ready to end hostilities. It's unclear if the message was sent before or after reports were publicized revealing the Americans' plan of action to "scour and burn the country" as they rounded up Lukban's army "for final extermination." Maybe Lukban believed the menacing reports pronouncing the Americans' plans to force the Filipinos' surrender: "Samar island will be made a desert where birds cannot live."

Lukban was captured in February 1902, and at least one newspaper recognized the lucrative economic impact the end of armed fighting would have on American businesses. A headline in March said it all: "Insurrection at End on the Isle of Samar, Trade Conditions for America Are Promising." The *Lincoln (Neb.) Evening News* explained, "Governor Taft looks for a large increase of American trade in canned goods, cotton and machinery. The outlook, he says, 'is for a considerable income from customs, duties, etc.'" And in April, Miguel Malvar surrendered (by some accounts at the urging of his wife). American newspapers reported his surrender statement: "While I have heretofore been a firm believer in absolute independence for the Filipino people, I am now convinced that I was mistaken. I firmly believe that independence under American protection is best for my people."

It's unclear how influential the Women's Peace League was in bringing about the end of the fighting, but the *Philadelphia Ledger* newspaper offered an opinion: "If the Filipino women are anxious for peace, the Filipino men will not stand out much longer." In July 1902, the Americans declared the war in the Philippines concluded.

Constancia Poblete's work as a reformer and activist continued. This angel of peace remained a guiding force long after the wars ended. In 1909, she launched the first national magazine for women, which "became the mouthpiece of early feminist sentiments." Through its pages, *Filipina* "urged women to speak out and support their favorite political candidates" despite being denied the vote.

JESSIE AGNES SCHLEY: "MEDDLESOME MAID FROM MILWAUKEE"

Growing up in a wealthy Milwaukee, Wisconsin, family Jessie Schley had always been an enigma to other young women her age. Her rich friends reveled in the glitter and glam of the lively social scene in the city. But Jessie wanted none of it. She preferred to work among the "poorest and unfortunate." While her friends spent their days shopping at the Gunther department store for fur hats and capes, Jessie worked at a community center, caring for children whose mothers were "compelled to work for a living." During the economic depression following the Panic of 1893, as wealthy society women experienced little disruption in their lives, continuing to furnish their homes with china, cut glass, and etchings, Jessie led efforts to establish soup houses in Milwaukee.

But in the summer of 1898, Jessie ventured far beyond the city of Milwaukee, and she found herself thrust into the international arena. Before she was finished with her adventures, generals, European royalty, ambassadors, and government officials in Spain and the United States were well aware of the movements and opinions of this woman from the American heartland. It was Jessie's unpopular ideas about war that drew attention to her. She didn't like war and had no compunction about stating her opinion. With the United States newly entered into war with Spain, Jessie couldn't keep quiet.

Jessie Schley *LOS ANGELES HERALD,*
OCTOBER 2, 1898.

"Spartan women used to urge their men to war. It is for American women to urge their men to peace," Jessie explained when asked about her resistance to the Spanish-American War. She intended to do her part to bring about world peace, but her questionable sentiments prompted newspapers across the country to run stories about the "meddlesome maid from Milwaukee." The more charitable labeled her "curious" and "odd." Some excused her bizarre behavior as the rantings of a "hysterical young woman." The more outrageous accusations painted Jessie as a traitor.

When war broke out between Spain and the United States in April 1898, Jessie had been studying art in Europe. "I feel terribly about this war," Jessie wrote her parents back home in Milwaukee. As her strong antiwar, peace-at-all-costs feelings converged with her belief that it was up to women to act in the name of peace, she vowed to set up an organization of women to "protest publicly against" the conflict between Spain and the United States. She sprang into action and by July had established the Women's International League for Peace. Within three weeks, Jessie claimed membership had soared to 3,000. The group held a peace convention in Paris, attended by five European peace organizations. It was here that Jessie was chosen to travel to Madrid to implore Queen Regent Maria Cristina of Spain to sue for peace immediately.

"I was elected a committee of one to go to Madrid and inform the queen regent and Señor Sagasta that they were whipped," Jessie said. (Práxedes Mateo Sagasta was the Spanish prime minister.)

By July 22, Jessie was in the Spanish capital. Word spread quickly about this "self-appointed dove of peace" from the middle of America.

Newspapers around the world carried articles about Jessie. The *New York Times* was not impressed, calling Jessie "the delegate from nobody." The *Philadelphia Inquirer* reported that the deeds of this "hysterical young woman" were "criminal." A German newspaper, *Der Deutsche Correspondent*, insisted the troublesome American was simply a "rebellious girl" who had committed a most inappropriate transgression—disobeying her father.

Jessie was forty-six years old at the time—hardly a girl or a disobedient child. Still, reports began to circulate indicating Jessie had made the trip to Madrid against the wishes of her father, Charles Schley. Her escapades had become an embarrassment for the Schley family. Commodore Winfield Scott Schley, commander of the U.S. naval forces at the Battle of Santiago in Cuba, was a cousin of Charles Schley. It didn't look good—a female cousin leading an antiwar group topped off with her gutsiness in seeking a meeting with the enemy.

A New York newspaper published a letter from Charles in which he stated, "I do not endorse her course in regard to this. She will come home immediately."

However, Jessie, the "Joan d'Arc of the peace cause," had no intention of returning to Milwaukee until she had completed her mission. Armed with a document outlining a path for peace, Jessie was determined to meet with Spain's cabinet members as well as the queen. And while some viewed Jessie's undertaking a "mission of mercy" and an effort to "save life rather than killing and destroying," others called it criminal. They went so far as to accuse her of treason—violating a federal statute specifying that any American citizen who "carries on any verbal or written correspondence . . . with any foreign government . . . with an intent to influence the conduct of any foreign government" was subject to a fine of "not more than five thousand dollars and imprisoned not more than three years."

As reports of Jessie's maneuvers in Europe began to circulate, newspaper publishers printed stories with outrageous details of her quest for peace. The *Kansas City Journal* predicted on July 26 that "neither the queen regent nor any responsible personage will receive her." The *Chicago Tribune* dramatically claimed she was "practically ordered out of the country." A headline in the *Asheville (N.C.) Citizen-Times* stated, "Jessie Schley's

Mission: She Has Failed and Must Leave Madrid." But other reports challenged some of the negative press. Charles Schley disputed the *New York World* story about his demand that his daughter return home. "I had never written a letter in connection with this matter," he said. It was an "audacious forgery," he charged. The Committee of the Universal Peace Union berated the newspaper: "It shows how the press of the day will invent and circulate falsehoods for the sake of selling the papers."

In early August, the *Chicago Tribune* offered a less gloomy version of Jessie's accomplishments. By means of a "special cable" to the paper, the *Tribune* had learned that despite previous reports, Jessie indeed met with Queen Regent Maria Cristina, who "received her kindly, talked to her, and encouraged her." Jessie presented the queen a document that offered suggestions for peace. According to the report, the queen told Jessie, "I am deeply touched by these beautiful resolutions in favor of peace; but I am a constitutional sovereign, and I cannot take the initiative in any matter without my Minister." The queen suggested Jessie visit with her secretary of state, Duke Almodovar del Rio, to present the petition to him as well. According to reports, Jessie succeeded in meeting the duke, who reinforced his support through a letter: "The generosity and energy which have prompted you to make this long excursion . . . convinces me that you will be a powerful and beneficent influence in the United States."

For weeks, newspapers around the world had carried articles about Jessie's adventures, but many contained conflicting and inaccurate information. Finally, Jessie offered her own version of her experiences in Madrid. She composed a letter printed by newspapers across the world and addressed to "The American Press" in which she claimed victory. "We women, especially we American women, made peace between Spain and our country," she wrote. And while it remained unclear from Jessie's account that she met with the Spanish queen, she provided details of her movements and accomplishments. She indicated that on her arrival on July 22, she immediately began "visiting and conferring" with "prominent officials." On July 23, Duke Almodovar del Rio asked her to "put in writing the matter I desired to convey to him," which she did on July 25. According to Jessie, she read in a local newspaper that the queen's cabinet—including the duke—met and discussed her "communication."

Jessie went on to report that on July 27, she was "hurried out of Madrid" when officials feared a riot against her. And she quoted from a letter she claimed to have received from the duke on the afternoon of her departure: "Your letter of yesterday has received my fullest attention and had preference to my other pressing business."

Jessie conceded that her interaction with Spanish officials was only partially responsible for Spain ending the conflict with America. She noted that Spain had intended to continue to fight in Cuba and the Philippines but that her document had played a pivotal role in their decision to end the war. "It was only a straw, but still 'the straw that broke the camel's back,'" Jessie wrote about her visit. And in her letter to the press, Jessie gave some hints about the content of her negotiations with Spanish officials. She admitted to calling the U.S. involvement in the conflict "foolhardy." She stated that she advised the Spaniards in negotiating a peace settlement, suggesting they turn over one or two Cuban coal stations to the United States as a peace offering. "Strictly speaking," Jessie wrote, "we should not take even that, as we had begun the war 'in the name of humanity.'" Later, Jessie admitted that perhaps she'd been too "blunt" in calling the United States "foolhardy." But the actions of her government at the end of the conflict convinced her that her original statement had been accurate. "I was certain my country would act honorably," Jessie wrote, "so you may imagine my mortification and chagrin to find we are trying to grab all we can." Jessie closed her letter admitting that she expected to be the recipient of "a storm of abuse" for her opinions. But she was resolute in defending her patriotism. There was no one "who has made greater sacrifices to maintain the honor of our grand country," Jessie wrote in describing herself.

While Jessie received a great deal of attention for her efforts in Spain, she also became a sensation for her activities in Cuba. After leaving Madrid, she sailed to Havana on the steamer *Lafayette*. Arriving in early September, she intended to help with relief work there. Her work running soup houses in Milwaukee would serve her well in Cuba, where it was reported that soup kitchens in one city served more than 1,000 rations daily. A newspaper claimed those efforts were instrumental in removing beggars "who littered the streets." However, relief work was delayed when a cargo transport from America was held up with customs problems in the port of Havana. The *Comal* was laden with 2,000 tons of rations for the people of Cuba. But controversy about who would pay duty on the contents prevented the unloading and distribution of the badly needed resources. In addition, there was a disagreement about who would distribute the contents. The Americans insisted that Red Cross personnel should take on the distribution responsibility. However, some Cuban officials believed they should oversee the work of distribution. That led to accusations by the Americans that some unscrupulous Cubans merely "wanted their pound of flesh," leaving those Cuban people who needed the supplies empty-handed.

Only days after her arrival in Cuba, Jessie heard about this latest injustice and knew she had to take control of the problem. It didn't mean her injection into the situation was any more welcome than her work in the peace process in Spain had been. By now, Jessie had a reputation as a "celebrity"; however, the title did not afford her any special treatment. When she visited customs agents to negotiate a solution to the duty payment and distribution problems of the supplies on the *Comal*, she was met with skepticism. Criticized for being a "monomaniac," a person suffering from an "excessive concentration on a single object or idea" according to *Merriam-Webster*, her credibility was also called into question—because of her *appearance*. "Instead of being the slim, fair young girl of twenty that her photograph showed, she is a rather stout woman of about forty-five, with hair slightly gray," a newspaper decried.

When officials questioned her ability to resolve the problems, Jessie reminded them, "You know I brought about peace." And although they refused to allow Jessie to take any part in resolving the distribution issue, the Cubans told her to do what she could to have the duty removed. They recommended she start with the secretary of the treasury, Marquis Rafael Montoro. It was reported Jessie "went away and made all sail" for Mr. Montoro in an attempt to "argue him into releasing that duty." And although the duty was eventually lifted, it's unclear that Jessie had anything to do with it. The *Evening Star* newspaper reported that she may have. The paper indicated that Montoro, out of desperation to rid himself of this monomaniacal American woman, finally said, "If you'll just quit, I'll take off that duty."

Late in September 1898, Jessie returned to her home in Milwaukee. The *Chicago Daily Tribune* reported the "self-appointed dove of peace" was "about through with her fluttering." The paper predicted she would "retire to the sylvan shades of Milwaukee to recuperate and count her laurels." By the first days of October, it was clear the *Tribune* was wrong about Jessie. In an interview for a local paper, she indicated she planned to continue her work as a peace advocate. She said she would work to hold America to its word in terms of its postwar treatment of Cuba.

"This government of the United States is in honor bound to give them a trial at self-government, after it has promised it to them, else we will disgrace ourselves in the eyes of the civilized world, and history will scorn us," Jessie promised.

In addition to her political activism, after her return from Cuba, Jessie became a prominent figure in the art community in Milwaukee. When she put out a call for a woman with "powdered cheeks and flashy attire" to model for her portrait of Mary Magdalene, the fallen woman of Bible fame, she said, "I am looking for a model who must be beautiful, a blonde, and bad." She asked the local police to help identify a woman who would fit her description (most likely the "bad" characteristic), and when they declined, she was forced to continue her quest for a model through other channels. She drew the ire of the Society of Milwaukee Artists when she publicly criticized a jury of members for refusing to include two of her paintings in an upcoming Chicago art exhibition. Ultimately, she was expelled from the Society of Milwaukee Artists when they voted to rescind her membership for her efforts to "discredit the society in public opinion."

5

War Correspondents
"The Swish of Journalistic Petticoats"

"I was determined to go to war. . . . So I hurried to New York and tried to get an appointment as correspondent from some of the magazines there, but none of them would send me. They said it was no sort of work for a woman and I couldn't possibly do it." After multiple rejections, including one publisher who said her request was "positively absurd and foolhardy," Elsie Reasoner made one more attempt to get to Cuba to report on the war, and this time she was successful. "After all the others, I went to *McClure's*. The outlook was not promising for my getting there, I must confess; but I was bound to go. When I saw Mr. McClure and made my proposition to him, he refused point blank to send me. 'Why it's foolish. You can't get through; and even if you should, you might not come back alive. I won't take responsibility. But if you do go, I'll be glad to take whatever you write.'"

Fortunately for American newspaper and magazine readers, Elsie found her way to Cuba and delivered in-depth narratives of what she witnessed. Landing with Clara Barton and her Red Cross workers on the ship *State of Texas*, Elsie described her arrival: "As the 'State of Texas' steamed into port, we sighted on our starboard bow four gray, sinister battleships. . . . Massive cruisers and blunt-nosed torpedo boats were about us." Elsie made her way to Siboney, where Americans and Spaniards clashed in the first days of the war. "Soon after the soldiers had faced fire, word was received that boys of Uncle Sam had been fighting on empty stomachs, and that there was little prospect of their getting anything to eat unless

Elsie Reasoner *TRAVEL: AN ILLUSTRATED MONTHLY MAGAZINE*, 1896, P. 308.

the army rations, which were still where they were thrown from the landing place, were carried over the rough roads to them," Elsie wrote. Elsie described Clara's response: "Quickly and skillfully she had the supplies that had been transferred from the Red Cross ships to the land loaded on carts drawn by mules and sent to the men." From the battle-fields, Elsie wrote, "I was present at a number of skirmishes; near enough to the firing line to hear the music of the Mausers and the crack of the rifles our boys carried. Indeed, I got just as close to the firing line as the command-ing officers would permit me to go." When Elsie returned to the United States and someone asked about her intense interest in going to the war in Cuba, she recalled a Civil War general: "I had read what General Sherman said, that 'war is hell,' and I was seized with a desire to investigate on my own account, and see if he really knew what he was talking about." And, based on her firsthand experiences, Elsie had drawn her own conclusion about Sherman's "war is hell" statement: "I was near enough to see some of the horrors of war, and to realize that doubtless General Sherman had it about right."

Elsie was one of numerous women who reported from war zones in Cuba and the Philippines. Teresa Dean wrote for *Frank Leslie's Weekly* and for the magazine *Town Topics* under the pen name "The Widow." In July 1898, she wrote from the U.S. Army training camp at Chickamauga, Georgia, where she enjoyed a meal with some soldiers from Illinois: "I was not exactly invited, but it was not my fault; I did all that I could to get an invitation, and then, failing, invited myself." She concluded that the stew the men were served was "not bad," and she reported that the men were in need of these supplies: towels, soap, handkerchiefs, safety pins, black shoelaces, sewing needles, and pajamas. Later, in August, Teresa reported from Fortress Monroe, where wounded and sick soldiers were being treated. She wrote about a young soldier whose body was being buried at the post cemetery: "The hearse, draped with flags, stood outside. A military band and a company of artillery were there as an escort. Passing through the hall were the soldier pall-bearers. . . . There were no relatives, no tears. . . . A little later I could hear the three volleys fired over the grave. The soldier had committed suicide."

Kate Masterson may have snagged one of the biggest scoops of the war in Cuba when she interviewed the infamous Spanish General Valeriano Weyler, otherwise known as "The Butcher." Masterson refused to sugarcoat her questions for the general: "In the United States an impression prevails that your edict shutting out newspaper correspondents from the field is only to conceal cruelties perpetrated upon the insurgent prisoners."

"I have shut out the Spanish and Cuban papers from the field, as well as the Americans," Weyler replied. "They are a nuisance."

"Then I can deny the stories that have been published as to your being cruel?" Kate asked.

"Some of them are true, and some are not. War is war. You cannot make it otherwise, try as you will," Weyler replied.

Kate's articles covered an array of topics—housekeeping practices on the American warship the *Terror*, where sailors, in the absence of women, were responsible for cooking and cleaning, and conditions at a Cuban dynamite factory where a guard at the entrance warned, "Well, drive in; but be careful, or you may be taken out on a shovel." When she inquired about the peculiar layout of the grounds—multiple small structures with noticeably wide gaps between buildings—the manager explained, "We don't want to blow up too many people at one time. That would put our orders back." Her reporting on Cuban children joining their parents in the fight to dislodge the Spaniards from their island must have shocked some readers. "There is no more pathetic feature in the war between Cuba and Spain than the actual presence of children upon the battlefield," Kate wrote. "There are little ones in the insurgent camps today whose playthings

Margherita Arlina Hamm SCHOMBURG
CENTER FOR RESEARCH IN BLACK CULTURE,
JEAN BLACKWELL HUTSON RESEARCH AND
REFERENCE DIVISION, NEW YORK PUBLIC
LIBRARY DIGITAL COLLECTIONS, CATALOG ID
B11718203.

are cartridge shells, whose lullaby is the trumpet call and the noise of battle. Some of them die on the field, where they march beside their fathers with tiny hands clasping some implement of war. Others are stricken down with machetes or trampled upon by horses' hoofs in the wild charges of the insurgent army."

Margherita Arlina Hamm was one of the most prolific writers during the Spanish-American War and the Philippine-American War eras. Her articles appeared in newspapers and magazines throughout the United States, and her books reflected popular topics of the time: *America's New Possessions and Spheres of Influence, Dewey, the Defender: A Life Sketch of America's Great Admiral,* and *Greater America: Heroes, Battles, Camps, Dewey Islands, Cuba, Porto Rico.* Her photographs were featured in *Photographic Views of Our New Possessions,* published in 1898. In a nod to her support of the freedom fighters' cause, she dedicated her book *Manila and the Philippines* to Filipino leaders José Rizal and Emilio Aguinaldo.

Margherita fulfilled dual roles in going to Cuba in the summer of 1898—a representative of the New York National Guard Women's Auxiliary and a war correspondent. In her Women's Auxiliary role, she assessed needs of American service members in Cuba—large safety pins to repair suspenders and belts and to fasten bandages, mosquito netting for hospital beds, and needles to reattach buttons on their uniforms. She emphasized the need for large needles rather than smaller ones: "The average man cannot thread them; they simply draw blood and profanity." She reminded readers that the men appreciated letters from home—preferably lighthearted ones that would uplift homesick soldiers. She offered an example—a soldier had received a letter from a family member recounting the story of a little boy whose dog had died after suffering from mange. The boy insisted on a proper funeral for his beloved pet, and as the body was lowered into its grave, the boy was heard to say, "Remember the mange," a play on words related to the popular chant at the time "Remember the Maine"—the sinking of the USS *Maine*, which sparked the Spanish-American War. She recognized early on that America's new possessions were economic assets, writing that the Philippines, with its abundance of rich natural resources, would provide lucrative commercial prospects. "The conclusion is that very soon the archipelago will be the most wonderful scene of energy and industry the history of commerce has ever known," she wrote. And writing from Puerto Rico, Margherita described economic opportunities there: "Our troops were no sooner landed when the missionaries of progress appeared upon the scene in the shape of promoters, speculators, brokers, agents and adventurers." Examples are the American businessman who sold American flags to locals for five times their value after convincing reluctant buyers that American officials would protect only those who displayed American flags and the Wisconsin investor who came to Puerto Rico to erect a monument and "drop a tear upon the graves of two Wisconsin chums" killed in battle on the island. "He may have dropped a tear, and he may at some time put up a monument, but he certainly bought up the best mineral spring on the island, which burst from the earth a short distance from where the Wisconsin braves made their last flight," Margherita wrote.

Readers of newspapers and magazines during the wars in Cuba and the Philippines were often surprised to see female bylines attached to articles. Headlines boasted about the activities of female journalists: "Plucky Woman War Correspondent" and "The First Woman War Correspondent to Go to the Front." Those women who were bold enough and resolute enough to become wartime correspondents faced more than a few challenges as they fought for their rights as journalists. "The swish of the journalistic petticoat," as one male correspondent wrote, was also unnerving to male journalists. "Time was when the war correspondent had only men to contend against, men—and censors. But with the advent of woman came sorrow," he wrote. He recalled an encounter he had with a Canadian war correspondent, Kathleen Blake Watkins, in the early days of the Spanish-American War as impatient journalists waited in Florida for transportation to Cuba. "A lady war correspondent! The idea was too comic. We could not believe it," the male correspondent remembered. His exchange with the woman should have caused him to reconsider his skepticism.

"And so you are thinking of going along to Cuba with us?"

"Oh, yes, I know what you think; you think it is ridiculous, my being here; that's the worst of being a woman. But just let me tell you. I'm going through to Cuba, and not all the old Generals in the old army are going to stop me."

Any reporter armed with that spirit of determination certainly could pose intimidating competition for headlines if she ever reached the war zone. And Kathleen Blake Watkins did—along with other dogged female journalists.

ANNA NORTHEND BENJAMIN: DELIGHTED BY DANGER

Anna Northend Benjamin wrote from Tampa, Florida, in June 1898 about conditions on the military transports preparing to carry American soldiers and animals to the conflict in Cuba: "The quarters of the mules are as uncomfortable as those of the men. I do not know which to pity most. Eight hundred of the poor creatures are to be stowed away on board." As a correspondent for *Frank Leslie's Weekly* magazine, the adventurous twenty-three-year-old writer, box camera slung across her shoulder, had arrived in Tampa, hoping to hitch a ride on one of those transports to the war zone on the island less than 100 miles away. Things didn't develop as she planned when General William Shafter of the U.S. Army refused her space on board due to the policy forbidding women on military transports.

The travel delay gave the ambitious journalist an opportunity to seek out stories at the military camps in the city. Although she couldn't travel on the transports, she was permitted to tour the sleeping quarters where bunks were stacked "like the tenement lodging-house double deckers"

Mules Being Loaded for Cuba at Tampa, Florida STROHMEYER & WYMAN, UNDERWOOD & UNDERWOOD, CA. 1898, LIBRARY OF CONGRESS PRINTS AND PHOTOGRAPHS DIVISION, WASHINGTON, D.C., LC-USZ62-92731.

except that they were "triple-deckers." They allowed six men to occupy a space about five by six feet—cozy quarters with only about two feet of passage space between each row. She noted that many were located near the engine, making for extremely hot sleeping conditions.

When she began hearing stories about shortages of rations for the men, Anna decided to investigate. "Haven't you been given any rations to-day?" she asked a soldier from New York. "Oh, we had some crackers that ought to be used for paving-stones, coffee that you could hardly call by that name, and some fearful beef!" the soldier replied. When the Rough Riders arrived in Tampa from Texas, Anna took the opportunity to ask them about the rations they had been supplied by Uncle Sam for their journey. They complained they had rations enough for two days, but the trip was a four-day jaunt. "We stole pigs and chickens and everything we could lay our hands on," one of Teddy Roosevelt's men admitted. Their notoriety was so renowned that "their fame spread before them," and when they reached Tampa, their commanders were asked to contain the Rough Riders within the army camp. According to Anna's reporting, Teddy Roosevelt's men had rightfully earned the nickname "Teddy's Terrors" for their outrageous behavior. She wasn't the first or last to attach the label to Roosevelt's men. But it was notable that the term stuck even before the Rough Riders had left the United States for their legendary adventures in Cuba.

Anna ventured from Tampa to Key West as she waited for transportation to Cuba. Her article written on July 7 from Key West described in vivid detail the arrival of a troop transport, the *Iroquois*, with wounded from the early skirmishes in Cuba. "Most of them could walk or hobble, and these were marched to the street-cars in squads and driven to the hospital," she wrote about the men. "Some of them walked all the distance." As the bedraggled men in their bloodstained uniforms walked through the streets, crowds watched in silence. "There are some emotions which cannot be expressed in cheers," Anna wrote. "The other ships containing wounded men already on the way from Santiago are to be turned aside to Tampa. There are only ninety extra beds here now, and they would hardly accommodate the four or five hundred desperately wounded who are on the ships," she wrote.

Determined to get to the war, Anna located a coal collier about to leave for Cuba and pressed the captain to accommodate her. He told Anna it wasn't possible, as his vessel had been chartered by the U.S. government to carry coal. "Were the cabins under charter too?" Anna asked. He admitted there wasn't a word in his government contract about the cabins, and Anna was on her way to Cuba on the slow-moving, dirty collier.

Arriving at Guantanamo Bay—held by the Americans after marines had defeated the Spanish there three weeks before—she penned another article on July 15 for the readers of *Leslie's Weekly*. "It is a fine harbor, and just what we want for coaling and repairing, so the United States flag flutters high up on the hill in the midst of the camp of the marines, and we make ourselves very much at home," she wrote in her article titled "A Woman's Point of View." From the harbor, she could see the American marines' camp on a hilltop and a Cuban refugee tent camp nestled at the bottom of the hill. Despite the American victory, thousands of Spanish troops remained in the area but posed little threat; many interacted with the Americans conversing in a combination of Spanish and English. The next day, she anticipated her move to Santiago. "The last mines are being fished up out of Santiago harbor, and tomorrow, probably, our great battleships will steam in and take possession," she wrote. That afternoon, Anna left on the *Aransas*, a government transport loaded with freight, horses, and mules for Siboney and Santiago. She wrote from Siboney, "It is literally the calm here after the storm. There is plenty of work ahead, but no more fighting in this part of the country." The *Aransas* spent a few days waiting for orders—frustrating for Anna and her fellow writers—described by one observer as "woe-begone war correspondents, ragged and tired and ill, with their extra clothes, if they had any, tied up in a poncho or a blanket." Cheers went up when the transport finally received orders to ship out to Santiago. *Leslie's Weekly* published Anna's article written on July 19, only days after the Americans had secured the city of Santiago. "We glided into the glassy water of the large inland harbor—and the city of Santiago lay before us," Anna wrote. But when they arrived, word spread among the correspondents that General Shafter had issued orders to them—anyone who ventured off the ship and into Santiago would be shot. And that deterred the correspondents but only for a short time. "We had been coming to the conclusion that if we left the ship nobody would shoot us, and we were now at the point where we did not care if they did, if we could see the city first," Anna wrote. "So we simply left the ship in twos and threes and marched on the town."

She offered a stark scene of life in the city, where the residents had been living under Spanish occupation with dwindling amounts of food and water triggered by an American blockade. Anna reported the Cuban residents were "on the brink of starvation," resorting to eating horse meat. American correspondents could get a meal at the Café Venus for an astronomical price of $14. However, Anna wrote, "the wealthiest citizens could not manufacture food with their gold and silver." She described little Cuban boys, many dressed in rags, who greeted the Americans and showed less interest in the money tossed at them than precious bread and hardtack. Refugees who had left the city before the siege were beginning to return—"a surging mass of humanity," according to Anna. The American Red Cross ship *State of Texas* was unloading desperately needed supplies, and Cuban families streamed to the distribution site. Most of the defeated Spanish army was confined in a camp outside the city; however, some roamed freely in Santiago, interacting with the Americans through Spanish and English supplemented with gestures. Their guns had been confiscated, but some of the Spaniards were selling their machetes to American souvenir hunters for as much as $6. Anna purchased one herself from a Spanish soldier who seemed amused that she would spend money for such an item. Although they were rusty and dented, many sported bone or silver handles. Anna ventured outside the city to explore the surrounding battlefield and picked up a bag of Mauser cartridges from a box lying on the ground near the Spanish trenches. "Standing there on a hill-top," she wrote, "one may read the tragedy."

Leaving for the United States on July 30 on the *Aransas*, Anna helped nurse sick and wounded soldiers on the transport. Over the next months, she embarked on a lecture tour, giving talks about her experiences punctuated with photographs she had captured. She attracted crowds all along the northeast part of the United States. By June 1899, Anna was on her way to the Philippines to cover the fighting between the Filipinos and their new American occupiers for the *New-York Tribune* and the *San Francisco Chronicle*. This time, she had somehow convinced the government to permit her to travel on a military transport, the *Sheridan*, with 2,000 troops. Her article describing life aboard the vessel was filled with anecdotes and interesting details. There were the three little stowaways discovered in the depths of the ship shortly after leaving the port of San Francisco—they were put to work washing dishes after spending a few hours in the brig. (The oldest was ultimately hired as a crew member for $5 a month.) Again, she focused on the troops' sleeping quarters—heavy canvas stretched over iron tubing three tiers high, causing most men to sleep on the deck or anywhere other than those close quarters, including atop the tables in the mess. And there were the amusing tug-of-war competitions raging on the deck. When the *Sheridan* reached Honolulu for coaling, some of the men went ashore to purchase musical instruments thanks to donations from the ship's officers. From Hawaii to the Philippines, there were nightly band concerts. The only glitch was that the band members were treated to beer and cigars during intermission—much to the dismay of the troops in the audience who were denied these luxuries.

Anna's articles from the Philippines covered a variety of topics. On August 14, she reported the Filipino fighters had been "tracked and beaten" within a radius of forty miles of Manila. Writing that many of the American troops were impatient with their generals, who were viewed as too cautious in their pursuit of the Filipinos, Anna wrote that more

Anna Northend Benjamin *FRANK LESLIE'S POPULAR MONTHLY,* SEPTEMBER 1899.

troops were needed to put down the Filipino fighters, whom she described as "in every way inferior to us." She blamed anti-expansionists in America for strengthening the resolve of the Filipino independence advocates. Her writings were frequently insensitive and racist—"Filipinos at times seem much like monkeys," and "Concentration for any length of time is not a national characteristic." Rather than showing appreciation for the backbreaking task of loading coal onto the American ships, she ridiculed the work of the Chinese workers, or "coolies," while complaining about the "native jabbering which drives you to place your hands over your ears."

In September, Anna decided to see a little of the Philippine countryside outside Manila and took a train north to Dagupan about 130 miles. "I was the only woman there, and rather expected to be put off, but I got through the lines," she said. Newspapers reported an attack by Filipino fighters who derailed the cars and killed two U.S. soldiers. Anna escaped unharmed. "I was forced to make part of the trip in Army wagons, burned flat cars and cattle cars. But it was a great experience, and I don't regret it," she said. In December, she reported on the death of Captain Bogardus Eldridge of the 14th Infantry, who had been killed at a battle at the town of Bacoor. She wrote that the death was a reminder for everyone who had become complacent about the situation in the Philippines that "Filipino bullets can kill and can send a heartache to America, more than ten thousand miles away."

Later, when Anna recalled receiving her coveted assignment from *Leslie's Weekly* to cover the war as a "full-fledged war correspondent," she admitted, "It was a dangerous honor, but one that filled me with delight."

MURIEL BAILEY: A WOMAN WHO KNEW SOMETHING ABOUT WAR

It seems strange that the Filipinos have retained any faith in humanity—that there is not more bitterness and fear and hatred and treachery in their hearts. Small wonder that they spring up when the hand of oppression is removed and feel mighty enough to rule the world!—
"At Home with Aguinaldo," Muriel Bailey, 1899

"Within even a savage is born an undefined idea of liberty, and that is what has been awakened in the Filipinos in the last few years," Filipino leader Emilio Aguinaldo cautioned American reporter Muriel Bailey during her interview with the man who had fought for years for Filipino independence. It was an uncertain but critical time in Philippine–American relations. Together, the Americans and Filipinos had succeeded in defeating the Spaniards—signifying for the Filipinos the end of 400 years of Spanish occupation. The peace treaty between the United States and Spain, signed on December 10, 1898, had resulted in the United States acquiring the Philippines. Many Filipinos, including Aguinaldo, believed it was time for self-government. At the time of the interview (likely in the final days of December 1898 or sometime in January 1899), Aguinaldo and Muriel, like the rest of the world, wondered what the United States intended in terms of dealing with the newly acquired islands and its inhabitants. And the world anxiously watched Aguinaldo, speculating about *his* intentions for his homeland. The interview took place at

Aguinaldo's headquarters in Malolos, a two-hour train trip from Manila for Muriel. From the train station in Malolos, she traveled in an oxcart to Aguinaldo's home, along the way witnessing remnants of Spanish rule—clusters of crude huts where Filipino farm families had been moved and detained as the Spanish confiscated their lands—a "shining example of the reconcentrado rule," according to Muriel.

Arriving at Aguinaldo's house, she described the leader as "short and slender—not handsome even in the Oriental type; but his narrow eyes are very brilliant, and his manner is easy and his air deliberate." She had been invited to share a meal with him and a group of his generals. When Muriel complimented her host, telling him she found the Philippines a beautiful country, he remarked, "It could be made so. It would be the richest country in the world with proper cultivation. You Americans understand that. We have been sadly handicapped." He explained how the Spaniards had forced Filipino farmers into villages where they lived in confined areas (*reconcentrados*) but were allowed to travel the five miles or so to their farms to work the soil—the reconcentration policy in which people were forced to leave their homes in the countryside and crowded into designated towns where they could neither feed themselves nor expect the government to feed them, evidenced by Muriel on her trip from the train station.[7] But they had to pay tolls to enter and exit the village, eating up two-thirds of their profits. Many eventually grew tired of the arrangement and gave up the land to the Spaniards. Throughout the meal, Aguinaldo, who ate little and consumed no alcohol, enlightened the American reporter, complaining that the Spaniards had treated his fellow Filipinos as slaves, denying them education, self-government, and basic human rights. Muriel challenged the leader, who in December 1898 had resigned as president of the new Filipino government that had been established to replace Spanish rule: "And you, having led them so far, are resigning them?"

"No, I have resigned as President, but that is because they will not agree to the terms of the Americans," nodding to the generals, who would

---

7. The reconcentration policy was started by the Spaniards in Cuba and the Philippines and continued under American occupation in the Philippines.

consider nothing short of "absolute independence," Aguinaldo said. "I do not agree with them, and therefore I resign."

And when he left the room for a few minutes to get his wife and mother, Muriel observed "nothing but sullen silence" among the men who remained with her. After meeting the women and enjoying an afternoon of music, eating, and drinking, Muriel was escorted by Aguinaldo himself in his personal carriage to the train station. On returning to Manila, she learned of skirmishes that day in outposts where an American sentry had been wounded by a Filipino soldier. Muriel mused that this had occurred "as I sat in Aguinaldo's palace," and "I have been wondering how much of this Aguinaldo knew!"

By early February, the world no longer wondered about Filipino–American relations, as the Filipinos made it clear that they would resist the Americans' plan for occupation of their land. And the Americans made it clear that they would quash the Filipinos' attempts at independence. Aguinaldo and his freedom fighters were now targets of American bullets, and they returned the fire. Muriel was ready to see the fight firsthand and to relate to the American people in news articles the scenes she witnessed on the battlefields.

"It does make one's blood boil to see a strong, manly fellow crossing the way in the full light of the sun, whistling oftentimes and taking firm, free steps—a picture of health and manliness—and then to see him fall suddenly and lie still, all his strength gone in a breath. You can't help wanting to fight after that, even if you're a woman," Muriel wrote for the *San Francisco Examiner*. "It fills you with a hatred and longing for revenge that is almost an exaltation. It carries you into the clouds and makes you forget danger and death in desire." Her perspective from the battlefield, first at Caloocan on February 4–5 and again on February 22–24, appeared in American newspapers across the country—chilling words that certainly triggered anguish for families with loved ones fighting in the Philippines.

"I have seen men die, I have watched the surge of battle," she wrote in her article titled "A Woman's Picture of the Battle of Caloocan." "I have heard the crash of bursting shells. I have ducked my head at the menace of the eager Mauser ball. I have felt the sullen murder desire—the shriek of the soul for revenge. But apprehension of some nameless, insistent horror is the worst of battle and siege."

Describing her five-mile ride from Manila to Caloocan in a carriage, she wrote, "We carried our pistols in our hands that night as we drove, and many a bullet sung as it sped past to do damage to something further on." Muriel described the scenes along the route to Caloocan. Soldiers from Montana looking "grim and business like" as they leaned on their guns, a Colorado battalion waiting for action, and the signal corps stretching telegraph lines. "And then I knew I was in the presence of the enemy. The thought sent little tremors up and down my back." Passing American entrenchments formed from piles of earth and sandbags, from hilltops she spotted the enemy's trenches and witnessed valley after valley of Mauser and Springfield fire. "Six miles of firing lines between myself and the bay, and we were getting it on two sides," she wrote.

She marveled at the courage of the American soldiers. At the end of her first experience on the battlefield, Muriel approached wounded soldiers being carried on litters to the field hospital. "They say that women have no place in battle, but they may be allowed to speak to the wounded," she wrote. She met a lieutenant colonel who recalled his encounter with the enemy: "It was a Mauser. Caught me in the left side and took a piece of my lung and went out at the back. Nothing to speak of. I'm all right." Then she came on a fellow whose leg had been splintered. He smoked a cigar and joked with the hospital men who carried him: "Not dead yet. But I'm sorry it isn't my arm so that I could go back again."

Recalling the eventful night, she wrote, "I ducked my head with the rest when the bullets went by; discussed the already wounded and the possibility of getting hit myself; wished urgently for daylight, so that the fight with the 'niggers' might be begun in good earnest, hoped for the enemy's slaughter with right good will, and did not discover until I started home that I had put on a dark gown and forgotten to change a pair of white slippers when I started to war."[8]

---

8. Muriel used the term "nigger," which was in line with a "racist ideology in which white Americans characterized Filipinos as they did African-Americans: as inferior, inept, and even subhuman," according to Scot Ngozi-Brown in his article "African-American Soldiers and Filipinos: Racial Imperialism, Jim Crow and Social Relations." E. San Juan Jr., in "An African American Soldier in the

Muriel returned to a hotel in town for a short respite. The next morning, she directed her driver to move in the direction of the beach, where she could see the crew and gunners on an American battleship and observed "the errands of destruction" caused by their shelling. Meanwhile, the infantry fire from both sides continued relentlessly. She watched the 4th Infantry and soldiers from North Dakota, California, and Kansas engage in heavy battle before her eyes. "I could not realize that we were all facing death in that very spot or that my eyes were witnessing deeds of courage as great as any history has recorded. It began to be horribly real," she wrote.

The *San Francisco Examiner* ran a story from Muriel with the dateline "In the Trenches before Caloocan, February 18," in which she chronicled events in two days of fighting, again near Caloocan: "The fortune of war has changed the once green wood into a brown patch with green edges. The strong, upright trees are pierced by shells, the bamboos are cut with bullets and the broad banana leaves are torn and twisted and the large bunches of luscious fruit are cooked black."

She watched as soldiers from Pennsylvania, Montana, Kansas, and Utah held their positions against the enemy. She described Mauser bullets grazing past, falling like hail as hundreds of American heads ducked simultaneously. At night during a pause in the fighting, men retreated to their camp to rest, eat, and share a few yarns. She wrote about a sentry setting out for guard duty: "He is liable to be driven in during the night." And when he did return, Muriel noted the young fellow stumbled into camp muttering "expressions not learned in Sabbath-school." She added, "But then he wasn't taught outpost duty there either."

The next morning, with Filipino fighters 300 yards to the front in a clump of trees and a sharpshooter in a bamboo tree directing steady fire

---

Philippine Revolution: An Homage to David Fagen," stated, "The general sentiment of the occupying army was captured by one volunteer: 'We all wanted to kill 'niggers'. . . beats rabbit hunting.'" And a news article in the *San Francisco Call* on August 21, 1902, titled "Filipino 'Niggers,'" explained, "The American public has become accustomed to hearing the Filipinos spoken of as 'niggers.'" The article cited Jamas A. Leroy from the *Atlantic Monthly*: "He says it is the usual thing for Americans there (the Philippines) who imbibe a contempt and dislike for the natives to betray in common conversation their estimate of the Filipinos to be based upon the popular notions at home as to the incapacity and shortcomings of the negro."

Guard at Caloocan LIBRARY OF CONGRESS PRINTS AND PHOTOGRAPHS DIVISION, WASHING-
TON, D.C., LC-USZ62-80472.

at the Americans, Muriel wrote, "Now and then the bullets fly so fast and thick that everyone has to crouch down and lie still a few moments while the things sing over your head and make you afraid to speak." The "lonely singing of strong and spent bullets about our hearts, will live in memory as long as life," she added.

Muriel's talent for capturing riveting battle scenes and voices of intriguing figures during the war in the Philippines was revealed again in October 1899, when the *San Francisco Examiner* published her feature article about Major General Elwell Otis. Muriel first met Otis in September 1898 after he had been in the Philippines only a couple of months and shortly after he was appointed commander of the American forces. By the time her 1899 profile ran in the *San Francisco Examiner*, Americans had already come to know him through anecdotes, newspaper articles, and gossip. His reputation as a "fussy, pompous micromanager who obsessed over every minute detail of his command" was reinforced by Muriel, who recounted her interview with him on a typical day at his headquarters. His exchange with a staff officer was revealing:

"'Some things wanted in the commissary, sir.'

'What are they?' Otis inquired.

'One dozen cans tomatoes, six cans clam broth, six cans chicken soup, six cans—'

'Wait!' said the General. 'Did you say a dozen cans of tomatoes?'

("The great man with the weights of war and of state upon his shoulders pondered a moment in deep thought, while a cablegram marked 'important' slipped to the floor," Muriel wrote.)

'Send them sixteen, and send them four cans of clam broth instead of six.'"

"I was wondering how a Major-General in command of the Eighth Army Corps of the Philippine islands, could have acquired such an intricate knowledge of the price of canned goods," she wrote.

In her article, Muriel recalled an earlier meeting with Otis in December 1898 shortly after the signing of the peace treaty ending the war between the United States and Spain at which he insisted he anticipated no trouble with the Filipinos. When asked if he believed Aguinaldo to be friendly to the Americans, Otis had replied, "Oh, yes! Perfectly friendly." Muriel continued, "Two weeks afterward I began to wonder why one's friends should purchase guns and shut one up in a city surrounded by trenches and poke impudent-looking cannons up under one's very nose."

Muriel also questioned the major general's military acumen. She had been on the battlefield of Caloocan where the Americans were initially restricted from firing on the enemy due to Otis's assurances that he had "the matter well in hand and the affair would be ended in ten days." Despite nightly volleys of Mausers and daily casualties, the Americans "waited anxiously for Otis' ten days to pass." When during her interview Muriel offered some military advice of her own, Otis expressed his thoughts about her value as a woman. "Women know nothing about war," the major general pronounced. Muriel may not have responded to Otis directly, but she closed her article with this: "We all know that! How many mothers, wives, sweethearts and sisters could testify that all they know of war is the hours of dread suspense, the days of agonized waiting and the nights when, alone in the darkness, they try to realize the sorrow that has come upon them?"

FANNIE BRIGHAM WARD: AN INDEPENDENT WOMAN

Fannie Brigham Ward offered graphic words to readers of *The New Era* newspaper in Lancaster, Pennsylvania, in an article titled "The Story of

Cuba's Woes" in March 1898: "Words fail in attempting to describe the soul-sickening sights that day—emaciated wretches, the swollen legs and bursting feet, in the last stages of starvation; dying men, women and children, imploring a morsel of bread . . . the dreadful smells and cries and groans that everywhere pursued us. . . .With our tears was mingled burning indignation that such a state of things would be permitted to exist near the end of the nineteenth century within a day's journey of the United States." It was one of several American newspapers that carried Fannie's byline under her far-reaching chronicles of life in distant lands as well as locations only miles from American shores. Her proposal submitted years earlier in 1886 to provide syndicated columns as she traveled throughout Central and South America to newspapers across the United States had been accepted by *The New Era* as well as about forty other publications. So, by the time she arrived in Cuba to report on the situation there as Cuban freedom fighters took up arms against their Spanish oppressors, she had a loyal following of readers and the endorsement of influential newspaper owners.

When she described circumstances in Cuba in the spring of 1898, the United States had not yet declared war on Spain, and her observations may or may not have helped steer public opinion as American politicians contemplated going to war. It's likely some of the headlines attached to Fannie's articles were intended to tug at readers' emotions: "Fannie B. Ward among the Reconcentrados," "How Valeriano Weyler Has Murdered Two Hundred Thousand People by Starvation," and "A Tale of Horrors." Her words would have touched at least some of her readers, "Fancy being simply turned out of your own homes in Lancaster, with only what you could hastily collect and carry in your hands, the rest being burned before your eyes," she wrote. Fannie was referring to the policy of reconcentration in which the Spaniards relocated Cuban citizens from their farms and homes to concentrated areas where thousands died of disease and starvation. Fannie echoed the words of many others when she labeled the practice a policy of "extermination."

As Fannie traveled across Cuba in those days before American intervention, she provided windows into the lives of average citizens and specifically the *reconcentrados*. There was the young woman who had sought refuge in a hospital in hopes of receiving relief. On a visit to the facility, Fannie was drawn to the woman, writing, "Nobody in the hospital knew anything about her, except that she was a Reconcentrado . . . she held aloof from the rest during the terrible march, sleeping in the fields and slowly starving." But the woman was beyond saving. "While we stood beside her the breast ceased to move. Death had set its inscrutable seal on her lips."

A five-year-old boy "with the big head and the pipe-stem legs" who had been found lying on top of his dead mother caught Fannie's attention when she toured an orphanage. He sat motionless on his bed day after day. She described "the first human emotion" he displayed when given a furry toy dog with black bead eyes. That night, he slept with the dog tightly clasped in his arms. At Matanzas, Fannie and her friend Clara Barton of the Red Cross toured a hospital operated by the Spanish. "I believed that no more dreadful sights could be found in the sin-cursed world than I had already witnessed in Havana," Fannie wrote. Yet she was disturbed by conditions in Matanzas, where the hospital was nothing more than a shabby shed with crude stretchers resting on dirt floors and where patients were offered little relief in terms of care, as few medical personnel were to be found. "I have seen misery in many lands, but never anything like this," Fannie informed her American readers.

Often traveling by train, Fannie witnessed signs of the war being waged by Cuban freedom fighters against their Spanish occupiers across the island. While the Cubans operated from secret camps throughout the countryside, the Spanish forces were visible everywhere. "Every train that passes this way has its strong guard of soldiers in an iron-clad car attached, a cattle-car, covered with iron plates, in which are looped holes for guns; each soldier standing at his gun, ready for instant action," she wrote of the Spaniards. Writing from Havana, Fannie described a city stringently under Spanish control yet under a cloud of uncertainty as its residents—Cubans, Spaniards, and Americans—waited for developments in Washington as officials debated America's next move. "I find an ominous quiet brooding over the Capital," she wrote from Havana. "It is the stillness that presages a storm." However, tracking down news from the outside world was nearly impossible, as the Spanish issued harsh penalties to anyone possessing foreign newspapers. American journals and maga-zines were banned from the Cuban postal system, and bundles of newspa-pers more times than not ended up at the bottom of the bay. Occasionally, brave American seamen smuggled papers into the island. But prison awaited offenders of the censorship laws, and spies were everywhere—servants in the kitchen, beggars at the door, and Spaniards who professed to be dear friends. The streets were teeming with Spanish officials and military. Fannie offered unflattering appraisals of the Spanish soldiers, "undersized, often manifestly underfed, slouching in gait and hang-dog in general appearance." Yet, she warned, "the Spaniards are certain to do wild things when the crisis comes." And although she admitted little was known about the movements of the Cuban fighters, everyone was aware they were scattered across the island waiting for word from their Ameri-can friends. She wrote that their campfires were visible in the hills sur-rounding Havana and that they were ready to "pounce" as soon as the U.S. Congress declared war. Soon enough, the wait was over, as America declared war on April 21, 1898.

As the United States joined forces with the Cuban freedom fighters to resist the Spanish, some news reports based on racist ideas painted dispar-aging pictures of the Cuban fighters. "The American soldiers looked with silent curiosity upon the ragged brown insurgents," one writer proclaimed. Americans were surprised to learn that many of the Cuban soldiers were Black. However, Black enslaved people had long been part of Cuban his-tory, as they had provided labor in the island's plantations since the 1700s, and throughout the nineteenth century, the slave trade had flourished. These Blacks and their descendants were as much a part of the movements for independence as any group. Although the Cubans had been fighting for years by the time the Americans joined the fight, countless narratives portrayed the Cuban fighters as substandard in comparison to the Ameri-can soldiers. "It is not safe to rely upon their fully performing any specific duty, unless they are under the constant supervision and direction of one of our officers," an observer commented. Another surprise awaiting Ameri-cans was the revelation that some Cuban fighting units included women.

"At first nobody really believed that there were women in the Cuban army, though the newspapers printed romantic tales of their exploits. The truth is that from the outset, female soldiers have played no unimportant part in the struggle for independence," Fannie wrote in May a few weeks after war between Spain and the United States had commenced. "Maceo, the mulatto insurgent leader, had more than 100 female soldiers (mostly colored) in his company. Gomez also had a good many and so has Calizio Alvarez, the chief from the eastern district of San Jago de Cuba," Fannie wrote. Many of the women, who "transformed into avenging furies," carried machetes and revolvers and were wives or daughters of independence advocates, according to Fannie. She added, "They fought shoulder to shoulder with the men, led daring raids and applied the torch in a thousand places; and some of them now sleep in unmarked graves."

While Fannie had not shied away from exposing conditions brought about by the Spanish during their rule, she continued to seek out mismanagement and ineptness on the part of the Americans as they became involved in Cuban affairs. She warned against the threats of yellow fever, dysentery, typhoid, smallpox, and leprosy. "Spanish bullets are not the only dangers our boys in Cuba will have to encounter," she wrote in June. She accurately predicted that these threats would "eventually cost more American lives than the war." From Santiago in August after the Americans had taken control of the city, she wrote that "to encounter a corpse or two, stretched across the sidewalk or lying on its face in a doorway, is no uncommon occurrence." She continued, "Decayed fruit, dead dogs, cats and mules, all manner of filth and carron lies wherever it happened to fall, festering in sun and rain, to quickly become a mass of living, wriggling abomination." Fannie placed blame for the horrific conditions squarely on the shoulders of Major General William Shafter. "The wonder is that some bullet, aimed by a revengeful hand, does not cut short his career in these lawless times, as he rolls about town in his carriage, or his great bulk is carried from camp to camp on a litter," she wrote about the American commander. And any grievance not assigned to Shafter she laid on the U.S. Army's chief medical doctor, Surgeon General George Sternberg. "Men are dying by hundreds because of somebody's criminal neglect . . . a good deal that properly belongs to . . . Surgeon-General Sternberg," she wrote. "The Sternbergian theory is directly responsible for at least half of the three thousand deaths which have occurred since July 2, to say nothing of the hundreds now dying from subsequent unnecessary hardship and exposure," Fannie wrote. Sternberg's policy toward female nurses on the battlefield was at least partly to blame, according to Fannie. "Surgeon-General Sternberg announced in the beginning that he had no use for 'women's work and women's tears, and on the other day reiterated that he did not want any female nurses in the army. Therefore, he has opposed the Red Cross in every way, refusing to permit it to follow the army," Fannie wrote. She sang the praises of her friend Clara Barton and the Red Cross workers who had injected themselves into the field hospitals despite Sternberg's resistance. "Thus hundreds of mother's boys were saved, who in a few hours more of Sternbergism would have been beyond mortal aid," she wrote.

While Fannie's readers came to rely on her firsthand reports about societal and military aspects of the Cuban situation, many valued her insight into economic issues. Her travels throughout Cuba had provided her with knowledge about business endeavors and economic conditions on the island. She had written about plantations where thousands of workers produced hundreds of thousands of bags of sugar each year—making the owners wealthy and adding millions to the Spanish government's coffers in tax revenues. "No wonder Spain considers her rebellious colony a prize to fight for," she wrote. However, she cautioned that Cubans had paid a gruesome toll for their rich agricultural lands: "Heaven knows it ought to be fertile, with frequent baptisms of blood during four centuries. Within the last two years it has been enriched by upwards of 400,000 human carcasses." She wrote about American capitalists who had benefited from Cuban enterprises before the Cubans began their most recent war for independence against Spain in 1895. There was the sugar plantation owned by a New York firm and a Connecticut family who had lived for generations on the rich profits from their Cuban sugar plantation. And she wrote about the Louisiana businessman who was unhappy with the yield of crop from his Cuban sugar plantation, which had been exhausted by years of repeated use until he discovered a source of unlimited fertilizer: the long-forgotten caves at the end of his estate where years and years of bat guano provided a source of rich fertilizer. She wrote about American firms that owned iron ore mines in Cuba, including the Sagua

Iron Mining Camp in Cuba, 1899 LIBRARY OF CONGRESS PRINTS AND PHOTOGRAPHS DIVISION, WASHINGTON, D.C., LC-DIG-STEREO-1S20328.

Iron Company, held by a Philadelphia firm, and the Juragua Iron Company in Santiago province, a subsidiary of the Bethlehem Steel Company. And she identified refineries in New York and Pennsylvania where Cuban sugar was sent for processing.

Only days after Congress declared war on Spain, Fannie predicted lucrative opportunities for financiers who might invest in an independent Cuba: "Speculators have already turned their eyes that way. . . . Somebody will, no doubt, be making money out of Cuba's ruined homes and mills within the next few months." She had received letters from American businessmen inquiring about potential business prospects after the war ended. "A man with eyes in his head and the business instinct of the average American will see avenues for profitable investments of money and labor in every direction as soon as peace is restored on the island," she wrote. There would be properties and houses as well as farming equipment and machinery for sale at bargain prices, according to Fannie. "It seems a pity to take advantage of other people's misfortunes, but many are the fine old casas in Havana and other cities which will be bought for a song," she wrote. She recognized that the United States would benefit handsomely from an independent Cuba when she wrote in late June 1898, "Soon as hostilities are ended our commerce will, of course, be greatly stimulated—free trade, absolute commercial reciprocity and all that sort of thing being established with the independence of Cuba."

Over the years, many readers were surprised to find a woman's name attached to Fannie's articles when they appeared in newspapers across the country. From the start, when she described scaling mountains on a burro in Mexico and South America or when she wrote from war-torn Cuba, readers were taken aback to learn of this woman who had "done what few women have undertaken" and engaged in activities "from which the average woman would shrink." One newspaper owner cited Fannie's "vigorous style" of writing that led readers to remark it was "too masculine to be the work of a woman." But Fannie had an answer for those who questioned her lifestyle: "All my life I have gone on my own independent way, regardless of who might disapprove of my course."

6

Sisterhoods of Support

"WOMEN AS WELL AS MEN REALIZE THAT IN UNION, THERE IS STRENGTH." Bell Merrill Draper of the Daughters of the American Revolution wrote about the admirable work of the women of the organization during the Spanish-American War in 1898. Her words could have applied to countless Cuban, Filipino, and American women who showed little reserve when fighting for their ideals, families, and causes while appealing to likeminded women to help tackle problems, accomplish lofty goals, or simply step in to fill a void.

Cuban exiles in the United States were far from quiet in the years before and during the war and relied on well-organized and dedicated groups to sustain the fight for independence in their homeland. The *Cuba Libre* (Free Cuba) movement—consisting of a network of institutions, civic and political committees, newspapers, and revolutionary clubs—encouraged the formation of women's clubs to help accomplish their goals. In New York by 1898, there were close to 100 women's organizations dedicated to the cause. Through concerts, dances, banquets, and monthly membership dues, the women accumulated funds to buy supplies for the freedom fighters in Cuba. One was *Hijas de Cuba* (Daughters of Cuba)—raising $10,000 in the span of three years. Membership dues of $1 per month in addition to fund-raising events filled the coffers, allowing the purchase of arms, ammunition, food, and medicine for the Cuban fighters. Membership consisted largely of women whose relatives had been active in the revolutionary cause for years. Laura de Zayas Bazan had spent most of her childhood in Paris and contributed her acting and singing talents to fund-raising events, Frances Molina had been imprisoned in Cuba by the Spanish, and Carmen Mantilla was one of the few unmarried women in the *Hijas de Cuba*. The club had formed before the United States joined the fight, and part of their mission was to make Americans aware of the Cubans' struggle for independence from Spain. When the United States finally declared war on Spain in April 1898, the *Hijas de Cuba* were relieved that their burdens would be lightened somewhat. "We do not have to furnish arms any longer, because the United States government is attending to that; but we still have to help the poor, fugitive *reconcentrados* who have come to this country destitute of everything but liberty," Laura de Zayas Bazan said.

Florida was another hot spot of Cuban exile activity, where *Hijas de la Libertad* (Freedom's Daughters), *Hijas de la Patria* (Fatherland's Daughters), and *Obreras de la Independencia* (Women Workers for Independence) supported the freedom fighters through parades, picnics, and raffles. Florida's proximity to Cuba made it a frequent destination for prominent independence leaders who were welcomed by crowds often organized by women of the communities. The large Cuban exile population in the state created a hefty pool of financial contributors to the cause, and the leaders were welcomed into homes where they enjoyed generous meals and comfortable accommodations usually provided by the female members of the household.

American women were swift to mobilize as the threat of war loomed. In New York, Ellen Hardin Walworth sounded the alarm in early April before the United States declared war. Maybe it was her years with an unstable husband that propelled her to prepare for the worst by establishing a network of female volunteers. By the time men throughout the country began to board trains for military training camps and transports for war zones in Cuba and the Philippines, women in small towns and big cities had already formed committees to sew pajamas, preserve fruit, and assemble care packages for soldiers. The Women's Christian Temperance Union (WCTU) in Louisville, Kentucky, assembled and sent comfort bags containing spools of thread, needles, and buttons to their servicemen. Each bag also contained Bible verses and abstinence pledge cards—signers pledging "to abstain from the use of all intoxicating liquors" and "to employ all honorable means to encourage others to abstain." The WCTU in New Mexico had done the same for their soldiers stationed at Whipple Barracks in Arizona, and it resulted in the return of forty-seven signed pledge cards. In Buffalo, New York, the Women's Auxiliary to the Citizens' Aid Committee formed to provide food, shelter, and clothing to needy families of service members, and Defenders' Aid Auxiliary in Brooklyn, New York, sent packages of books, magazines, pencils, paper, handkerchiefs, and underwear to servicemen. They oversaw the shipping of canned goods, jellies, clam broth, preserved fruits, barrels of raspberry vinegar, and condensed milk to training camps. The Ladies' Auxiliary of the Detroit Patriotic Association implemented a program in which women greeted every returning soldier at the train depot, and they expanded the program to include soldiers and sailors from other states who passed through the station on their way home. They met with the mayor to identify women in Detroit who needed employment due to a husband's absence.

While many women's groups were motivated by patriotism and enthusiasm for the war, nothing triggered a response faster than word of mismanagement and waste by officials: gallons of milk spoiling in the hot sun at a train station due to a shortage of wagons to transport the precious liquid to typhoid patients in a nearby hospital and seriously ill men lying on the floor of an army hospital tent despite a supply of cots sitting for days at a station only two miles away waiting for someone to locate trucks to transport the beds. Women's groups around the country refused to accept such carelessness and neglect when it affected the country's soldiers, sailors, and marines. A group of Morristown, New Jersey, women supplied the local navy hospital and hospital ships with nightshirts, handkerchiefs, underwear, and blankets as well as tasty homemade treats for the sailors. When a group of wealthy Maine women inquired about the lack of ice on some hospital ships and learned that only the large vessels carried the cherished commodity, they chartered a schooner and shipped ice for use on smaller ships. The Women's Auxiliary in Pottsville, Pennsylvania, sent a special train stocked with milk, ice, and medicine to Camp Meade in Middletown, Pennsylvania, to bring local soldiers suffering with malaria and typhoid fever to the Pottsville Hospital. Red Cross groups in California, Oregon, and Seattle sponsored nurses and sent thousands of dollars of supplies to hospitals in the Philippines.

When reports of unprepared or disorganized government officials reached the homes of families who had offered up their men for the service of their country, it prompted frustration and anger. However, many Americans agreed with the assessment of one reporter who wrote in August 1898 as the fighting in Cuba wound down, "A number of women with kind hearts and willing hands have been at work doing what the government should have done from the start."

And while fighting had tapered off in Cuba and a peace treaty between the United States and Spain would be signed in December, war would continue in the Philippines as Americans replaced the Spanish occupiers. As Filipinos realized independence was again being denied (this time by the Americans), they turned to influential American women's groups to lend support to their call for self-government, and they were not disappointed. The WCTU at their annual convention in Seattle in late 1899 passed a resolution supporting independence for the Philippines: "We deeply deplore the attitude taken by our Nation with respect to the Philippine islands . . . we protest against the policy which would compel a foreign people to submit to the rule of the United States." A committee of women from the Anti-Imperialist League sent a petition to President William McKinley, asking him to "cease at once this war of criminal aggression" in the Philippine islands. They appealed to women across the country to sign similar letters to the commander in chief. And when an influential Filipina sought support for the cause of self-government for her people, she appealed to women of the Anti-Imperialist League and the Women's Suffrage Association and an ensemble of female academics from a prestigious women's college to help advocate for her cause.

Early in the war effort, many women recognized the efficiency of working in groups to identify needs and pool resources—both material and human. By organizing around common goals and inserting themselves into a sometimes broken and dysfunctional system, women's groups demonstrated the priceless value of determined, focused, and resilient groups of people.

Paulina Pedroso: Woman with a "Heart of Gold"

In August 1968, workmen were in the process of demolishing the old Flagler Building in Tampa, Florida, when they spotted an impressive-looking bronze plaque unceremoniously resting in the old boiler room. It bore the likeness of an African American woman and the name "Paulina Pedroso." Residents of Tampa in 1968 were generally puzzled by the identity of this woman, who must have been someone of consequence, considering the substantial quality of the fifty-pound object, and when a local historian came forward to reveal the story behind Paulina Pedroso's remarkable life, the mystery was solved.

The woman memorialized in bronze turned out to be one of the most influential individuals in the *Cuba Libre* (Free Cuba) movement living in exile in Ybor City, Florida, in the 1890s. As a Black woman living within an ethnically and racially diverse community in a southern region of the United States at the time, Paulina undoubtedly confronted a wide range of experiences every day. Despite her banishment to the basement of the Flagler Building in the 1960s, her stature within the Cuban émigré community in the 1890s was unquestionable and renowned.

Paulina, born to enslaved parents, grew up in Pinar del Rio, a tobacco-growing region of Cuba, where as a young girl she married Ruperto Pedroso. As young adults, the couple moved to Havana, and in 1892, they moved to Florida, a short journey geographically but worlds away from the unrest and uncertainty of Spanish-ruled Cuba with its undercurrents of revolution close to the surface of everyday life. While Ruperto and Paulina had escaped the physical dangers of war when they left Cuba, they did not run away from their responsibilities as supporters of independence for their homeland. The two ended up in Ybor City, where Ruperto went to work in a cigar factory and Paulina managed a boardinghouse where male boarders appreciated the clean rooms, hearty meals, and occasional political debate if they cared to partake.

By the time the Pedrosos arrived in Ybor City, the place had become home for working-class Cuban exiles seeking jobs and a secure way of life. Many had found employment in the numerous cigar factories in town, where it was a common practice for the owners to provide lectors who

A Reader in a Cigar Factory in the Early 1900s LIBRARY OF CONGRESS PRINTS AND PHOTOGRAPHS DIVISION, WASHINGTON, D.C., LC-USZ62-90209.

read to the workers as they toiled in their mind-numbing jobs as tobacco leaf strippers and cigar rollers. Workers voted on reading materials, and while they often chose popular works of fiction, at other times, they voted for political essays—some from the French Revolution. When the workers heard words such as "equality," "reform," "revolution," "distribution of power," "social justice," and "civil rights," they thought about conditions in their Cuban homeland, where friends and family suffered under some of the same injustices that prompted the French people to rebel against their monarchy in 1789. The Spaniards had suppressed the Cuban people for 400 years, so when young charismatic Cuban writer and revolutionary activist José Martí began visiting Florida in his efforts to rally support for the cause of *Cuba Libre*, cigar workers, as well as others whose families in Cuba were never far from their thoughts, were tantalized by his words. When Martí formed the Cuban Revolutionary Party in February 1892 as a vehicle to support the insurrection through money and resources, he attracted eager followers.

Political clubs for men and women formed in Cuban communities throughout Florida, including in Ybor City. Many workers embraced the idea of "el dia de la Patria," contributing one day's wages to the cause of independence for the homeland. Along with his passion for Cuban independence, Martí championed the ideals of social justice and equality for races and announced his intent to "create an interracial coalition on behalf of *Cuba Libre*." Through his efforts to do so in Ybor City, he worked with Paulina and Ruperto, whom he had first met in Key West in 1891 and where he had told Paulina, "You are going to help me a great deal here for Cuba."

Martí, of course, was not popular with Spanish authorities in Cuba, and as he became more influential, they sought ways to discredit him or worse. Spanish immigrants, as well as Cuban émigrés, constituted a sizable portion of residents of Ybor City, and some of those Spaniards favored Spanish rule in Cuba as passionately as the exiled Cubans endorsed independence. It wouldn't have been difficult for Spanish officials to employ some of their countrymen living in Ybor City to engage in a little espionage on their behalf. One day in 1893 as Martí was relaxing in Tampa, he became suspicious of the glass of wine someone placed in front of him. Fortunately, he refrained from raising the drink to his mouth, as it was laced with poison as he had suspected. After this incident, he began to make a habit of staying with the Pedrosos in their boardinghouse, where he knew he was safe. Ruperto became his bodyguard, and Paulina became his second mother.

The Tampa area became so important to the revolutionary cause that Martí referred to the cigar areas as the "civilian camp of the revolution." Paulina's home became a gathering place where Cuban activists exchanged ideas about the possibilities of revolt against the Spaniards and revolutionary leaders inspired and encouraged action. Paulina connected Martí to other influential African Cubans in the community. It may have been shocking to some residents of the town to see this young Cuban man out for a stroll with the Black woman as they shared thoughts of a future that involved a free Cuba. He welcomed Paulina's insight as an African Cuban woman. Martí's work in Ybor City included visiting cigar factories, where he hoped to raise awareness of the causes of *Cuba Libre* and to elicit emotional as well as financial support from the hardworking men and women in the factories. And when José arrived at a cigar factory one day to deliver a speech to the workers, the sight of Paulina at his side may have caused some to look twice at the pair. It might have been a spy hired by the Spaniards to infiltrate the factory who shouted "bandit" at José when he reminded workers of his request for part of their wages for *Cuba Libre*. But it was Paulina who responded, "Gentlemen, if any of you is afraid to give his money, or go to the Savannahs to fight, let him give me his pants and I will give him my petticoat." The apparent attack on their manhood motivated the men in the group to give generously.

José was instrumental in convincing the Pedrosos to work with the Tampa League for Instruction, a spin-off of a similar group in New York offering classes in Spanish grammar and the French language as well as a library of the works of the great philosophers. Black businessman Cornelio Brito had established the Tampa League at the urging of Martí. An education center supporting the *Cuba Libre* movement, the Tampa League reached out to local African Cubans. Classes were offered in math, English, writing, history, and world geography.

Paulina and other Cubans in Ybor City and locations across the globe had talked about and planned for Cuba's liberation from Spanish rule for years. So when word reached Florida on February 24, 1895, that the revolution had been launched by freedom fighters on the island less than 100 miles away, Ybor City crowds gathered in the streets to celebrate the long-anticipated step toward liberty. The exuberance turned to sorrow a few months later in May, when José Martí, who had joined the freedom fighters, was killed. Paulina must have been heartbroken to learn the young Cuban, who had thumbed his nose at racism by walking arm in arm down the sidewalks of a southern city with a Black woman, had given his life for the cause of freedom. Many Ybor City groups and individuals had supported the cause of Cuban independence with financial resources before the revolution, and they continued over the next three years, when the Americans joined the fight by declaring war on Spain in April 1898. Community organizations raised money through parades, picnics, fiestas, and raffles, helping to purchase arms, ammunition, food, clothes, and medicine for the freedom fighters. Paulina and Ruperto themselves contributed substantially to the cause.

In 1910, years after the Cubans had defeated the Spaniards, Paulina and Ruperto moved back to Cuba, where they were given the use of a house and Ruperto obtained a job as a doorman at a Havana police station. When Paulina died in 1913, American newspapers used a racist term of the era—"aged mammy"—for this prominent business owner and powerful political activist, who "gave all she had to aid the cause" of a free Cuba. Others recognized her humanitarian qualities of humility and selflessness. At some point, a group or an individual decided to pay tribute to this "bronze woman with a heart of gold" by constructing the plaque uncovered by the workmen all those years later in 1968. It was reported that Paulina's plaque had probably hung on a wall in the old Flagler Building, which had been a Cuban consulate until 1961, when the United States and Cuba broke relations. As memories of the struggle for independence in the little island off the coast of Florida faded, the contributions of this generous woman became diluted by the passage of time. The discovery of the plaque prompted a new generation to revisit them.

ELLEN HARDIN WALWORTH: "MOTHER OF THE CAMP"

Dr. Russell Childs testified to the scene he witnessed at a New York City hotel in June 1873: "I found a body lying on the left side with its head against the washstand; I felt the pulse; it was barely perceptible; the respiration was very feeble; the wash-basin had water in it; blood had spurted into the water; under the bed was quite a pool of blood." The body was that of Mansfield T. Walworth, and no one disputed that the four bullets piercing the body and ultimately causing death had been delivered at the hands of Walworth's son, Frank, who had voluntarily surrendered to the police after the gruesome encounter. His murder trial commenced in the fall and captivated New York City residents; it wasn't every day that New Yorkers were privy to the intimate details of a prominent family torn apart by internal strife. Especially intriguing was the bizarre twist that brought a son to kill his own father.

"My father treated my mother very cruelly for years. . . . About three years ago he beat my mother cruelly. . . . I was troubled about leaving

ELLEN HARDIN WALWORTH,
CHAIRMAN OF THE COMMITTEE ON TABLETS,
SARATOGA MONUMENT ASSOCIATION.

Ellen Hardin Walworth WIKIMEDIA COMMONS, FROM *BATTLES OF SARATOGA, 1777.*
THE SARATOGA MONUMENT ASSOCIATION, 1856–1891. SCANNED FROM ORIGINAL PUBLICA-
TION IN SARATOGA SPRINGS PUBLIC LIBRARY.

my mother without a protector," Frank explained. He spoke about sleeping outside his mother's bedroom door to defend her from "the family persecutor."

The accused's mother, Ellen Hardin Walworth, testified on behalf of her son, recalling an incident in which Frank had saved her from Mansfield's wrath: "I had been subjected to physical violence, which compelled me to scream; my scream brought in Frank; I showed a severe bruise on my arm." She described her life with Mansfield as one of sporadic abandonments, letters filled with threats to herself and her children, and her eventual divorce. She recalled the births of her eight children and the death of her youngest as a newborn, whom her husband had never troubled himself to visit.

Despite a vigorous defense for insanity, the teenage Frank was convicted of second-degree murder. Sentenced to life in prison, he was initially incarcerated at Sing Sing prison north of New York City, later transferred to Auburn prison, then declared insane and sent to an asylum. However, in 1877, Frank was pardoned and released.

Throughout the ordeal of her son's trial, observers commented on Ellen's indifference to the proceedings. Nothing seemed to faze her as she appeared each day at the trial and as she testified in her son's defense. Friends encouraged her to show a little emotion as she appeared in court. They said it might help her son's case, yet she remained stoic. "I can do nothing for effect. I was never an actress, and my sufferings have taught me self-control," she said. It was that same resilience and straightforward approach that sustained Ellen in years to come as she organized a sisterhood of support for American veterans returning from the battlefields of the Spanish-American War and as she faced another personal tragedy that shattered her world.

—◦—

"In view of the crisis through which our country is now passing and of the imminent presence of war, it is fitting that the patriotic women of the country should prepare, as our government is preparing, for the possibility of war," Ellen wrote in a letter to various women's clubs in early April 1898. It would be three weeks before the United States officially declared war against Spain, but Ellen's sense of history prepared her for what she saw as an inevitable future. "As patriotic women our duties are distinct and clear in the event of war, for again history enforces the fact that in every war through which our nation has passed on to victory, the efforts, the sacrifices, and prayers of women have been efficient aids to the attainment of such victories," she wrote. She called for women and even children to volunteer in any way they could. Calling on existing women's groups in cities and small towns to take the lead, she encouraged them to create lists of reliable volunteers within their communities. "Men are organizing in armies to fight, women of the country will organize to help the suffering," she predicted as the country careened toward war.

Late in April, Ellen and a group of wealthy socialites, including former First Lady Julia Grant, formed the Women's National War Relief Association (WNWRA) in New York. It wouldn't be the first time Ellen established a women's club—in 1890, she and three other women had formed the Daughters of the American Revolution to celebrate their heritage and to perform good works in their communities. The WNWRA was founded with the goal of acting as a booster club of sorts to the army and navy during the Spanish-American War. Members signed a pledge declaring "allegiance to the United States of America and . . . to contribute to the general welfare, health, and comfort of the men engaged in the military and naval service of the republic in the present war." With a membership fee of twenty-five cents, women across the land joined the cause. A special drive was implemented in public schools to encourage volunteerism among young children who joined with a ten-cent membership fee. One of the group's first projects was to outfit the hospital ship *Relief* with twenty-five electric fans in the patient wards, and in early June, they sent $600 to the surgeon general of the army to aid the comfort of soldiers and sailors. Over the next several weeks, the women sent supplies to American military camps in Florida and Georgia as well as to American military hospitals in Cuba.

By August, a truce had been called in the fighting, and thousands of American soldiers and sailors were about to come home—many with wounds and many more with deadly contagious diseases. Newspapers began to publish troubling articles about the conditions these returning fighters endured both on their journey in military transports from Cuba (some "little better than pig pens") and on their return to American soil. At times, soldiers were dropped off at train depots or shipping ports—left to walk to the local military facility if they were in any shape to do so. There were reports of serious overcrowding on the ships, lack of fresh drinking water, spoiled food, and absence of quarantine quarters for men with highly contagious and deadly diseases. And as the men disembarked back home in America, in many cases, the military camps were poorly organized or unprepared for the influx of large numbers of war-weary, wounded, or sick veterans. Often, men who could barely walk were sent home for thirty-day furloughs simply because there were no beds for them in military hospitals. "It is rather a sad homecoming for the soldiers. They had gone away strong and full of enthusiasm, ready to fight and to die for their country. They had come home with health gone and maimed and, instead of being well received, had been practically told to go home, get well, and then report back," the *New York Times* reported.

The U.S. government had leased a spot of land on the tip of Long Island on Montauk Point about 125 miles east of New York City with plans to hastily construct a temporary demobilization and quarantine facility for the thousands of troops returning from Cuba. From the start, there were accusations of mismanagement and disorganization at the facility named Camp Wikoff. The camp was far from ready when troops began to arrive. On the evening of August 13, a transport, the *City Gate*, sat in the water off the tip of Long Island loaded with 550 men eager to disembark, but word came from Camp Wikoff that they must stay on board until the camp was ready to accommodate them. Workmen scrambled, working throughout the night to complete storerooms and hospital facilities. A camp doctor had gone out to the ship to assess the health of the men and found cases of dysentery, malaria, and typhoid fever. The next morning as the men began to filter into the camp, the disorganization became evident. Water was an immediate predicament. Two wells providing drinking water offered a limited supply, and water stored in a large tank that had previously held oil had to be distilled to eliminate the unpleasant flavor. A new 30,000-gallon storage tank was still under construction.

Boys of the 71st New York at Montauk Point Returning from Cuba LIBRARY OF CONGRESS PRINTS AND PHOTOGRAPHS DIVISION, WASHINGTON, D.C., LC-D4-21292.

Food at the camp was another concern. Standard military fare—beans, bacon, and hardtack—were ready and waiting for consumption by the returning men. While not especially appetizing for healthy men who had recently delivered a resounding military victory for the American people, it was simply inedible for men battling serious maladies such as yellow fever and dysentery. Reporter Mary E. Leonard didn't mince words when she issued her opinion: "With a carelessness and stupidity, which it must be confessed our army officials have recently become noted for, the sick soldiers were dumped on the barren end of Long Island, known as Montauk Point, and left to recover and recuperate on army rations. They do very well for men who are strong and hearty, but typhoid patients do not thrive on such a diet. The war department intends to treat humanely men who captured Santiago, but good intentions do not make fried bacon taste like chicken broth." The *New York Times* reported that although some order had been established after the first few hours of operation, "things still appear to be in a chaotic state." And, according to the paper, the camp's chief surgeon had received a message indicating five more transports had sailed from Cuba on August 9 and were expected to arrive at Camp Wikoff within days if not hours—only adding to the confusion.

Fortress Monroe, Virginia H. C. WHITE CO., 1901, LIBRARY OF CONGRESS PRINTS AND PHOTOGRAPHS DIVISION, WASHINGTON, D.C., LC-DIG-STEREO-1S07952.

When news of the situation reached Ellen and the members of the WNWRA, they sprang to action. Ellen had already spent several weeks at Fortress Monroe, Virginia, learning firsthand the needs of military camps, and the first thing she tackled was the kitchen. She asked the camp doctors to recommend healthy diets for men suffering from typhoid and other diseases. Outraged that sick soldiers were served regular army food rather than a special diet, she committed $100 per week to the purchase of supplemental food. In addition, she arranged to place a French chef, Julien Duché, in the fort kitchen. He provided healthy, easily digested broths and soups as well as special delicacies to tempt the sick men. The military cooks benefited when the chef taught them some of his skills. And when Ellen learned about the situation at Camp Wikoff in early August, she packed her bags and headed to Long Island, where she hired a private cook for $60 per month and an assistant for $50. She arranged the delivery of 800 bottles of beef extract, fifty pounds of cocoa, three cases of assorted jams, and sixty dozen eggs, and one day after driving twenty miles in a rainstorm to get milk for the sick men, she arranged to have thirty gallons brought into the camp each day. In addition, the WNWRA arranged to send furnishings, including oil stoves, rugs, slop pails, feathers dusters, and commodes, to the camp. The camp kitchen benefited from the WNWRA's generosity when the women had frying pans, saucepans, coffeepots, ladles, corkscrews, and dish soap delivered. The women, appalled to see dirt floors in hospital tents, purchased lumber and hired carpenters to install more substantial floors. As Ellen wrote, "The business of the Women's War Relief struggled on amid the heap of confusion and general discomfort of the place and time."

Several military hospitals operated in Camp Wikoff to serve 25,000 men in tents, and Ellen visited each regularly, using a horse and carriage to travel between locations. She soon became known as "the mother of the camp." When Ellen moved to Camp Wikoff, she asked her daughter, Reubena, who had been working as a nurse in the typhoid ward of Fortress Monroe, to join her. Reubena's degree in art from Vassar College may not have prepared her for medical work in the camps, but she had taken an emergency nurse training course when the war broke out and became a beloved nurse at Fortress Monroe. She soon became indispensable at Camp Wikoff. Working in the dreaded Detention Hospital, where typhoid fever cases were treated, she was isolated for weeks with the sick men.

It soon became apparent to the women of the WNWRA of the need for a transitional facility for returning soldiers—men treated and released from Camp Wikoff and other military facilities or men waiting for transportation to their homes or their next military assignments. So the WNWRA established a convalescent home in a residence at 316 East 15th Street in New York City where the soldiers could relax for a few days. The home offered a lounge, reading room, clean beds, and healthy meals. It was a place the men could have a smoke and enjoy a game of cards with other men. Philanthropist Helen Gould donated $25,000 to the operation, and the house was named Camp Walworth in honor of Ellen. The first lodgers, fourteen men who had disembarked at Camp Wikoff, arrived with Ellen on September 8, and over the course of the next few months, more than 2,000 men took advantage of the hospitality at the home. Some came for a few hours as they passed through the city; others spent several nights. The women kept meticulous records about the men who passed through Camp Walworth, cataloging their names, regiments, and physical and financial conditions and the names of friends and family. At the end of the war, the women proudly produced a chronicle of the invaluable service they had performed for the war heroes.

Late in September, it was reported that Reubena was seriously ill and had left Camp Wikoff. Her mother admitted her to New York City's Presbyterian Hospital, where doctors diagnosed her with typhoid fever.

A month later, she was dead. People who had served with Reubena at Fort Monroe and at Camp Wikoff spoke lovingly of her. A doctor who had served with her marveled at the work she performed, carrying buckets of water, cooking meals, and feeding the patients. A former patient said, "I was one of the first among the wounded soldiers who came to Monroe from Cuba, and in those long and weary days that followed, when we lay there suffering from wounds and fever in Ward 1, her bright face and cheering words and tender nursing were the sole means of bringing many of us back to life and health. She will never be forgotten by any of the boys who were there." A soldier whom she had tended at Camp Wikoff said, "Never a doubt has crossed my mind that I owe my life to the gentle, careful nursing that she gave me. Her death was that of a patriot and heroine."

Reubena Hyde Walworth WOMEN'S NATIONAL WAR RELIEF ASSOCIATION, *WOMEN'S NATIONAL WAR RELIEF ASSOCIATION; ORGANIZED FOR THE EMERGENCY OF THE SPANISH-AMERICAN WAR*, 1899, HTTPS://WWW.LOC.GOV/ITEM/99003434.

Reubena's devotion as a fearless nurse was honored at the time of her death, but her insight into the shameful situation that greeted returning veterans was reflected in a poem she wrote shortly before her death as she stood on a hill at Montauk looking over the open graves of fallen soldiers and the tents filled with her patients. Her mother shared it after Reubena's death. A reporter described the poem as "the warning note of an angel of mercy":

> We're burying our boys whom the cannon passed by,
> Whom care might have saved, we have brought home to die.

We're burying the victors who trampled on Spain;
Oh, Nation, awake! Right the wrong, fix the blame!

As relief efforts wound down and people looked back at missteps by the government and impressive accomplishments by women's groups, the work of the WNWRA was touted as one of the most efficient. As one newspaper reported, "There has been no reckless blowing in of its funds, no senseless waste and no misapplication of the supplies provided." In the final report issued by the WNWRA, the women reminded readers of the promises they had made at the start of the war and proudly reported that they had fulfilled those promises. Ellen included a stark assessment of the situation she had witnessed at Camp Wikoff: "Except for the boundless generosity of nature in an atmosphere unsurpassed for purity, there would hardly have been a person able to escape from that poisoned spot to tell the tale of its miseries. The suffering endured there is a blot on the history of the nation."

Laura Drake Gill: "Full of Positive Energy"

At noon on June 9, 1899, a group of distinguished men gathered for lunch at the Lawyers' Club in the Equitable Building on Broadway in New York City. Lunches at the exclusive location, prepared by a French chef who imported Hungarian flour for his homemade bread, were served with red and white wine imported from Paris. A specially built zinc-lined storeroom had been constructed for the prized flour as American mice gravitated toward the delicacy, and no one at the club wanted to see mouse droppings in their bread. The group that gathered on June 9 was there to discuss a situation in Cuba, where conditions were critical for children who had been left parentless and homeless in the War of Independence. Much of the blame was assigned to General Valeriano Weyler, the Spanish general who had herded innocent families into camps where thousands had died from overcrowding and hunger. The men meeting at the Lawyers' Club, all wealthy entrepreneurs, military officers, philanthropists, financiers, and physicians, had decided to create the Cuban Orphan Society, whose object was "the care and education of orphans and other destitute children of Cuba." The men would serve as trustees

Cuban Orphans, 1899 LIBRARY OF CONGRESS PRINTS AND PHOTOGRAPHS DIVISION, WASHINGTON, D.C., LC-DIG-STEREO-1S20253.

securing funds and overseeing the operation. They hired Laura Drake Gill as superintendent to oversee the day-to-day work in Cuba. She had a stellar educational background, and her experiences during the Spanish-American War provided her with insight about Cuba as well as practical skills in assessing needs and providing people to address those issues.

Laura had earned bachelor's and master's degrees at Smith College and studied in Germany, Switzerland, and France before becoming a mathematics teacher at a school in Massachusetts. When the Spanish-American War broke out in the spring of 1898, she joined the American National Red Cross Auxiliary No. 3 for the Maintenance of Trained Nurses. This organization, funded through private donations and organized by a group of wealthy New York women, committed to supplying as many as 200 nurses for the war effort at field hospitals and on the battlefield. These women were not only rich; they were determined. When they heard the army was not interested in using female nurses, they were not deterred. Individuals, businesses, and community organizations contributed amounts ranging from $1 to hundreds of dollars. A women's sewing class donated $1, while Grace Vanderbilt donated $1,000. Not to be upstaged by the White Plains Presbyterian Church's $125 donation, the White Plains Episcopal Church committed $215. Some contributors, such as the New York and Brooklyn Ferry Company and Chilton Manufacturing, committed to monthly subscriptions. By early July, Auxiliary No. 3 for the Maintenance of Trained Nurses had raised nearly $7,000. They would need it and every additional dollar they could raise as expenditures to maintain the initial 100 nurses came in at about $5,000 per month.

The auxiliary hired Laura to coordinate certain aspects of the nursing program. It's unclear whether she ever served as a nurse herself, but she oversaw the logistics of placing and transporting the nurses secured by the agency. In early July 1898, Laura had traveled to Tampa, Florida, with a group of a dozen nurses who had been hired to work in military hospitals treating wounded soldiers who had been brought from Cuban battlefields. She then returned to New York to bring an additional twenty-seven nurses to Florida. And while in Florida, she sent a telegram back to the New York agency that more nurses were needed to tend to wounded soldiers and those sick with malaria and other diseases. By late July, Surgeon General George Sternberg, after much trepidation, had begun to allow female nurses to tend to his soldiers. Laura was sent to the army camps at Chickamauga, Georgia; Fortress Monroe, Virginia; and Jacksonville, Florida, to interview military authorities about living arrangements for the nurses. Auxiliary No. 3 for the Maintenance of Trained Nurses was paying for living expenses, but before they sent nurses to the camps, they wanted to ensure that accommodations were suitable. Within a few days, Laura traveled with ten nurses to Camp Thomas, the army training facility at Chickamauga, where the nurses would work at the Leiter Hospital. The auxiliary's female nurses served admirably during the war, and by the fall of 1898, Surgeon General Sternberg had only good things to say about them: "I desire to express my high appreciation of the valuable services rendered to the medical department of the army by this organization."

By August, a truce had been called in the fighting in Cuba, and in December 1898, a peace treaty had been concluded between the United States and Spain. Cuba was now a protectorate of the United States, and that meant the U.S. military and other officials remained in Cuba until 1902, when the Cubans established their own government. Plenty of controversy surrounded the continued presence of the United States on the island. "Cuba for the Cubans" was a popular slogan among the native people. A Spanish newspaper expressed an opinion held by many about the new occupiers: "The Americans have converted the beautiful park into a camp. There they eat, there they drink and there they wallow freely like hogs in a creek on a summer day." Cubans and the Americans began to adjust to an uneasy new life together.

As an employee of the newly formed Cuban Orphan Society in May 1899, Laura rose above political issues. She was there for the children. Her wealthy New York trustees had sent her to the island as their agent to provide an accurate and unvarnished assessment of conditions as they finalized their plans for their philanthropic work. And as Laura traveled, she could only confirm what one Cuban newspaper had reported about the orphans: "The suffering which war and blockades bring fell upon their innocent heads with awful force."

From Sancti Spíritus, she wrote back to the New Yorkers that the suffering was worse than any she had seen. More than 400 children were in dire need. Some "mere little skeletons" made her wonder "whether it was any kindness to help them to live a few years longer." From Remedios, one of the island's oldest cities, she reported people were dying in the hospital from lack of food and medicine. The facility averaged seventy deaths per month. In the town of Santa Clara, she discovered "at least 250 children right in the city who need care"—and certainly there were many more in the tiny villages outside the city. She reported there were reliable accounts from Santiago that as many as 1,500 children were in immediate need. Laura concluded her letter, "I wish that I might have between $30,000

Refugees on Street Corner in Remedios, Cuba, 1899 LIBRARY OF CONGRESS PRINTS
AND PHOTOGRAPHS DIVISION, WASHINGTON, D.C., LC-DIG-STEREO-1S20270.

and $40,000 placed in my hands for fitting up asylums and running them until the 1st of November." The men of the Cuban Orphan Society were quick to respond by issuing a public statement: "The need is urgent. We appeal for aid, generous aid." They also made $10,000 available to Laura immediately. As business owners and entrepreneurs, they viewed the money as a prudent investment: "If the children are properly cared for now, they in turn will later care for Cuba." They hoped their statement would touch the hearts of Americans, and it did.

By the end of July, almost $22,000 had been raised from generous individuals and groups. Boys at the Episcopal High School in Alexandria, Virginia, had sent a dollar; numerous churches had donated;

countless individuals whose names were published in New York news-papers contributed; and others listed as "a friend of the cause" or "anon-ymously" gave to the orphans. In addition, the Cuban Orphan Society had sent Laura a variety of supplies—sewing machines, calico, mus-lin, bedding, linen, shoes, stockings, needles, pins, writing paper, pens, pencils, condensed milk, and beef extract—on the transport *Kilpatrick*. Operating from her headquarters in Remedios, she informed the trust-ees in New York that the local government was refitting the old hospital building for use as a school and that one of her assistants traveled to Havana twice a week to help set up a kindergarten there in connection with the Widows' Home. She reported that the American military offi-cers had been supportive of their efforts, providing a horse and carriage for the women as they traveled free of charge anywhere on the island. "This will make a tremendous difference in expense for me, and I value it on this account as well as for the feeling of cordial support which our military authorities are giving to the work," Laura wrote. In Cienfuegos, the local Cuban government had established three large orphanages, and Laura and her teachers opened a kindergarten, providing classes in modern teaching methods for the city's teachers. Similar work was also being done at Guantanamo.

In December, Laura and her assistants—American and Cuban women—had established a kindergarten in Santa Maria del Rosario. She reported that it had become a center of curiosity for the locals. The Cuban mayor had set aside a plot of land plowed with the town oxen, and the American women, hoping to teach lessons about sound nutritional eat-ing, had supplied garden tools and vegetable seeds. Although the main goal of the orphan society was to educate young children, Laura helped set up clinics and nurses' training classes at Santa Maria del Rosario and Remedios. In the spring of 1900, new subscriptions to the Cuban Orphan Society had totaled about $37,000, and Laura had secured the services of twelve American teachers who had come to the island to teach at the orphanages. They taught kindergarten as well as sewing and agri-culture to older students. And some of the Cuban students were pre-paring to become teachers themselves. The ideas Laura and the Cuban Orphan Society implemented in Cuba were very similar to the efforts of the Settlement House Movement that had been established in New York City at about the same time—educational and social services for new immigrants that included kindergartens and adult education classes.

Back in New York City, the trustees of the Cuban Orphan Society, from the headquarters on Fifth Avenue, continued to supplement their coffers through the formation of women's sewing bees during Lent when women made items that would be sold at a National Easter Festival held April 16–21, 1900, at the 71st Regiment Armory. The weeklong event sold items that every New Yorker could use, and the proceeds went to the Cuban orphans. A permanent store had been set up at 15 Astor Place, and a loft in the streetcar barns at Park Avenue and 32nd Street housed supplies for the agency. Telephones and printing materials were provided at no cost to the society, and although the clerical staff received wages, all other work was completed by volunteers.

In April 1900, the *Detroit Free Press* published an article of reflections by a Michigan businessman who had vacationed on the island. As a business owner, he was highly interested in Cuba's postwar economy, but he also was greatly impressed with the work of Laura and her assistants. Visiting some of the orphanages with her, the American businessman wrote about the partnership between the Cuban Orphan Society and the local and central governments. The city of Remedios had given the orphanage a five-year lease on the school building along with 100 acres of land, while the central government had granted $16,000 for renovations of an old Spanish army barracks for use by the orphan organization. And in May, a reporter from Boston ran across Laura in Cuba and reported that she was acting as an ad hoc adviser to the U.S. military in matters concerning the welfare of children. "Young, self reliant, original and full of positive energy" is the way the reporter described her as she toiled in an "unattractive and laborious" field.

In the summer of 1900, Harvard University in Cambridge, Massachusetts, offered a unique opportunity to 1,500 Cuban teachers to attend six weeks of school at no cost to them. In addition to classes in teaching methods, history, English grammar, and literature, the students had the opportunity to visit local manufacturing businesses and enjoy nature excursions at local attractions. Classes were taught by forty American

Spanish-speaking instructors hired by Harvard and brought in from all over the country. A Harvard librarian taught a class about books and libraries. A teacher from Chicago taught government. And the university had convinced Laura to spend the summer in Cambridge to lend her unique insights to the project as an interpreter and consultant. The War Department supplied four transports to bring the Cubans to America, and Harvard students acted as guides. Although by most accounts the summer program was a successful enterprise, some of the women were annoyed that they were required to have chaperones when they were out and about, and they were required to be back to their rooms by 10:00 each night. The male students were free to come and go as they pleased at any hour—which on one occasion caused some young American men to be arrested as they helped the Cubans "see the city by night."

From the beginning, Laura and the Cuban Orphan Society perceived the orphanages as temporary solutions to the problem of large numbers of homeless children. They intended that the children would find permanent homes with Cuban families. And they viewed their methods as valuable models for future enterprises, especially in the realm of education. By January 1901, Laura had accepted a position back in the United States as dean of Barnard College. Again, influential leaders had recognized Laura as an individual whose positive energy would be a timeless asset.

Clemencia Lopez: "We Like You, but Not When You Come as Conquerors"

"Gen. Bell Tired of the Lenient Treatment of Filipinos"

"Gen. Bell Herding Natives in Towns and He Will Carry on a Policy of Confiscation"

"Gen. Bell Driving Filipinos in Batangas Like Sheep"

The headlines in American newspapers may have been reassuring to some Americans; however, they must have had a terrifying effect on Filipinos such as Clemencia Lopez, a young woman whose life would be significantly impacted by General Bell and his ruthless policies. News reports throughout 1900 delivered stark reality to bolster the headlines. In April, General Franklin J. Bell, American commander in the province of Batangas, issued a proclamation promising relentless retaliation until the Filipino fighters ceased their resistance. Threatening to take drastic measures to weed out the freedom fighters, including burning to the ground towns that harbored Filipino fighters, the general had already sent troops to complete their gruesome errands—"leaving the field strewn with dead" at one location and cornering and shooting fifty Filipinos in a river, "the bodies floating away." But the Filipinos were just as determined as ever and continued their fight for independence throughout 1900 and 1901. By December 1901, as the general had become increasingly frustrated with the fighters, he was much more specific in his warnings notifying the residents of Batangas province of what was to come. The Americans would begin the process of concentrating all residents in enclosed neighborhoods or zones of the towns. Some of their livestock and some food would be moved into the concentrated areas, and anything outside the area would be confiscated. Bell targeted the province's richest residents: "The wealthy and influential are those against whom the most energetic efforts should be directed." By January 1902, the Americans reported what they perceived as progress in their efforts. Many of the people of Batangas had packed up their belongings and left the area, those who had not fled had been herded into *reconcentrado* camps, and "the arrest of members of the wealthy Lopez family" had taken place.

By the time General Bell had arrested brothers Lorenzo, Cipriano, and Mariano Lopez, their sisters, Clemencia and Maria, had arrived in Hong Kong, where another brother, Sixto, lived in self-imposed exile. Initially, the visit simply may have been a joyous family reunion, but it soon evolved into a more dramatic conclave with the three siblings developing a plan to save their family. Sixto had spent the previous months touring in the United States as an outspoken advocate for Philippine independence. Some of the statements he made were labeled treasonous by Americans, who celebrated the acquisition of the Philippines in the peace treaty ending the Spanish-American War. "It is certain that permanent peace will never be established until Philippine independence is obtained," Sixto had

Clemencia Lopez FROM THE COLLECTION OF VICTORIA LOPEZ, LOPEZ OF BALAYAN,
BATANGAS FOUNDATION.

said. He rankled some when he expressed his opinions about Protestant missionaries who viewed Philippine Catholics as potential converts: "The Filipinos have had more than enough of missionaries. But we should be glad if the missionaries would give some other country a turn—Hawaii, for instance." And when he refused to sign an oath of allegiance to the Americans who occupied his homeland, it was advised he stay away— thus his exile in Hong Kong.

Shortly after their arrival in Hong Kong, the Lopez siblings heard about the arrest of their brothers and the confiscation of their property back in the Philippines. It was decided Clemencia would travel to the United States to petition President Theodore Roosevelt to intercede for the family. It didn't seem like such an outrageous idea because George Curry, a former Rough Rider with Teddy Roosevelt in Cuba, had been appointed chief of police in Manila and agreed to write a letter in support of Clemencia's plea for her brothers' release.

Ultimately, in March 1902, Clemencia did visit the White House and asked President Roosevelt to look into the troubling events in the Philippines, where, in Clemencia's opinion, his general had blatantly abused his power by arresting the Lopez brothers without affording them their civil rights and by illegally confiscating Lopez properties. Roosevelt was gracious and promised to give the situation some attention. In April, Clemencia received a letter from the president's secretary stating that Roosevelt "does not think anything can properly be done" and that there was consensus that "no injustice was done." It's unclear whether Clemencia's visit to the White House had any impact on her brothers' situation, but it was reported that their living conditions in the prison improved somewhat. And they were eventually released—in May after the resistance by Filipino fighters had essentially ended.

After Clemencia's visit to the White House, she continued to advocate for her brothers' release, but she also took advantage of her situation as a celebrity of sorts in America. For years, policies such as Manifest Destiny and the conquest of indigenous lands, which embraced ideas of racial and cultural superiority, had been part of American life. Inhabitants of the Philippine islands were characterized as uncivilized savages and referred to as "little brown brothers" by American officials and, according to a president, were people who needed to be educated, uplifted, and civilized. Beginning in December 1898, the policy of benevolent assimilation had been promoted by American leaders. President William McKinley had issued a proclamation explaining to the Filipino people that their new colonizers would afford them individual rights and liberties and that the mission of the United States was "one of benevolent assimilation." The proclamation explained that this included maintaining "the strong arm of authority, to repress disturbance and to overcome all obstacles to the bestowal of the blessings of a good and stable government upon the people of the Philippine Islands under the free flag of the United States."

As newspapers began to run articles and photos of Clemencia and as influential people such as anti-imperialists Fiske and Gretchen Warren, who shared the Lopez family's belief in independence for the Filipinos, befriended her and introduced her to other powerful people, some Americans began to develop a different impression of Filipinos and questioned some of the ideas implemented by American policymakers. Clemencia made speeches about life in the Philippines, telling Americans about the ugly side of benevolent assimilation that she and her family had witnessed. She explained that her family had welcomed Americans into their home in Batangas and looked forward to a peaceful resolution to the situation in her homeland—including independence or at least a form of self-government.

Clemencia had acquired a solid education in the Philippines, and when she was offered the opportunity to attend Wellesley College during an extended stay with the Warrens, she enrolled as a special student. At Wellesley, Clemencia was in the company of female political scientists, economists, historians, writers, and activists. It was here that she honed her English skills and "spent some of my happiest hours in this country." Her economics professor, Katharine Coman, said, "We have found Senorita Lopez a most delightful, courteous, charming and responsive student." As her English skills improved and as Clemencia gained confidence, she continued to speak out for causes such as Philippine independence.

In the spring of 1902 as Congress debated the Philippine Organic Act laying out the governing framework for the new American territory, politicians haggled over details of education, economic, and justice systems; trade guidelines; and governing bodies in towns and provinces as well as other facets of Philippine society. Clemencia and the Anti-Imperialist League struggled to be part of the process. It was hoped that Clemencia would speak to a Senate committee, but in the end, the Committee on the Philippines simply accepted written documents from her.

However, the New England branch of the Women's Suffrage Association invited her to speak in June, and she delivered a memorable talk: "I believe that we are both striving for much the same object—you for the right to take part in national life; we for the right to have a national life to take part in." She talked about her homeland and her fellow Filipinas as they struggled to adjust to life after war: "I should like to say a word about the patriotism of the women. This is a delicate subject, for to be patriotic to our country means that we must oppose the policy of yours. But patriotism is a quality which we all ought to be able to admire even in an opponent." She wanted American women to understand the importance of self-government to Filipinas: "I should have reason to be ashamed if I had to come before this association with the admission that our women were indifferent to the cause of their country's independence. You would have a right to despise me and my countrywomen if we had so little love for our native land as to consent that our country should be governed by foreign hands. You ought to understand that we are only contending for the liberty of our country, just as you once fought for the same liberty for yours." On July 4, 1902, President Theodore Roosevelt proclaimed the Philippine-American War over, and Clemencia and her fellow Filipinos had not won their independence or self-rule. Despite what must have been a heartbreaking setback, Clemencia continued to speak out. And many Americans refused to abandon hope that one day Filipinos would enjoy independence.

On the afternoon of May 13, 1903, anyone walking past the Hotel Bellevue in Boston may have heard strains of orchestra music drifting from one of the banquet halls. About 150 members of the New England Anti-Imperialist League gathered for a luncheon and to hear Clemencia speak. Several speakers shared their thoughts on a range of topics related to the recently concluded Philippine-American War—the cost in financial terms as well as in human capital and the group's hopes for the future. "The very badness of the situation in the Philippines affords hope of a change for the better," one speaker said. And another said, "I think that at heart and in their sane senses the people of America are opposed to aggressiveness and injustice." Another concluded, "Let us continue rubbing in these facts and figures until all the people get them through their heads."

Then it was time for the featured speaker. "Who would imagine that barbarity and cruelty would disgrace American troops in the Philippines! You know how towns were destroyed by fire; people left homeless; Filipinos thrown in prison and shot without proof of any crime. I cannot place the loss of life, due directly or indirectly to the American occupation, at less than 1,000,000 souls," Clemencia said. She called for a commission to travel to her homeland to "ascertain the real situation and the real sentiments of the Filipinos." She concluded, "The Filipinos have no natural dislike of Americans. We like you when we visit you in your own country or when you visit us in ours, but not when you come as conquerors."

A Farewell Luncheon

IN HONOR OF

SEÑORITA CLEMENCIA LÓPEZ,

OCTOBER 5, 1903,

IN THE ROOMS OF

THE TWENTIETH CENTURY CLUB.

Pamphlet from Farewell Luncheon for Clemencia AUTHOR'S COLLECTION.

Of course, those remarks couldn't go unnoticed. At least one newspaper took offense and printed an editorial about the gathering of the anti-imperialists. "The Boston anti's may have their little lunches and dinners and make as much as they like of any little Filipino lions or lionesses that they can get hold of as sensations, but their antics merely amuse the people at large," the *Statesman Journal* (Salem, Ore.) opined.

In the fall of 1903 as Clemencia made plans to return to her native Philippines, the Anti-Imperialist League held a farewell luncheon on October 5. It was a bittersweet afternoon as one speaker after another apologized to Clemencia for the occupation of her homeland by the Americans. It was "one of the great national crimes of history" under the guise of benevolent assimilation, which was nothing more than a "pious fraud," a speaker proclaimed. Another empathized with Clemencia that she would be returning to a home where a foreign country "which boasts of a government of the people, by the people, for the people" would "conduct business, frame the laws, exact the penalties." A "foreign soldiery enforces submission," and "a Christian civilization has been introduced at the mouth of the cannon!" Speakers expressed pleasure in learning more about the Philippine people through their interactions with Clemencia: "She has told us of a Christian and civilized people, traduced as savages, in order that another people, professedly and boastingly Christian, might 'civilize' them by fire, famine and slaughter, pillage their property, imprison their able leaders, fetter their trade, interfere with their religion." Others pleaded with Clemencia to assure her fellow Filipinos that not all Americans agreed with the policies of the American government. "I beg our injured friends in the Orient to bear in mind that unnumbered American hearts beat in sympathy with them and for their aims to establish self-government," a speaker said. Another speaker reminded the audience that America's struggles with racism toward Black people continued and had transferred to the people of the Philippines. "The doctrine that brown men have no right to be free applies with equal force to Black men, and the attempt to conquer eight millions of Filipinos threatens the freedom of ten million American citizens," the speaker said. "In the struggle to maintain the rights of our colored citizens the rights of the Filipinos will be won." Finally, Sixto Lopez took the stage, thanking the members on behalf of his mother and himself for cordially receiving Clemencia in America.

Clemencia implored the audience to understand that although the war had ended, many Filipinos continued to suffer in the aftermath. The racism that had victimized Black people in America persisted. "Now it is the brown," she said. "I have found that the majority of Americans have good intentions in regard to the Philippine Islands . . . and deplore the conduct of the representatives of the government of this country . . . and [am] convinced that justice demands the independence of the Philippines." She described the situation in her home province of Batangas, where there existed "a picture full of gloom." Afterward, one of the attendees said, "We were indignant at the wrongs [toward] the Filipinos before; but now our feeling is less impersonal; it goes deeper and is more intimate."

As the early years of the 1900s transitioned to the midway mark of the decade, Americans tried to put the Philippine issues behind. Newspapers carried few articles about the faraway islands and instead focused on the day-to-day happenings of ordinary citizens. In Abingdon, Virginia, T. W. Preston & Co. real estate advertised a nice three-room house for sale for $300; the family of Philip Hagerman mourned his loss in Ukiah, California, when he died from a large pepperwood tree limb striking the back of his head; and in Winona, Minnesota, bowling leagues battled for first place with the Exchange, taking three games from the Gophers at the Philharmonic alleys. People may have wondered if General Bell was thinking of Clemencia when he encouraged the army to allow soldiers' wives to go to the Philippines with their husbands, as they might have an impact on Filipinas and have "more influence on public opinion than the men of the islands." General Bell's military career took an upward trajectory despite the bad press he had received after the army released a report of devastating conditions in Batangas province as a result of the general's policies. President Roosevelt appointed him army chief of staff and promoted him to major general. Sixto Lopez remained in exile in Hong Kong as he persistently resisted that oath of allegiance to the Americans who occupied his homeland. Clemencia carried on her fight for just causes, resuming her role as a valuable spokesperson for Philippine independence and the anti-imperialist movement. In 1905, she was one of a group of women who founded the Philippine Feminist Association, "committed to social service and reform . . . and women's civic participation" in society. They called for reform in women's education, labor, and prisons, among other areas of concern for women.

7

Women of the Arts Reflect the Times

"To Pay the Tax"

She sits alone in the window seat,
Watching the soldiers who throng the street.
A tear clings fast to her gentle eye,
Her bosom heaves with a sudden sigh,
And her slender fingers that clutch the sill
Wave a proud adieu with a royal will.
But her mouth in its motions never slacks
O'er the gum she cheweth to pay the tax.

There are women who go to the battle front,
Women in hospitals bearing the brunt,
Women who serve 'neath the Red Cross sign,
Women whose mission seems half divine,
But Annabel sits at the window high,
She cannot go where the bullets fly,
But steadily onward through packs and packs,
She cheweth the gum to pay the tax.

WHEN THE U.S. CONGRESS BEGAN TO CONSIDER THE MOST LUCRATIVE way to raise money to support the war in Cuba and the Philippines in the spring of 1898, the Ways and Means Committee mulled placing taxes on certain items that were likely to bring in some serious money. It was the hope that the taxes would raise sufficient revenues at the very beginning of the hostilities to equip and operate an army "capable of crushing the enemy in short order." Three items rose to the top of the list: beer, tobacco, and chewing gum. And when word about the possibility of a tax on one of America's favorite treats—chewing gum—spread, creative types, such as songwriters and poets, quickly turned their attention to the issue. The anonymous writer of "To Pay the Tax" was one example, and T. C. Harbaugh's "The Chewing Gum Tax" was another:

"The Chewing Gum Tax"

> Start the factories to going,
> Let the gum brigade advance.
> It will chew old Spain to ruin
> If they only get a chance;
> Every Yankee girl stands ready
> To eclipse the sword and drum,
> And the Spanish won't be in it
> When we put a tax on gum.

As one newspaper pointed out, "As every war furnished its own heroes, so does every war furnish its own song." And the Spanish-American War was no exception. Poems and song lyrics about the war flowed from writers' pens as the country veered toward conflict with Spain. Ella Randall Pearce penned this:

"To the Women of America"

> If you cannot in the army
> Serve to march against the foe,
> You can send your loved ones thither,
> Firmly, bravely bid them go.
> You can show them faith and courage,
> You can lend them cheer and might,
> You can hold them to their duty,
> You can help them win the fight.

Jennie R. Anderson wrote "A Song of '98," commemorating the sinking of the USS *Maine*:

Our eyes have seen fair Cuba with four hundred thousand slain,
We have seen our slaughtered seamen, we have seen the stricken *Maine*.
And the hand that wrought the ruin, was the dastard hand of Spain,
Our host is marching on.

Songwriter and composer Hattie Moulton dedicated her composition "Our Boys" to the men in Company G, 1st California Volunteers. The Zeno Mauvais Company of San Francisco sold the sheet music of this inspirational composition describing the departure of the lads for the Philippines. The accomplishment by the young lady was somewhat remarkable considering Hattie was a sixteen-year-old student at John Swett Grammar School.

Other young people were recognized for their songwriting abilities during the war. Eleven-year-old Florence Wentz Adams wrote "The Soldiers' Saying":

Our flag is near us,
Some brave hearts to cheer us,
We know that we fight for the right.
Onward we'll go,
Never fear the foe,
Even if we they smite.

And another eleven-year-old, Anna Cleveland, wrote this:

"Manila, May 1, 1898."

There lay the Spanish ships
All splendid in array,
None of the captains even dreamed
Their fleet would burn that day.

There lay the Spanish ships
Their captains ne'er would say,

"We were licked by the Americans
Upon the first of May!"

The war also inspired new dances—the military two-step, the cadet lancers military square dance, and a line dance named the "volunteer skirmish." Waltzes were out of style; while two-steps—more suitable to marching music—were very much in vogue. In the spirit of intense patriotism, small American flags were incorporated into dance moves as participants passed the flags from dancer to dancer.

Surprisingly, the popularity of war dances and songs failed to result in brisk sales for music-related businesses in America. Sheet music seller J. M. Christian of Philadelphia complained that while there was a flood of war songs on the market, Americans were not buying them, choosing instead more lighthearted music. A music publisher said his customers were not buying the new patriotic songs either, although sheet music sales for the old favorite "The Star-Spangled Banner" were robust. "When I say that the popular-song business is dead until the war is at an end I do not exaggerate," he said. "Theaters are popular during a war, for people want to be amused, and one would think that songs that interested them in times of peace would interest them in war times; that they would applaud them in public and play them in their homes. Personally, however, I find that the opposite is the case."

And as the exasperated music publisher expressed, war-themed plays *were* undecidedly fashionable. One, simply titled "Cuba," featured a plot rife with conspiracies and characters sure to attract audiences—female spies, Rough Riders, the Red Cross's Clara Barton, and dying soldiers. In "Old Glory in Cuba," a character wraps an American flag around himself, shouting at a Spanish soldier, "Fire upon this if you dare." All ends well with the playing of "The Star-Spangled Banner." Playwright Lillian Lewis's "For Liberty and Love," a romantic military drama centering on "the loves and losses and sorrows and strife" of wartime Cubans, includes the "palpitating vibration of fife and drum" and "weeping and laughter, brave deeds, brave women," all for liberty and love. And what theater-goer could resist a play titled "Red, White and Blue" with its themes of love and war laced with American courage, Spanish intrigue, fiery battle scenes, and a gallant defense waged by American women to protect their wounded countrymen, all neatly tied up by the end of the play with the arrival of an American man-of-war driving the Spanish into the sea—causing audiences to break into loud hissing at some of the performances? If theater audiences preferred lighter fare, there were plenty of war comedies to ease the pain of wartime America. "For the Flag" featured a hero who was a daredevil fighter as well as a "picturesque lover." The play "A Milk White Flag" was described as "hilariously illustrating the follies and foibles current among our popular militia" and "creating a comic sufficiency that drives dull care away." Playwright Lottie Blair Parker's four-act comedy-drama titled "A War Correspondent" featured Burr McIntosh in the lead, lending a unique perspective to the role, as he had been a news correspondent in Cuba. And the female lead, Grace Filkins, was the real-life wife of navy Lieutenant Commander Adolph Marix, who had survived the explosion on the USS *Maine*. For as little as twenty-five cents, a person could enjoy an evening at the local opera house in most small towns and cities across the country. Better seats ran seventy-five cents to as much as $1.

Two new wax exhibits were introduced at New York City's Eden Musée in May 1898 just as the war heated up. One portrayed a scene on Admiral George Dewey's warship the USS *Olympia*. Three gunners stripped to the waists stood by the ship's big cannon, which was about to be fired as an officer and assistant in uniform waited nearby. The other new exhibit replicated naval heroes Admiral Dewey, Rear Admiral William Sampson, Commodore Winfield Scott Schley, and Captain Charles Sigsbee with the army's General Nelson Miles, Lieutenant Colonel Theodore Roosevelt, and Major General William Shafter. Overhead, a wax war balloon held other officers and implored visitors to "Remember the Maine." The Musée's cinematograph had been sent to Havana to capture authentic scenes of war—the USS *Maine* entering the harbor, the crew at work on the deck, divers working on the sunken hulk, burial of the sailors, and war correspondents rushing to the telegraph office. The moving photographs were shown hourly during the day and evening. Admission was twenty-five cents. In July, when his ship the USS *Saint Paul* stopped in Tompkinsville, Staten Island, for coaling, Captain Sigsbee visited the

Musée, experiencing an eerie feeling at the sight of his life-size wax figure. "It's a right novel sensation this meeting yourself face to face for the first time," he said. "I don't know that I quite like it." He remarked on the skill of his tailor who had made the coat for the wax doll: "Either the doll is better built than I am or else that tailor knows his business. The coat fits like a glove. The wax doll rather had the best of me." The hero said the moving pictures were shocking. "At first sight it's most alarming. It gave me a cold chill," he added.

Political cartoons were rather predictable during the war with Uncle Sam typically portrayed as a tall, lanky figure and his honest, kindly face with a "joke rollicking somewhere about his eyes or mouth." Many depicted pointed political commentary such as the one of a grim-faced Uncle Sam striding forth to war with a gun slung over one shoulder, while a plump lady "with a Wall Street-broker face" and named "Business Interests" clung to his neck pleading, "Oh don't go to war, Sam; it would kill me." Spanish newspapers also had their versions of political cartoons—Uncle Sam's face was portrayed as homely rather than jolly, and more times than not, he was a fat, ugly pig.

American citizens were given plenty of opportunities to witness the personages and events of the war through art in local newspapers and national publications. The *Journal Times* (Racine, Wisc.) offered a series of paintings of war scenes titled "Our Nation in War." *Leslie's Illustrated Monthly* gave away three proofs of original drawings with a three-month subscription to the magazine for $1.25. Charles Nelan, an artist with the *New York Herald*, came out with a book titled *Humorous War Sketches*. The Paris Exposition showcased war pictures of Black American soldiers at the Afro-American exhibit. And for those who could not make it to Paris, tramps riding the train throughout Illinois had tastefully decorated train cars with patriotic pictures and sentiments in colored chalk.

Thomas Edison's moving pictures were the rage across the country. In Boston, patrons at the Pitts-Kimball Company's third-floor exhibition hall could enjoy a matinee of Edison's kinetekinetoscopes in a room cooled by a new ventilation system that changed the air in the room every minute—comfortable as the seaside. In Hope, Kansas, patrons experienced Edison's living, moving pictures—"the greatest wonder of the

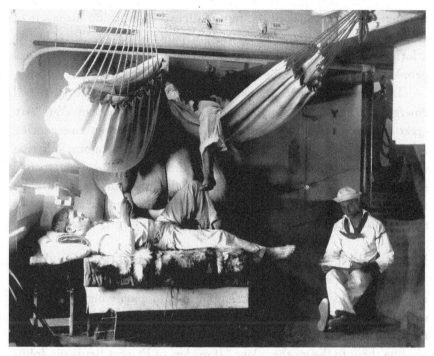

Sailors in Their Quarters on the USS *Olympia*, Captured by Photographer Frances Benjamin Johnston LIBRARY OF CONGRESS PRINTS AND PHOTOGRAPHS DIVISION, WASHINGTON, D.C., LC-DIG-PPMSCA-38990.

age"—at the opera house, where management claimed, "We strive to please, and do please."

By the time peace between the United States and Spain was on the horizon late in the summer of 1898, the art community, like other facets of American life, was looking toward the postwar era. As the *Washington Post* mused, "The conquest of Spanish territory has been so easy that it is perhaps natural that quick speculation as to the material results of that conquest should follow. . . . And while politicians are surveying their grounds for a place in the premises, while missionaries are girding up their loins for civilizing tasks in the new territory, and while manufacturers of everything possible of exploitation in the new climes, from patent medicines and unpatented beverages to ice-making machines, are taking account of demand and means, it is pertinent to inquire what the transferred colonies may in the future offer to enterprising managers of amusements." At the same time, the newspaper admitted, "There is also a lot of balderdash being printed about what the American theatrical people are going to do in the newly acquired Spanish colonies."

The *Kansas City Star* offered a unique critique of war art that had emerged during the brief months of the Spanish-American War: "Art, great as it is, much as it does for mankind, fails in certain emergencies. And perhaps it is well. Perhaps it is better that terror, agony, suffering cannot be preserved on canvas, bronze, or marble, to remain a perpetual spectacle. None may reproduce 'the groan, the roll in dust, the all-white eye turned back within its socket.' And thus the years of peace overgrow and hide the years of war and man is privileged to forget."

FRANCES BENJAMIN JOHNSTON: "A GENIUS FOR HARD WORK"

"Pure white striped with dark chocolate . . . crimson with a pouch of soft rose . . . a series of hairy blotches upon its drooping wings, reveling in striped green and brown petals with a cinnamon brown lip. The twin blossoms looked like two great bumblebees tugging away from the stout cords binding them to the mother plant." If readers of Frances Benjamin Johnston's article "Some White House Orchids" in *Demorest's Family Magazine* in June 1895 couldn't envision the lovely blooms so artfully depicted in the writer's words, their curiosity was sated by the breathtaking photographs tucked among the words. Her gift for seeking out titillating topics to spark readers' interests—peeks inside the homes of the wealthy or mysteries of money making at the nation's mints—coupled with her journalistic and photographic genius made Frances a sought-after professional by newspaper and magazine publishers. Readers were drawn to her portrayals of woodwork "cut and enameled to give the creamy richness of ivory" and her crisp photographs of women workers trimming and stacking currency sheets at the Bureau of Engraving and Printing.

Frances lived in Washington, D.C., with her parents Anderson Doniphan and Antoinette Benjamin Johnston, who provided their only child with invaluable advantages in terms of education and social exposure, including art school in Paris. Her father's position as an employee of the U.S. Treasury Department and her mother's job as a correspondent

Florence Benjamin Johnston, 1896 LIBRARY OF CONGRESS PRINTS AND PHOTOGRAPHS
DIVISION, WASHINGTON, D.C., LC-DIG-PPMSCA-38981.

for the *Baltimore Sun* newspaper, where under the pen name Ione she
was touted as "Our Washington Lady Correspondent," aided Frances in
immeasurable ways. An aunt, Elizabeth Bryant Johnston, was a talented

writer, penning several editions of a visitors' guide to Mount Vernon and a definitive book cataloging the history behind the original portraits of George Washington. Bolstered by the support of her well-positioned family, Frances certainly entered the world of journalism with obvious advantages. However, her success as an entrepreneur and her renown as an internationally acclaimed photographer came about as a result of clearly defined characteristics that Frances identified in a piece she wrote in the *Ladies' Home Journal* in 1897. In "What a Woman Can Do with a Camera," Frances encouraged readers to consider photography as a career: "Photography as a profession should appeal particularly to women, and in it there are great opportunities for a good-paying business—but only under very well-defined conditions." She provided a list: "good common sense, unlimited patience to carry her through endless failures, equally unlimited tact, good taste, a quick eye, a talent for detail and a genius for hard work."

Although Frances had initially found satisfaction in painting, she eventually became interested in photography, studying at the Smithsonian and acquiring a Kodak camera. And though her early writings were illustrated with her drawings, she transitioned to using photographs. Her talent as a photographer and her access to Washington society presented her with opportunities to earn a living as a portrait photographer for government officials, including cabinet secretaries as well as the presidents and first families. In early 1897, she photographed First Lady Frances Cleveland and the wives of the cabinet at her studio at 1332 V Street "fitted up in artistic effects with draperies, old armor, and a cozy open fire." Her experience photographing the officials of the federal government earned her the title "court photographer of Washington." She captured photos of magnificent buildings and statues in Washington and served as an official photographer at the Chicago world's fair in 1893. She was hired to photograph students at Hampton Institute in Virginia, where Booker T. Washington had gone to school. Those photos became the backbone of the "American Negro" exhibition composed by W. E. B. Du Bois for the Paris Exposition in 1900. She did a series of photos at the U.S. Naval Academy, documenting phases of cadet life at Annapolis. She also photographed ordinary people as they went about their work—a milkman with his cart and dog, breaker boys in Pennsylvania coal mines, women working at a shoe factory in Massachusetts, and men working in salt mines.

Her work was featured at galleries and museums in the United States as well as abroad. When Philadelphia's Academy of Fine Arts organized the first Photographic Salon in this country, Frances was one of the artists asked to showcase her work. The United States National Museum (later known as the Arts and Industries Building at the Smithsonian) sent her to study photographic exhibits in the museums of Europe. Three hundred American photographers applied to show their work at the "IV Exhibition of the Photographic Salon" of London, running from September to November 1896, but only nineteen were selected. One woman—Frances Benjamin Johnston—was selected to participate. In 1898, three of Frances's photographs were featured at the Paris Photographic Salon.

When the United States became enmeshed in war with Spain in 1898, cameras and moving picture machines injected war scenes into the lives of everyday Americans—fueling either hunger for more or disdain for America's imperialistic tendencies. Frances was one of the photographers who played a role in documenting historic events and people related to the conflict. The French ambassador to the United States, Jules Cambon, helped negotiate peace between the United States and Spain, and when his official photo appeared in newspapers, often Frances's name ran under it as a credit. In August 1898, the war officially ended with the signing of a peace agreement—captured in photos by Frances. In January 1899, when President William McKinley formed the Philippine Commission, a group of five men charged with studying conditions in the islands and making recommendations for life after Spanish rule, Frances was asked by the president to take an official photograph. Admiral George Dewey, the American naval commander who had defeated the Spanish navy in the Philippines, was a member. It would not be the last time Frances would interact with the admiral.

In June 1899, Admiral Dewey began his journey home. Traveling on his flagship, the *Olympia*, Dewey left the Philippine islands on June 1 on a westward route that would take him through Asia, the Middle East, and Europe before arriving in the United States. Throughout the three-month journey, Americans were kept abreast of the admiral's progress through newspaper reports, telegrams, and messages sent by the admiral. Victory celebrations were planned for the war hero as soon as he was back on American soil, so planners kept in touch with Dewey as he neared the shores of his homeland. All along the way at ports around the world, Dewey and his crew were greeted with salutes and visitors who came aboard to meet the naval hero—government leaders, American ambassadors, tourists, and ordinary citizens who wanted to meet the man whom everyone was talking about. In Hong Kong, Singapore, Ceylon, Egypt, and Austria, curious people crowded the docks when news of the arrival of the *Olympia* spread. In Colombo, Ceylon, although his arrival was not marked by any official ceremonies, he was enthusiastically received by crowds in the streets when he ventured ashore. Near Aden, Arabia, the *Olympia* encountered rocky waters as monsoons tossed the ship about. During a coaling stop in Port Said, Egypt, the crew voluntarily quarantined, then sailed for Trieste, Austria, where they were greeted with a twenty-one-gun salute and a visit from the U.S. ambassador. On August 5, the *Olympia* arrived in Naples, Italy, where they were again greeted by salutes, officials, and tourists. A musical troupe was invited aboard and entertained with Italian ballads for two hours.

Dewey's popularity made him the man of the hour, and news agencies were eager to feature him in their publications. They knew their readers would buy newspapers and magazines that carried details about the intriguing naval commander, and photos of the returning war hero on board his ship only enhanced the story. Much was made of a photo session the admiral sat for at the request of an Italian photographer who was reportedly the official photographer of the king of Italy. And American publications were frantic to capture the story and the photos. *Harper's Bazaar* weekly magazine ran a full page featuring the pets living on the *Olympia*—Prince, a "shaggy, good-natured" collie pup; Maria, a cat that was mother to forty-nine kittens; and Sagasta, a Filipino pig that the crew named after Spanish Prime Minister Práxedes Mateo Sagasta. But it was Frances Benjamin Johnston who obtained some of the most iconic images of Dewey and his crew experiencing day-to-day activities on the *Olympia*.

Frances B. Johnston and Admiral Dewey on the Deck of the USS *Olympia*
LIBRARY OF CONGRESS PRINTS AND PHOTOGRAPHS DIVISION, WASHINGTON, D.C., LC-J689-5.

Frances worked for George Grantham Bain's news service, which provided photos and news stories to the country's major newspapers, and it was likely the Bain's Correspondence Bureau that sent her in July 1899 to track down Admiral Dewey as he traveled home from the Philippines. She wasted no time in embarking on her mission. While the country's newspapers were running articles outlining the admiral's itinerary, they were sometimes days late and not always accurate as delays occurred and weather affected the ship's progress. Frances's first challenge was to calculate where the admiral would be on any given day. However, within forty-eight hours of receiving her assignment, she was on her way to Paris from New York. She was surprised to find that although Americans were enamored with the admiral, Europeans were not as avid fans, and when she inquired about the possible whereabouts of the American admiral, she was frequently met with blank stares. Eventually, she learned that the *Olympia* would dock at Naples on August 6, and she booked train passage from Paris to Naples. Within twenty-four hours, she had reached

Sailors Dancing with Each Other Aboard the USS *Olympia* LIBRARY OF CONGRESS
PRINTS AND PHOTOGRAPHS DIVISION, WASHINGTON, D.C., LC-USZ62-47558.

Naples, arriving in the evening but immediately gaining access to Admiral Dewey. She found herself being warmly welcomed by the admiral, whom she found a "modest, courteous gentleman." She was invited back to the ship to begin her photographic journey of the admiral and crew set for 8:00 the next morning. Spending the day documenting the crew and Admiral Dewey in their natural environments brought the images to life as she photographed the men eating at tables in the mess, relaxing in their bunks (canvas hammocks suspended from braided ropes), and dancing with fellow crew members in the absence of female partners. She followed the *Olympia* when it made its way to the next stop in Leghorn, Italy, and showed Dewey the proofs of the photos she had taken the day before. He was pleased, and Frances sent the photos off to New York. *Harper's Bazaar* called the collection "a piece of energetic work, that does credit to men, as well as to women."

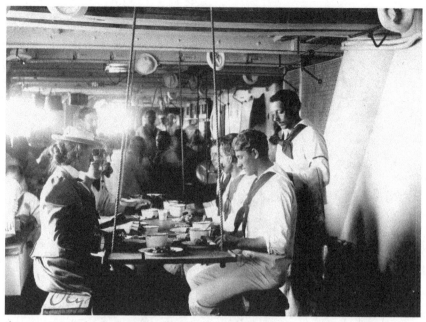

Frances Sharing a Meal with the Crew on the USS *Olympia* LIBRARY OF CONGRESS PRINTS AND PHOTOGRAPHS DIVISION, WASHINGTON, D.C., LC-DIG-PPMSCA-38989.

Frances carried on an illustrious career as a popular and highly regarded photographer throughout her lifetime. She died in 1952 at the age of eighty-eight. Over the years, many tried to put into words the essence of her art. One of the most eloquent was this: "They are like fine engravings, with the soft finish of satin in the delicate outlines."

JEAN MAWSON: "A GIRL OF MORE THAN ORDINARY PROMISE"

The *Boston Home Journal* described playwright and actress Jean Mawson as "a girl of more than ordinary promise" in April 1899. At the time, she was making a splash with her new production, *A Daughter of Cuba*, a play she had written and was starring in. The *Washington Post* declared her "still young and pretty." And a Grand Rapids, Michigan, newspaper offered this: "Graceful as a fawn and slender as a silken thread."

And while audiences were attracted to *A Daughter of Cuba* for a chance to witness the enchanting Miss Mawson in action, it was the topic of the play that drew crowds in most locations around the Midwest and Northeast

Jean Mawson METROPOLITAN MUSEUM OF ART, NEW YORK, ART RESOURCE.

in the late fall of 1898 and throughout 1899. When the play debuted in late 1898, Americans were celebrating a resounding victory against the Spanish in Cuba. Although fighting continued in the Philippines, people couldn't stop reveling in the glory of the American troops who had served in Cuba and especially any who had played any part in the capture of San Juan Hill—an experience immortalized by Teddy Roosevelt and his Rough Riders. *A Daughter of Cuba*, described as a comedy war drama, centered on the experiences of the 71st Infantry Regiment from New York—volunteer National Guardsmen who fought in Cuba at San Juan Hill along with the Rough Riders. But it also was a love story with Jean playing an American woman named Adele and her love interest Jack Price played by William H. Hallett. When he enlisted in the 71st, Adele rebuked her leading man, crying, "You care more for glory than you do for me." His girl's criticism failed to deter Jack, and he boarded a transport from New York, arriving in Siboney, Cuba, just in time to march toward Santiago via El Caney and San Juan Hill, where fierce fighting with the Spanish troops resulted in Jack being wounded. The fictitious Jack was unaware that his girlfriend was also in Cuba. The theatergoers, however, had learned of Adele's plan to travel to Cuba when she turned to the audience after berating Jack and confided, "I too can be brave, I too shall go to war." And she did—as a Red Cross nurse who happened to serve at Siboney. Imagine the audience's delight when Jack and Adele discovered each other in the hospital tent— Jack a wounded soldier and Adele his caring nurse.

As much as audiences and critics relished the love story, they were more enamored by the thrilling battle scenes artfully designed by Jean's scene artist, who had accompanied her to Cuba on a mission to see firsthand what Jack and Adele would have encountered. Working from sketches and authentic photographs from the war, the artist had created "plenty of atmosphere" to captivate the audience. And not one reviewer failed to mention the mighty Maxim machine gun that "will belch forth death and smoke to the infinite delight of patriotic ones in the audience." The scenes took place in New York as the 71st boarded transports, in the encampments and trenches of Cuba, on the crude roadways and valleys of Cuba as the Spanish fired on the advancing Americans, and in the hills and thick forests as the Spanish retreated.

A Daughter of Cuba opened on September 19, 1898, at People's The-atre in New York City, traveling to Wilkes-Barre, Pennsylvania, the fol-lowing week. In November, it ran at the Grand Opera House in Marion, Ohio, where seats sold for twenty-five to seventy-five cents apiece. In Boston in April 1899, soldiers from Massachusetts's regiments who had returned from service in Cuba appeared onstage as extras. When it ran in Washington, D.C., at the Academy of Music in the spring of 1899 the-atergoers marveled at the playwright's "insight into human nature" that came through in the writing and acting.

Most of the reviews were positive. The *Washington Times* remarked at the "fine flow of wit" displayed by Jean's writing and her ability to write lines that "alternately bring tears of laughter and of sympathy." The *Morning Call's* theater critic in Allentown, Pennsylvania, described *A Daughter of Cuba* a "pure and wholesome" play "filled with human interest, mingled with comedy." And one critic called attention to the playwright's talent for constructing a story illustrating the somber realities of war as well as the occasional humorous incidents that punctuate even the most solemn events in life. Of course, not all the reviews were favorable. Washing-ton's *Evening Star* christened *A Daughter of Cuba* "a dismal failure" and reminded readers that in fact the 71st Regiment may not have had a ster-ling reputation in terms of their performance on San Juan Hill. The good-bye scene in New York as the volunteers departed from their sweethearts, mothers, and sisters was "long, tedious and agonizing" in the reviewer's opinion—which resulted in "the almost unanimous exodus of the male part of the audience for stimulants." And Jean's portrayal of Adele was not immune from this relentless critic, who described the character "about which all the rest of the play turns with much literary creaking" as "barely passable." The critic concluded that Jean Mawson would have been wise to follow the "example of the lawyer who waived his argument and made a motion for a new trial before his case went to the jury."

Another reviewer of *A Daughter of Cuba* noted the contrast between the noisy, abrasive battle scene in the third act and the "charming" final act in which the heroes return home "wounded, fever-stricken and crippled" and with "a story in their hearts which will live with them to the end of time." In *A Daughter of Cuba*, Jean Mawson had produced a dramatic event meant to entertain, but it reflected reality in that many men and women returned from Cuba with wounds and diseases as well as memories that remained in their hearts and minds all their lives.

GEORGIANA "GEORGIE" FRANCK GREENLEAF: BOOKS OR BEER?

"Almost by the time the American soldier had stacked arms in the city a score of American saloons were opened." *Leslie's Weekly* claimed Manila's "air reeks with odors of the worst of English liquors" and called the saloon infestation the "worst possible kind of blot on Uncle Sam's fair name." According to the magazine, "The saloonkeeper sneaked in under the folds of Old Glory." Initially, it was the Spaniards and native Filipinos who engaged in the liquor trade and catered to the Americans; however, before long, American entrepreneurs arrived to take advantage of the business opportunities presented by the American presence in the Philippines.

In the fall of 1899, Georgie Greenleaf found herself in a position to do something about the threat facing American soldiers and sailors serving their country. As wife of army surgeon Colonel Charles Ravenscroft Greenleaf, she had supported her husband in his career as he mended limbs and saved lives in Cuba and the Philippines, and she might have devoted her days to teas and social events with other military wives in the San Francisco area, where the couple lived in late 1899. However, she chose to mend books and save men from the evils of alcohol as she devised a "counter-attraction to the saloon" problem in the Philippines, where American soldiers continued to fight the Filipinos. Her solution to the problem: offer America's fighting men a buffet of reading material and a place to consume it. And she enlisted the aid of influential people and patriotic organizations in her quest to accumulate a mass of bound books, paperbacks, magazines, and newspapers. Across the nation, through newspapers and by word of mouth, the call went out for donations: "Library for Soldiers" in the *Little Falls (MN) Weekly Transcript*, "An Appeal for Aid for This Patriotic Enterprise" in the *Los Angeles Times*, and "Books for Soldiers" in Honolulu's *Hawaiian Star*. Reading materials and financial support flowed in from around the country to designated collection centers set up by Georgie and women's groups.

When the Berkeley, California, branch of the Red Cross Society disbanded, there was a tidy sum of $350 in the treasury; hearing of Georgie's efforts to establish the library in Manila, the group donated the entire amount to the cause. The library at the University of California, Berkeley, became a collection center for contributions. Prominent Rabbi Jacob Voorsanger headed up a committee consisting of the very wealthy Phoebe Hearst, Stanford University's cofounder Jane Stanford, and San Francisco Mayor James Phelan to lend support to the campaign. The Sons of the American Revolution branch in Michigan sent books. The Chicago chapter of the Daughters of the American Revolution (DAR) collected books and magazines. In Ohio, each chapter of the DAR resolved to contribute to the library in memory of the state's men who had given their lives in the Philippine-American War. In San Francisco, more than 100 volumes sat in an office waiting for shipment to the men in the Philippines. Prominent heiress and philanthropist Helen Gould lost no time in sending books packed in handsome oak cases that could be converted into reading desks. A New York family with a son serving in the Philippines held a euchre party in their home to raise money for the purchase of books, and there was a Valentine's Day masked ball held in Fresno, California, with funds going to the library.

Transporting the books could have been an obstacle. However, military transports taking men and supplies to the Philippines from the United States made room for the many boxes of books, magazines, and newspapers. America's railroads and express companies donated time and space to carry the reading material from drop-off points to California ports for shipping. The International Express Company, with headquarters at 52 Broadway in New York City and offices in the Philippines, agreed to take books free of charge from New York to Manila. Georgie's enterprise was a well-organized, highly efficient endeavor reliant on the generosity of many determined individuals.

In December 1899, Georgie was on board the *Hancock*, a transport heading to the Philippines, intent on finding a home for the growing mass of books. As soon as she stepped off the ship, she began to organize committees to mend damaged covers and bindings, seek out a room or two to hold the volumes, set up shelves, and stock a reading room with books, newspapers, and magazines. According to *Brooklyn Daily Eagle* reporter Mary H. Krout, "The undertaking was one of the most praiseworthy that could well be imagined." And much of the credit was due to Georgie's "work and perseverance." Georgie had lost little time in hiring a librarian—Ellen "Nelly" Young Egbert, the widow of Harry C. Egbert, an army officer who had served in Cuba and died while in service in the Philippines. She proved to be a wise choice, as she remained with the library throughout the years as it transitioned into various forms.

In March 1900, Anna Beaver, chair of the San Francisco Library Committee, told the *San Francisco Examiner* she had received a letter from Georgie expressing the soldiers' appreciation for the library. At that point, she said the library had received 3,000 bound volumes, 4,000 paper books, and 12,000 magazines. Georgie reported the demand for newspapers was especially high, and she asked Anna to petition newspaper publishers in various sections of the country to mail their papers directly to the library in Manila.

In June, the *Los Angeles Times* published excerpts from a letter from Georgie: "We need financial aid now as well as books . . . I think I can with great economy, keep things going for a couple of months . . . my faith is strong that help will come." She wrote that when the U.S. military was unable to supply a building for the library, she had been forced to rent rooms to house the books and a reading room for the patrons, and she was paying high rent. She wrote that the men were urging her to keep the reading rooms open in the evenings as well as during the day: "But we cannot do this until we are able to put electric lights in the library, as coal oil is too dangerous in these flimsy buildings." But Georgie emphasized the value of the library project: "There is not an hour, day or evening when the rooms of the American Library in Manila are open that they are not crowded with men who are reading or playing games."

Ultimately, the American Circulating Library, which had launched with secondhand volumes and a desire to offer a wholesome gathering place and diversion for lonely American soldiers and sailors, became a center for literature in the Philippine capital city. As the library grew in size and popularity, it became a subscription library open to civilians as well as the military. A subscription of twenty-five cents per month granted users access to the reading materials and use of the reading rooms. Patrons borrowed two books at a time; for an additional fee, they could take more than two. Fines were charged for overdue books. By October 1900, it was reported there were 300 members. Books that were in poor condition were sent to hospitals and outlying military posts—a traveling library.

In 1901, the library was turned over to the civil government of the Philippines under the Taft Commission. After much discussion about the makeup of a library executive board, it was decided that one army officer, one naval officer, two Filipino citizens, and one American citizen living in the Philippines would make up the group.[9] Georgiana opposed including the Filipinos, as she feared that "natives would hardly be the proper person to promote" the original goal of the library as a memorial to Americans. Later, the library became a division of the Philippine government and combined with the Museo-Biblioteca de Filipinas, a library that had been established in 1887.

In 1905, when the American Library Association met for its annual meeting in Portland, Oregon, Nelly submitted a report on the Manila library, where she continued to serve as librarian under the Philippine government's Bureau of Education. She stated that the collection had grown to well over 20,000 volumes "given by the women of America." Five hundred subscribers, including Filipino students at the local normal school for teacher training, used an average of 1,600 books each month. "We have a large airy reading room, well lighted; fine reading tables, magazine racks, newspaper files made from the beautiful native woods, and the bays of books well lighted by electricity," she wrote.

And as testament to the idea that books could indeed deter the fighting Americans from descending into the perilous world of saloons, a soldier penned this letter to the editor of a local Filipino newspaper: "At one time there was little for us to do but spend our spare time in saloons

9. Bernadette Cheryl Beredo, in her dissertation "Import of the Archive: American Colonial Bureaucracy in the Philippines, 1898–1916," discussed the role that archives and libraries played in American imperialism.

The American Circulating Library Was Located in the Hotel de Oriente Building in 1904 UNDERWOOD & UNDERWOOD, *HOTEL DE ORIENTE WITH ITS TROPICAL SPANISH ARCADE. MANILA, P.I.*, N.D., GELATIN SILVER CONTACT PRINT, KEYSTONE-MAST COLLECTION, UCR/CALIFORNIA MUSEUM OF PHOTOGRAPHY, UNIVERSITY OF CALIFORNIA, RIVERSIDE.

or lying in our quarters. To break the monotony an American is forced to do something and the only thing on earth for a soldier to do was to visit the saloons. . . . It is much more different now, however, for there is plenty of opportunity of engaging the mind in more desirable and instructive recreation. The American library rooms can give a soldier the best evening's entertainment that can be found anywhere. I have spent most of my evenings there since it was opened, and I was impressed with the desire on the part of the management to make the boys in khaki feel at home."

8

Secret Agents

"They Know the Value of Silence"

ACCORDING TO REPORTS IN EARLY 1898, SPANISH GENERAL VALERIANO Weyler, "The Butcher," had lost his patience with his secret service agents in Cuba. They were charged with providing reports about conditions and movements of Cuban freedom fighters, but little valuable information was reaching the general. He believed that few women could resist the charms of a Spaniard, so he directed his men to seduce Cuban women who would in turn share what they knew. It's possible the Spaniards were successful in finding some women who were willing to betray their fellow Cubans. But without doubt, there were countless Cuban women who became involved in clandestine operations—in support of independence and in opposition to Spanish rule. Many of their names have been lost to history, but some have been preserved and honored for their heroism. And whatever was said about Cuban women who risked everything for independence could also be said about Filipinas. Those women were fearless, gutsy, and brave.

American journalist Fannie Brigham Ward wrote about the women she had encountered in her reporting from Cuba: "As a rule they are better conspirators than their fathers and brothers, because they know the value of silence." As messengers to the freedom fighters in the camps hidden throughout the countryside and high in the mountains, these women carried food in false pockets, hid letters in their clothing or hair, secreted medicine in umbrella handles, and concealed bandages in the lining of their garments. A young girl was nearly exposed when carrying dynamite carefully packed into eggshells. Disguising herself as a vendor, she was stopped by a Spanish soldier who confiscated her eggs and was about to prepare a tasty meal when he received a call from his commanding officer. Duty called, and the eggs were returned to the girl, who delivered them safely to her freedom fighter comrades.

Many Cuban and Filipina women served as messengers, spies, sentinels, and fund-raisers in the struggles for independence. Bold and courageous, these women were adept at deceiving and undermining their occupiers while planning for a future in which independence had been achieved. They toiled in secret—sometimes in plain sight through their women's clubs or innocent-looking social gatherings. Many were ultimately uncovered, arrested, imprisoned, and sent into exile. Still, some carried on their clandestine work from prison or from exile in Guam, Hong Kong, and the United States. In Cuba, Maria Luisa Mendive covertly gathered supplies, including food, medicine, and bullets, and transported them to soldiers in their hideaways, and Rosario Morales de los Reye oversaw the movement of a network of messengers between the towns and the camps. Maria Machado, who carried a special travel pass due to her father's position in the Spanish army, used her freedom to surreptitiously aid the freedom fighters. She supplied them with invaluable news regarding the location of forts, the numbers of soldiers who guarded them, and the positions of the Spaniards' cannons. Rita Suarez del Villar used her home to stockpile supplies for the fighters and arranged details such as transportation. In her memoirs, she recalled that she had committed to the cause of independence at the age of seven when she overheard her father and other family members conspiring against the Spanish government. "I listened to their conversations about the injustices committed against the poor patriots . . . and that experience affected me to the core of my being. Knowledge of the oppression in which my beloved Cuba lived produced in me great anguish. . . . This experience caused me to vow that as soon as I was old enough I would fight without rest until my beloved Patria became free and sovereign," Rita wrote.

Many of the Filipinas who worked in the underground network operated from their positions in the underground revolutionary society, the Katipunan, which had allowed the formation of a women's chapter in

1892. The women carried on a variety of activities, including charitable work and fund-raising for the revolutionary cause. Josefa Rizal, sister of the heroic independence leader Jose Rizal, became the president of the women's division known as La Semilla. In time, the women performed duties; the Cuban female revolutionaries served as couriers, food providers, military and political strategists, and nurses. Women across generations worked in the movement. Marina Dizon y Bartolome was only eighteen when she joined the group as record keeper and teacher/initiator for new members. In August 1896, the activities of the Katipunan were revealed by a traitor, and leaders paid the price. Marina's father and husband were arrested and imprisoned. Ultimately, her father was executed. As keeper of the records, Marina possessed dangerous information that the Spaniards would use to capture and torture her comrades. She moved from place to place using aliases as she avoided detection by the Spanish authorities and raised money to purchase bullets and weapons. After the Spaniards left the Philippines, the work of the revolutionaries continued as they battled the occupying Americans. Once again, Marina's husband was suspected of revolutionary deeds, and when the family learned that the Americans were about to arrest him, he fled to Hong Kong. This was a time when Marina likely thought of the advice she had often given new members of the Katipunan: "Be cheerful at all times; do not show fear of impending rebellion. Be prepared to be orphans and widows some day. Be brave and carry on."

The legendary Melchora Aquino, also known as Tandang Sora, became involved in the revolutionary movement when she was in her eighties. By then, she had been widowed for years and had raised six children on her farm, where she grew rice and sugarcane. Her home became a meeting place for the Katipunan, a place where they met to plot and plan for the revolution and where weapons and other supplies were stored. She also provided food, shelter, and medicine to the fighters. In August 1896, as a group had gathered for a meal at Melchora's farm, they were raided by the Spanish authorities. Her buildings were set afire, and she was eventually arrested and charged with sedition and rebellion. Some reports indicate Melchora was subject to violent interrogations at Old Bilibid Prison in Manila, where she was held, but in time, she was released and exiled to Guam.

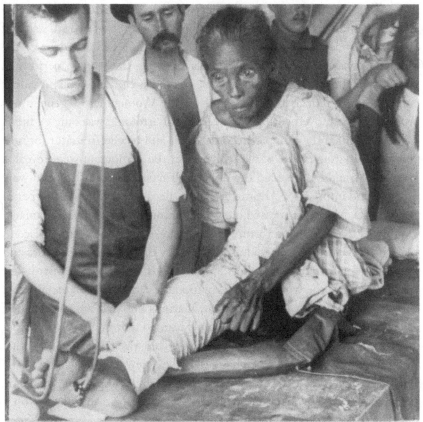

Old Woman shot through the leg while carrying ammunition to the Insurgents. In Hospital, Manila.

Filipino Woman Shot while Carrying Ammunition to the Fighters LIBRARY OF CON-GRESS PRINTS AND PHOTOGRAPHS DIVISION, WASHINGTON, D.C., LC-USZ62-66681.

A reporter for the *Chicago Times-Herald* in 1898 wrote about Cuban women's "success in discovering and transmitting information." His words could also be applied to women in the fight in the Philippines: "Every Cuban woman is, so far as she is able, a secret service agent for the insurgents. No fatigue is too severe, no hardship nor danger too great to be undergone in the service of their beloved Cuba."

PATROCINIO GAMBOA: "HEROINE OF JARO"

In April 1865, Fermin Gamboa and Leonardia Villareal welcomed a baby girl into their lives in the town of Jaro, Iloilo province, in the Philippines. They undoubtedly had ideas about the path their daughter would take as she grew to womanhood in a wealthy Filipino family; they may have dreamed of a traditional role for her in which she would marry and have children of her own someday. They intended to ensure that she had a quality education and a secure life in their beautiful home in Jaro. But chances are that the parents of Patrocinio Gamboa never could have imagined the journey their daughter would take on her way to becoming a heroine of the Philippine people and a historic figure celebrated for her role in the fight for independence.

As a young girl, Patrocinio attended school in Jaro, but her "rebellious nature" caused her formal education to end early. As she grew to young adulthood, she began to read newspapers and books that shaped her political and social conscience. In time, she began to read the works of Jose Rizal, Graciano Lopez-Jaena, Mariano Ponce, and Marcelo del Pilar—expatriates living in Europe and advocating Philippine independence from Spain. Their words were considered controversial and caused them to be targeted by Spanish officials in the Philippines. A newspaper called *La Solidaridad*—published in Spain—was one vehicle used by the men to transmit their progressive ideas. Rizal was a prolific writer of novels, plays, articles, and essays—all with a political message. Del Pilar, an editor at *La Solidaridad*, advocated armed revolt by the Filipinos. "Insurrection is the last remedy, especially

Jose Rizal, Marcelo del Pilar, and Mariano Ponce PUBLIC DOMAIN, WIKIMEDIA COMMONS.

when the people have acquired the belief that peaceful means to secure the remedies for evils prove futile," he wrote. Lopez-Jaena had practiced medicine in his native Philippines and was disturbed by the injustices he witnessed as a result of Spanish rule. When he published a biting satirical novel, *Fray Botod*, a devastatingly irreverent portrayal of a fictional Spanish priest, he decided it was in his best interest to leave the Philippines before Spanish authorities threw him in prison. He landed in Spain, working for a time as editor of *La Solidaridad*. He became well known for his charismatic skills as a speaker, and he used his voice from afar to encourage the Filipinos to demand social and political change. Rizal returned to the Philippines in 1892, and in August 1896, when Spanish authorities blamed him for an armed revolt that had occurred in Manila, he was executed.

The works of these men, who were considered heroes by many Filipinos, were not easy to obtain in the Philippines, as Spanish rulers had banned them, but Patrocinio somehow found secret copies in Jaro and devoured them. Something about these writings sparked her independent spirit. She became involved in secret revolutionary causes in her province, including in March 1898 an organization called the Conspiring Committee (*Comite Conspirador*), which later formed the framework for a revolutionary government in Santa Barbara, Iloilo, under the leadership of influential Filipino leaders Roque Lopez and General Martin Delgado. Tia Patron, as she became known by the locals, conducted clandestine activities, such as fund-raising and other undercover intelligence work, against the Spaniards.

In the fall of 1898, Lopez and Delgado issued a public proclamation about their new Filipino government being established in Santa Barbara. The "newly constituted government and the Generals of the liberating army" saluted the people of the region whom they hoped "will be a free nation . . . living peacefully under the shadow of the brilliant tri-banner and secure under the protection of Almighty God." And as plans developed for the inauguration celebration of the Provisional Revolutionary Government in November, the importance of symbols such as a flag were being discussed behind the scenes. By this time, the men were aware of the activities of the Jaro woman known as Tia Patron, and they turned to her to help with the design, construction, and transportation of the treasured symbol of their cause.

In Jaro, Patrocinio enlisted a group of women who furtively designed and sewed the flag that would be taken secretly to Santa Barbara and raised in the plaza on November 17 at the inaugural celebration. When the time came to get the flag to the Santa Barbara revolutionary government headquarters, Patrocinio volunteered to travel from Jaro through dangerous territory guarded by Spanish soldiers who were constantly looking for freedom fighters' activity. A Filipino soldier named Honorio Solinap offered to participate in the dangerous scheme. The two knew the chance of being stopped and searched by enemy Spaniards was highly likely, yet they were committed to the plan. No one knows who devised the idea, but it was decided that Patrocinio and Honorio would masquerade as a peasant couple traveling by horse and wagon with a load of grass in the wagon box. Somehow, the army lieutenant and the wealthy young woman from a prominent Jaro family pulled off an incredibly risky charade, duping easily amused Spanish soldiers.

On the day of the big event, the pair climbed into their wagon dressed as a typical farm couple. Patrocinio may have given the impression she was with child if anyone looked closely at her waist, but she and Honorio knew the bulge was caused by the precious flag concealed under her clothing. And they certainly must have been uneasy about the saber, a gift from Filipino leader General Emilio Aguinaldo to General Delgado, stashed under the hay in the wagon box. As anticipated, before the couple had traveled far, they spotted Spanish guards in the distance and prepared for a nerve-wracking encounter. Surely, they had rehearsed for the occasion, as they planned for the inevitable, but those are details that have been lost to history. Patrocinio launched into her role as a cranky, berating shrew, calling out her timid husband for some unknown offense. By the time the unhappily married couple reached the Spaniards, Patrocinio had resorted to cursing, pinching, biting, and boxing her unfortunate spouse. It all made for a hilarious distraction for the highly entertained soldiers, who erupted into laughter at the antics of the bickering couple. By the time Patrocinio and Honorio passed the Spaniards who hadn't given a thought to searching the squabbling Filipinos, they were safely on their

Patrocinio Gamboa COURTESY OF CASA GAMBOA.

way to delivering the precious cargo. Arriving just in time to hand over the flag for hoisting over the crowd-filled plaza, Patrocinio and Honorio were cheered as heroes that day. And they couldn't have known it at the time, but the story of their courageous caper would be passed down through future generations.

Of course, when the Spaniards were defeated by the combined efforts of the Filipinos and the Americans, there was no time for rejoicing for Patrocinio and her comrades. They quickly turned to fighting the Americans, who had become occupiers of the Philippine islands and barriers to Filipino independence. Patrocinio continued her secret work delivering military dispatches through enemy lines and raising money to purchase arms, ammunition, clothing, food, and medicine for the freedom fighters. The Americans, who were fooled by her reputation as a wealthy Filipina woman, overlooked the possibility that this refined, well-to-do woman could be carrying out any treacherous deeds. And she used that to her advantage. Patrocinio also acquired the role of nurse when called to help on the battlefield—for which she earned the title "Heroine of Jaro."

In time, the fighting ended, and Patrocinio continued to live in the Gamboa family home. She was offered a government pension for her contributions to the war effort, but she refused. "I do not ask for a pension. I give my services as a love offering to my country. I do not ask any compensation for those services," she is reported to have said. People said that throughout her life she filled the family home with mementos from the time of the revolution. One was a bust of Jose Rizal, the man who had inspired her revolutionary spirit when she was a young woman. It was said she always proudly displayed a Filipino flag on national holidays. When Patrocinio died in 1953, she was honored with a military burial in the local veterans' cemetery. In 1980, the National Historical Commission of the Philippines established a marker honoring Patrocinio in Jaro, and in 2015, a marker was installed in Iloilo City to honor her 150th birth anniversary. The home where she grew up has been preserved and is a museum, holding artifacts from her life and inviting visitors to recognize and honor the "Heroine of Jaro."

Magdalena Peñarredonda Doley: Keeping Silent and Speaking Out

The Spaniards had devised a devious and deadly defense system known as the trocha in their efforts to defeat the Cuban freedom fighters during the Ten Years' War (1868–1878), and most agreed it was quite effective. So, when the Cubans renewed their independence activities in the War of Independence (1895–1898), the Spaniards once again decided to make use of the original trocha and to build additional structures. The goal remained the same—eliminate the Cuban independence advocates by any means possible.

The fifty-mile-long trocha of the first war stretched across the narrowest strip of the island from Júcaro on the south coast to Morón on the north. The 200-yard-wide strip consisted of an assortment of barriers designed to deter or kill anyone who ventured into the perilous maze of defensive apparatus. First, the center was stripped of trees, and a railroad was constructed to carry the armor-clad cars of the Spanish military. Tree trunks, roots, and large branches stacked on each side of the beltway with barbed wire tucked in for added security formed yet another barrier. A series of forts were strung along both sides of the trocha with sentinels positioned in strategically placed blockhouses every half mile. Finally, explosives littered the strip at intervals. As the freedom fighters became bolder and more aggressive in the mid-1890s, the Spaniards expanded the trochas to villages and towns across the island where revolutionary activity was most pronounced. Only the most courageous or desperate individuals ventured into the areas peppered with the trochas, and those who survived unscathed were considered fortunate.

Magdalena Peñarredonda was one of those intrepid individuals who, on a daily basis, crossed the trocha near her hometown, Pinar del Río, where she had become involved in secret operations in support of the Cuban freedom fighters. Her involvement in political activities as an adult was a follow-up to events in her younger years, when she had cut her long hair in a show of support for the independence cause in 1851. It could not have been easy for the daughter and wife of a captain in the Spanish army to engage in revolutionary activities, but that's exactly what Magdalena did. Somehow, maybe from her French mother, she had acquired ideas about independence, and she refused to remain submissive to the Spaniards. Growing up on the family estate known as "El Ponton," Magdalena and her siblings were surrounded by meadows, acres of coffee and cornfields, and forests of ebony and cedar trees. Inside the family

Cuban Fighters in Trench Near Pinar del Río LIBRARY OF CONGRESS PRINTS AND PHO-
TOGRAPHS DIVISION, WASHINGTON, D.C., LC-USZ62-121719, STROHMEYER & WYMAN, 1899.

home, they were influenced by their mother's teachings and books about human rights.

Magdalena married Spanish merchant Jose Covielles at the age of fourteen and moved to Havana. She filled their large house with her paintings inspired by trees and flowers at El Ponton. And it was here that Magdalena as "a young lady who liked to talk" lived with "an older man that had nothing to say." Magdalena opened her house, hosting gatherings of Cuban intellectuals, politicians, activists, journalists, and playwrights.

In 1892, one of Magdalena's brothers was assassinated for his involvement in the fight for independence. And by the time Magdalena was risking her life crossing the trocha with supplies and secret messages, she had already caught the attention of Spanish authorities by writing what they considered subversive ideas in a national publication, *El Criollo*. It resulted in Magdalena's move for a time to New York, where she met Cuban revolutionary junta leaders in exile. When war broke out in Cuba in 1895, Magdalena was back in her homeland, separated from her husband and working as a secret agent for Cuban independence with leader Antonio Maceo—carrying information between Maceo and key independence leaders in Havana. Providing essential supplies to the freedom fighters in their hideouts required Magdalena to cross the trocha multiple times a day for a couple of years. Underwear, writing supplies, food, and critical supplies of medicines—all secreted into the camps by Magdalena concealed in her petticoats or her false-bottom satchel. In addition to conveying vital supplies and information, she was instrumental in transporting large sums of money into Cuba to be used in purchasing arms and ammunition. And when secret hiding places for valuable cargo such as explosives were required, Magdalena proved invaluable. It was not unusual for her to have fifty or sixty pounds of dynamite safely tucked away in her home. "Sometimes, with a gesture she would stop a visitor from sitting on a soft chair or from looking too closely at an artificial flower arrangement," an independence leader recalled. "The chair was full of bullets, or the flowers contained a secret chamber." She sometimes used aliases in her secret correspondences—"Benito Gomez," "Maxima Juarez," and "Maine" in reference to the American ship USS *Maine*.

Although Magdalena successfully carried on her clandestine activities for several years, eventually she was betrayed by someone posing as a trustworthy courier. Spanish authorities arrested her and sent her to the notorious Las Recogidas prison in Havana. According to friends and family members, initially she was given little food, forced to do menial labor such as floor scrubbing, and denied communication with anyone outside the prison. They claimed a jailer tried to extort money from them to ensure better conditions for Magdalena. When the family appealed to Spanish officials, her treatment improved, and they were allowed to send her a meal each day and provide a bed so she no longer had to sleep on piles of straw scattered on the floor. The family asked a local clergyman to intercede in negotiating her release. When Reverend Hammond English arrived at the headquarters of the Spanish government and met with an official, he came away with discouraging news. The clergyman described his meeting with the Spaniard: "He rang a bell and sent for a file of the

Las Recogidas Prison, Havana, ca. 1897 COURTESY OF THE GEORGE EASTMAN
MUSEUM, ROCHESTER, NEW YORK, WILLIAM H. RAU COLLECTION.

charges against Senora Peñarredonda, at least three inches high, which
contained upward of twenty accusations." Considering the volume of
charges against Magdalena, the official cautioned that her release seemed
unlikely.

Confinement in Las Recogidas may have prevented Magdalena from
carrying on her activities as a secret agent for the Cuban army, but it did
not quash her passion for advocacy on behalf of a cause that begged her
attention. Many of the inmates who were incarcerated with Magdalena
were disadvantaged women—some legitimate offenders, others political
prisoners, but all suffering from abysmal conditions in the facility. Before
long, Magdalena had organized protests among the women, demanding
better treatment from their captors. And her work on behalf of these
fellow prisoners earned their respect. "They only stop protesting and

complaining when they know I have a headache. Daily they consult with me and confide in me their sad histories," Magdalena said.

Ultimately, Magdalena was released from prison, and the Spaniards were defeated by the Cuban freedom fighters and the Americans. However, that did not signal the end of Magdalena's activism. She became increasingly alarmed by questionable actions of the Americans. Although she had favored American intervention in the war for independence against the Spaniards, she opposed America's continued presence after the war—especially when the Americans showed imperialistic tendencies. Magdalena joined other former Cuban revolutionists in opposition to tactics by some American military commanders, including General Leonard Wood, whom they viewed as extremely dictatorial in carrying out his duties. At one point, she organized a group to protest the appointment of an Italian—rather than a Cuban—as archbishop of Havana by the Catholic Church. Magdalena and others believed the Americans had influenced the appointment of a non-Cuban—one more example of their strong-arm tactics and an attempt to discourage Cuban nationalism. The protest group formed by Magdalena, known as the Popular Committee, was composed mostly of women and called for the resignation of the Italian clergyman.

Magdalena's actions throughout her lifetime appeared to be driven by her empathy for injustices committed against others who were vulnerable and less fortunate than she—especially women. After seeing the effects of the Spanish policy of *reconcentración*, essentially concentration camps for Cuban peasants established in 1896, she wrote a Cuban leader, "I have witnessed scenes that could not possibly be more horrible and moving in human suffering." She called the women in the camps "true heroines."

Magdalena was a woman who knew the value of silence when carrying out the work of a secret agent for the cause of independence; however, she also recognized the importance of speaking out when she saw wrongs in society.

Explanatory Notes

CHAPTER 1

"It has been": "A Brief Overview of NY in the Spanish American War April 25, 1898–August 12, 1898," New York State Military Museum and Veterans Research Center, https://dmna.ny.gov/historic/mil-hist.htm.

"Oh, true friend"; "life, liberty": "A Lament from Kentucky," *Woman's Journal*, February 25, 1899, 97.

"regular first-nighters": "Secretary John Hay," *Carlisle (PA) Evening Herald*, October 14, 1898.

"keen and incisive": *Marshfield (WI) Times*, September 2, 1898.

"I should welcome": "The Crucible," PBS, https://www.pbs.org/crucible/tl7.html; Howard Zinn, *A People's History of the United States* (New York: New Press, 2003), 219.

"War should never": "First Inaugural Address of William McKinley," Yale Law School Avalon Project, https://avalon.law.yale.edu/19th_century/mckin1.asp.

"I have been through": Stephen Kinzer, *The True Flag* (New York: Henry Holt, 2017), 34; Doris Kearns Goodwin, *The Bully Pulpit* (New York: Simon & Schuster, 2013), 222.

"destined to manifest": John O'Sullivan, "The Great Nation of Futurity," *The United States Democratic Review*, November 1839, 426–30.

"fulfillment of our manifest": John O'Sullivan, "Annexation,"

The United States Democratic Review, July/August 1845, 5.

"the United States should": William Deverell and Deborah Gray White, *United States History* (Orlando, FL: Houghton Mifflin Harcourt, 2012), R40.

America's imperialistic tendencies: Gerald A. Danzer et al., *The Americans* (Orlando, FL: Houghton Mifflin Harcourt, 2012), 549.

"an instrument": Ivan Musicant, *Empire by Default* (New York: Henry Holt, 1998), 16.

"the shapers"; "family paper"; "add(ed) their ablest": Display ad, *Anaconda (MT) Standard*, December 11, 1897.

"the man who must"; "as oil": "The Spirit of Fight," *Kansas City (MO) Journal*, May 12, 1898.

"a crying need": Carl N. Degler, *Out of Our Past* (New York: Harper and Row, 1970), 428.

"like having": Mariola Espinosa, "The Threat from Havana: Southern Public Health, Yellow Fever, and the U.S. Intervention in the Cuban Struggle for Independence, 1878–1898," *Journal of Southern History*, August 2006, 565.

"waste places"; "advancement of the race": Zinn, *A People's History of the United States*, 221.

"the Philippines might": Theodore Draper, review of *Empire by Default: The Spanish American War and the Dawn of the American Century*, by Ivan Musicant, *Los Angeles Times*, February 22, 1998, https://www.latimes.com/archives/la-xpm-1998-feb-22-bk-21801-story.html.

"the most disgusting"; "The only feature"; "the dirtiest city"; "falls far short"; "roughly paved"; "filthy, God-forsaken"; "a better"; "would either change"; "the grandest naval": "Havana Characteristics," *Asheville (NC) Daily Citizen*, April 7, 1898.

"The integrity of"; "look into our"; "evils"; "we concern"; "already dealt"; "We might also"; "buckling on"; "shouting themselves"; "the flower": "A Plea for Peace," *Asheville (NC) Daily Citizen*, April 11, 1898.

"nationalistic zeal": Goodwin, *The Bully Pulpit*, 226.

"hard choices": Goodwin, *The Bully Pulpit*, 225.

"weak and catering"; "natural and inevitable": "De Lome's Recall Is Demanded," *Twice-a-Week Messenger* (Owensboro, KY), February 12, 1898.

"destroyed by the": David J. Silbey, *A War of Frontier and Empire* (New York: Hill and Wang, 2008), online location 481.

"Remember the Maine": Anthony Depalma, "'Remember the Maine! To Hell with Spain!' How the United States Emerged from the Spanish-American War as a True Global Power," *New York Times Upfront*, February 18, 2013, https://www.questia.com/magazine/1G1-319811114/remember-the-maine-to-hell-with-spain-how-the.

"the cause of humanity"; "the very serious"; "menace to our peace": "April 11, 1898: Message Regarding Cuban Civil War," University of Virginia, Miller Center, https://millercenter.org/the-presidency/presidential-speeches/april-11-1898-message-regarding-cuban-civil-war.

"the most popular": Silbey, *A War of Frontier and Empire*," online location 570.

"Not one Spanish": Silbey, *A War of Frontier and Empire*," online location 566.

"Dewey our hero": No title, *Prescott (KS) Register*, May 27, 1898.

"exploitation and misrule"; Andres Bonifacio founded: Gregg Jones, *Honor in the Dust* (New York: New American Library, 2012), 43.

"officials at Washington": "Dorothea Dix Talks," *Times-Picayune* (New Orleans, LA), May 22, 1898.

"There are women": "Would Have Women Soldiers," *Camden (NJ) Daily Telegram*, May 12, 1898.

"brilliant, charismatic"; "the Bronze Titan": Musicant, *Empire by Default*, 41.

The army was: Evan Thomas, "Race and the Spanish-American War," *Newsweek*, March 24, 2008, https://www.newsweek.com/race-and-spanish -american-war-84171.

Some of the Americans: Thomas, "Race and the Spanish-American War"; Musicant, *Empire by Default*, 369.

"the colored troops saved": "A Nurse from Siboney," *Baltimore Sun*, September 20, 1898.

"American protectorate": Musicant, *Empire by Default*, 592.

"pretended that the Cuban": Zinn, *A People's History of the United States*, 226.

"None of us thought": Kinzer, *The True Flag*, 192.

"the town was fired"; "water cure"; "it was given by means": U.S. Congress, Senate, *Affairs in the Philippines*, Senate Document #331, Vol. 1, 37th Congress, 1st Session, 1902.

"How can the country": "A Lament from Kentucky," *Woman's Journal*, 97.

"A sweeter, nobler": "Ellen May Tower," *Livingston Democrat* (Howell, MI), December 14, 1898.

CHAPTER 2

Introduction

"Whatever you"; "There were": "The Days of the Martyrs," *Davenport (IA) Democrat and Leader*, September 5, 1898.

"fifty thousand": "Nursing in the Spanish-American War," *American Nursing History*, 5, https://static1.squarespace.com/static/5b3d0a 51c3c16a31624ce3f9/t/5b82e9601ae6cfab3d1cab35/1535306081429/ Role+Graduate+Nurses+S+A+War.pdf.

"I did not care": "The Army Nurses," *The Sun* (New York, NY), September 8, 1898.

"It was certainly": Anna C. Maxwell to Training School Committee, Board of Managers, Presbyterian Hospital: Report of her work at Sternberg General Hospital, October 31, 1898, https://www.ebooksread.com/authors-eng/american-national-red-cross-nursing-service/history-of-american-red-cross-nursing-ala/page-6-history-of-american-red-cross-nursing-ala.shtml.

Initially, each regiment: Musicant, *Empire by Default*, 643.

"covering fifteen": "The Days of the Martyrs," *Davenport (IA) Democrat and Leader*, September 5, 1898.

"A soldiers' camp": "Some Letters from the People," *San Francisco Examiner*, June 23, 1898.

"their qualifications ranged": Anonymous, *The American-Spanish War: A History by the War Leaders* (Norwich, CT: Chas. C. Haskell & Son, 1899), 440.

Nurses came from a variety: Mary T. Sarnecky, *A History of the U.S. Army Nurse Corps* (Philadelphia: University of Pennsylvania Press, 1999), 33.

"more or less": "Only Immune Nurses Will Go to Santiago," *Brooklyn Daily Eagle*, July 14, 1898.

There was also the racist view: Ingrid Gessner, "Heroines of Health: Examining the Other Side of the 'Splendid Little War,'" *European Journal of American Studies*, Special Issue: Women in the USA 2015, 16–17; Elizabeth F. Desnoyers-Colas, *Marching as to War* (Lanham, MD: University Press of America, 2014), 27; Lisa Tendrich Frank, ed., *An Encyclopedia of American Women at War* (Santa Barbara, CA: ABC-CLIO, 2013), 512.

"There is nothing": Sarnecky, *A History of the U.S. Army Nurse Corps*, 39.

"Patriotism at thirty"; "The fact"; "The colored women": "Matters Metropolitan," *Catholic Union and Times* (Buffalo, NY), July 28, 1898.

"appreciated"; "a smile"; "the nicest man"; "We're sort": "Off to Fight Yellow Jack," *The Sun* (New York, NY), July 20, 1898.

. . . located on the level directly below: "Quartered below Mules," *Boston Globe*, August 1, 1898.

"proved the utility"; "an endless"; "Everywhere their": "Women Nurses in War," *Anaconda (MT) Standard*, January 7, 1899.

"I am satisfied": *The American-Spanish War: A History by the War Leaders*, 442.

"When you": "Nursing in the Spanish-American War," *American Nursing History*, 4, https://static1.squarespace.com/static/5b3d0a51c3c16a31624 ce3f9/t/5b82e9601ae6cfab3d1cab35/1535306081429/Role+Graduate +Nurses+S+A+War.pdf.

Namahyoke Sockum Curtis

"supposed at"; "negro blood"; "colored persons"; "she appeared to"; "in a different"; "no prejudice": "Ejected on Account of Color," *Inter Ocean* (Chicago, IL), September 29, 1894.

"a woman of culture"; "a woman fair"; "full-blooded Indian"; "pure negro"; "The only charge"; "The agents were": "Negro Blood in Her Veins," *San Francisco Examiner*, September 28, 1894.

"It is the fundamental": "Cannot Disturb Mrs. Curtis," *Inter Ocean*, September 30, 1894.

"made a lively"; "a pleasant talker": "Purely Civil Service?," *Washington Bee*, March 12, 1898.

rotting carcasses: Musicant, *Empire by Default*, 509.

With a death; "It was the only": Musicant, *Empire by Default*, 510.

. . . it was reported half: Musicant, *Empire by Default*, 511.

"very accomplished": "Dr. Curtis and His Family," *Washington (DC) Bee*, April 30, 1898.

"worse foe than Spaniards"; "colored nurses"; "are less susceptible": No title, *Cawker City (KS) Public Record*, July 14, 1898.

"colored nurses"; "colored persons": "Troops in Peril," *Kansas City (MO) Journal,* July 13, 1898.

Although not a trained nurse; She made stops: Record Group 112: Records of the Office of the Surgeon General (Army), Entry 104: Case Files of Candidates Seeking Appointment as Army Nurses, 1898–1917, item number REP0006C, U.S. National Archives and Records Administration.

"colored college on St. Charles avenue": "Colored Women Nurses," *Times-Democrat* (New Orleans, LA), July 17, 1898.

There were conflicting: Mercedes Graf, "Band of Angels," *Prologue: The Journal of the National Archives* (Washington, DC: National Archives and Records Service, General Services Administration, 2002), 198; Anita Newcomb McGee, "Female Nurses in the American Army," *Proceedings of the 8th Annual Meeting of the Association of Military Surgeons,* delivered as a speech at Kansas City, Missouri, in September 1899. The Spanish-American War Centennial, http://www.spanamwar.com/Nurses .htm; and Anita Newcomb McGee, "Women Nurses in the American Army," *Proceedings of the 8th Annual Meeting of the Association of Military Surgeons,* delivered as a speech at Kansas City, Missouri, in September 1899.

"droves": "Gossip Gathered in Hotel Lobbies," *Times-Picayune* (New Orleans, LA), July 17, 1898.

"into a pitiful"; "In God's"; "suspect building"; "A sadder sight": "Santiago in War Time," *Washington (DC) Times,* August 28, 1898.

"Siboney!"; "The death rate"; "from ten"; "for further duty"; "Yes, decidedly": "Interesting Reminiscences by a Veteran of the Santiago Campaign," *Evening Star* (Washington, DC), September 24, 1898.

At least two; "on account of ill health": Mercedes Graf, "All the Women Were Valiant," *Prologue: The Journal of the National Archives* (Washington, DC: National Archives and Records Service, General Services Administration, 2014), 30.

. . . according to military records . . . : Record Group 112: Records of the Office of the Surgeon General (Army), Entry 104, 149, 150, Boxes 1, 2, 5: Case Files of Candidates Seeking Appointment as Army Nurses, 1898–1917, item number REP0006C, U.S. National Archives and Records Administration.

"It would be"; "What is to": "Peace Jubilee," *Washington Bee*, April 22, 1899.

Sarah Jane Ennies

"I, ____ the undersigned"; "women of superior": Freedmen's Hospital, Austin M. Curtis, Daniel Alexander Payne Murray, and Daniel Murray Pamphlet Collection, *Report of the Freedmen's Hospital to the Secretary of the Interior* (Washington, DC: Government Printing Office, 1899), 21, https://www.loc.gov/item/91898264.

"lifted its bow . . .": "Elbe Lost at Sea," *Chicago Tribune*, January 31, 1895.

"For three hours"; "An hour": "Our Soldiers Suffer Bravely," *Wilkes-Barre (PA) Times Leader*, July 1, 1898.

"as big as": "A Soldier's Talk," *Star-Gazette* (Elmira, NY), July 26, 1898.

". . . after a weary": "Cuban Aftermath," *Evening Star* (Washington, DC), July 30, 1898.

"One thought"; "The possibility": "Our Soldiers Suffer Bravely," *Wilkes-Barre (PA) Times Leader*, July 1, 1898.

"The trench around": G. J. A. O'Toole, *The Spanish War: An American Epic—1898* (New York: Norton, 1984), 321.

"Along the road": O'Toole, *The Spanish War*, 351.

"loaded with": Stephen Bonsal, "The Night after San Juan: Stories of the Wounded on the Field and in the Hospital," *McClure's*, December 1898, 122.

"delirious and shrieking": Bonsal, "The Night after San Juan," 125.

". . . colored persons": "Troops in Peril," *Kansas City (MO) Journal,* July 13, 1898.

Sarah's Army records; "first class"; "excellent"; "thoroughly satisfactory": Record Group 112: Records of the Office of the Surgeon General (Army), Entry 104, 149, 150, Boxes 2, 6: Case Files of Candidates Seeking Appointment as Army Nurses, 1898–1917, item number REP0006C, U.S. National Archives and Records Administration.

"I was glad"; "At our camp"; "secret marriage": Record Group 112: Records of the Office of the Surgeon General (Army), Entry 104, 149, 150, Boxes 2, 6: Case Files of Candidates Seeking Appointment as Army Nurses, 1898–1917, item number REP0006C, U.S. National Archives and Records Administration.

"colored nurses": "Santiago in War Time," *Washington (DC) Times,* August 28, 1898; "Work of Dr. J. S. King," *Daily Review* (Decatur, IL), August 24, 1898.

"untiring energy"; "esteem of": "A Popular Army Nurse," *Napa (CA) Journal,* May 23, 1900.

"Beloved by Soldiers": *Christian County Republican* (Ozark, MO), May 18, 1899.

"A Heroine of Santiago": *Sea Coast Echo* (Bay Saint Louis, MS), August 12, 1899.

"one of the happiest"; ". . . all my superior"; "to continue": Record Group 112: Records of the Office of the Surgeon General (Army), Entry 104, 149, 150, Boxes 2, 6: Case Files of Candidates Seeking Appointment as Army Nurses, 1898–1917, item number REP0006C, U.S. National Archives and Records Administration.

Della Weeks

Although she was not: Record Group 112: Records of the Office of the Surgeon General (Army), Entry 104, 149, 150, Boxes 6, 7, 21: Case Files of Candidates Seeking Appointment as Army Nurses, 1898–1917, item number REP0006C, U.S. National Archives and Records Administration.

Della Weeks arrived: "He Wants 'The Leader,'" *Des Moines (IA) Register*, June 26, 1898.

"wee morsel"; "would make stone-breaking"; "Every man"; "I didn't pull": "Only One Woman Nurse with the Manila Volunteers," *San Francisco Call*, July 17, 1898.

"If we could": "A Devoted Little Woman," *Des Moines (IA) Register*, July 24, 1898.

"She is worth": "Help for Miss Weeks," *Des Moines (IA) Register*, August 7, 1898.

"endeared her"; "forever in"; "deepest gloom": "At the Presidio," *Daily Iowa Capital* (Des Moines, IA), October 21, 1899.

"Many good men": "Importance of Corregidor," *Sioux City (IA) Journal*, December 13, 1899.

"noble work"; "useless form"; "The Iowa boys"; "The lives of": "Mothers of 51st": *Daily Iowa Capital* (Des Moines, IA), October 21, 1899.

"If the boys": "Calhoun County Spanish-American War News," Iowa Gen Web Project, http://iagenweb.org/calhoun/records/military/spanish -american/news.php.

"heat prostration": "Over 200 Iowa Boys Ill," *Sioux City (IA) Journal*, July 21, 1899.

"Miss Weeks must"; "a traitor"; "through the thoughtfulness"; "No good purpose"; "brutal to"; "The war does": "Correspondents Uphead," *Gazette* (Cedar Rapids, IA), July 25, 1899.

"hero in skirts": "A Hero in Skirts," *Daily Journal*, November 18, 1899.

Esther Voorhees Hasson

"Bravest of": "Nurses on a Hospital Ship," *Arizona Republic*, May 28, 1898.

"photo-micrographic appliances": "A Floating War Studio," *Morning Journal-Courier* (New Haven, CT), June 22, 1898.

"We had a"; "we rise": "On Board Relief Ship," *Morning Journal-Courier* (New Haven, CT), July 20, 1898.

". . . for three or"; "We were": "Two Interesting Letters," *Morning Journal-Courier* (New Haven, CT), August 8, 1898.

"I have entire"; "At first the army": "Letter from Miss Hasson," *Morning Journal-Courier* (New Haven, CT), September 20, 1898.

"When I entered": "Letter from Miss Hasson," *Morning Journal-Courier* (New Haven, CT), January 31, 1899.

"coffee was bad": "Esther Voorhees Hasson Journal," 1899, Henry Ware Lawton Papers, MMC-3815, Library of Congress, 19.

"glorious moonlight": "Esther Voorhees Hasson Journal," 22.

"they are the worst"; "absolutely malicious": "Esther Voorhees Hasson Journal," 48.

"after that": "On the Hospital Ship Relief, Journey to Manila and Return," *Morning Journal-Courier* (New Haven, CT), September 5, 1899.

"bullet floating": "Esther Voorhees Hasson Journal," 75.

"country boys"; "used to work and roughing it": "Esther Voorhees Hasson Journal," 63.

"The young and inexperienced": "Esther Voorhees Hasson Journal," 62.

"worthy of": "Esther Voorhees Hasson," Naval History and Heritage Command, https://www.history.navy.mil.

"many American soldiers": "Miss Hasson of the Nurse Corps," *New-York Daily Tribune*, September 6, 1908.

American Order of the Sisters

"Four Redskin": "Sioux Indian Nurses," *Lawrence (KS) Daily Journal*, December 8, 1898.

"in good condition"; "men looked well and healthy": "The Fourth Immunes," *Wheeling (WV) Daily Intelligencer*, October 3, 1898.

"the troops as a whole": "To Camp Cuba Libre," *Fort Wayne (IN) Daily News*, October 6, 1898.

"The very air"; "They are not taken": "Camp Cuba Libre," *Nevada State Journal*, October 5, 1898.

"Our work is": "From Camp Cuba Libre," *Detroit Free Press*, October 2, 1898.

"quite young"; "an ever ready"; "must act"; "very sturdy": "Nursed by Sioux Indians," *Sioux City (IA) Journal*, November 3, 1898.

"of Indian blood"; "accustomed to": "Indians to Act as Nurses," *Algona (IA) Republican*, July 27, 1898.

"work of the": "Nursed by Sioux Indians," *Sioux City (IA) Journal*, November 3, 1898.

"Poor old": "Second Louisiana," *Times-Picayune* (New Orleans, LA), December 20, 1898.

"We have not fought": "Our Boys in Garrison," *Gazette* (Cedar Rapids, IA), December 29, 1898.

"This is a beautiful": "Mt. Carmel's Soldiers," *Mount Carmel (IL) Register*, January 26, 1899.

"the old hatred": "Indian Nuns Are Sent from Cuba," *Journal News* (Hamilton, OH), March 14, 1899.

"was to promote"; "They wanted to send"; "established for the purpose"; "Everything went"; "We will remain": "Nuns Expelled from Cuba," *Nebraska State Journal*, April 23, 1899.

"She was much"; "Sister Gregory and myself": Thomas W. Foley, *Father Francis M. Craft, Missionary to the Sioux* (Lincoln: University of Nebraska Press, 2002), 131.

"thanks of the Congress": Congressman John Francis Fitzgerald, tendering thanks to Sisters of American Congregation, on February 28, 1899, to House of Representatives, House Resolution 379, 56th Congress, 1st session, *Congressional Record*, Vol. 33, December 4, 1899, 12.

"have proved": Thomas W. Foley, "Father Francis M. Craft and the Indian Sisters," *U.S. Catholic Historian*, Spring 1998, 54.

"we should give": "Mt. Carmel's Soldiers," *Mount Carmel (IL) Register*, January 26, 1899.

Chapter 3

Introduction

"These women soldiers": "The Cuban Women," *Wheeling (WV) Daily Intelligencer*, May 14, 1898.

Fierce warrior women: Adrienne Mayor, *The Amazons: Lives and Legends of Warrior Women across the Ancient World* (Princeton, NJ: Princeton University Press, 2016), 10.

The word amazon: Joshua Rothman, "The Real Amazons," *New Yorker*, October 17, 2014, 1.

There was the young woman remembered: Teresa Prados-Torreira, *Mambisas: Rebel Women in Nineteenth-Century Cuba* (Gainesville: University Press of Florida, 2005), 131.

"eleven women, colored": Murat Halstead, *The Story of Cuba* (Chicago: Cuban Libre Publishing Co., 1896), 327.

"The country needs": Halstead, *The Story of Cuba*, 326.

Fair Cuban Patriots: "Fair Cuban Patriots," *Pittsburg Press*, December 28, 1896.

Cuban Joan of Arc: "Cuban Joan of Arc," *Reformer* (Brattleboro, VT), July 3, 1896.

"riddled with Spanish bullets": "A Cuban Amazon Dies in the Ranks," *San Francisco Examiner*, March 27, 1896.

"I had no fear"; "I learned how": Gregoria de Jesus, "Autobiography of Gregoria de Jesus," trans. Leandro H. Fernandez, *Philippine Magazine*, June 1930, 18.

"raise her hand"; "armed with": "Mrs. Rizal Is a Spanish Joan of Arc," *Wichita (KS) Daily Eagle*, September 12, 1897.

"with reckless": "More Women Soldiers," *Pittsburg Press*, July 27, 1898.

"Astride a horse": Paolo Vergara, "Agueda Kahabagan Was Our First Woman General. But Do You Know Her?," *Scout*, March 29, 2019, https://www.scoutmag.ph.

Trinidad Perez Tecson, admired for her: Christine Doran, "Women in the Philippine Revolution," *Philippine Studies* 46, no. 3 (1998): 367.

"patriotic amazons"; "soldier maids"; "could do severe"; "a snake"; "daring horsewomen"; "shoot a Spaniard"; "quite as expert": "Women in War," *Tribune* (Scranton, PA), May 23, 1898.

"with bullets flying"; "For the first time": "Not Afraid of Filipinos," *Record-Union* (Sacramento, CA), May 3, 1899.

Evangelina Cisneros

"I had many fantastic": Evangelina Betancourt Cosio Y Cisneros, *The Story of Evangelina Cisneros Told by Herself* (New York: Continental Publishing Company, 1897), 196.

"Every drop": Cisneros, *The Story of Evangelina Cisneros Told by Herself*, 126.

"Father, I am": Cisneros, *The Story of Evangelina Cisneros Told by Herself*, 130.

"short, ugly": Cisneros, *The Story of Evangelina Cisneros Told by Herself*, 157.

"I did not know": *The Story of Evangelina Cisneros Told by Herself*, 188.

"You have some fine": *The Story of Evangelina Cisneros Told by Herself*, 187.

"I would die"; "Then everything was dark": *The Story of Evangelina Cisneros Told by Herself*, 195.

"was implicated"; "she herself in": Wilbur Cross, "The Perils of Evangelina," *American Heritage*, February 1968, 5.

"My plan is": *The Story of Evangelina Cisneros Told by Herself*, 73.

"We will soon": *The Story of Evangelina Cisneros Told by Herself*, 200.

"As if I needed": *The Story of Evangelina Cisneros Told by Herself*, 206.

"I might have been his grandmother": *The Story of Evangelina Cisneros Told by Herself*, 209.

"We are from Havana": *The Story of Evangelina Cisneros Told by Herself*, 210.

"I never could get": *The Story of Evangelina Cisneros Told by Herself*, 214.

"must have winked"; "absurd": W. Joseph Campbell, "Not a Hoax: New Evidence in the New York Journal's Rescue of Evangeline Cisneros," *American Journalism*, Fall 2002, 5.

In the preface of: Prados-Torreia, *Mambisas*, 141.

According to other reports: Karen Roggenkamp, *Narrating the News* (Kent, OH: Kent State University Press, 2005), 101.

"magnificent farce": Willis J. Abbot, *Watching the World Go By* (Boston: Little, Brown, 1933), 215; Campbell, "Not a Hoax," 1.

"cursed the whole": Abbot, *Watching the World Go By,* 216.

Wilbur Cross in an article: Cross, "The Perils of Evangelina," 4.

. . . a group of exiled: Prados-Torreia, *Mambisas*, 138.

"The truth is": Prados-Torreia, *Mambisas*, 139.

"so-called autobiography": Prados-Torreia, *Mambisas*, 140.

. . . and much later in an interview; she replied that: Eleanor Andersen, "Helpless Martyr or Hardened Mambisa: Race, Gender, and Agency in the Cisneros Affair," *Perceptions* 5, no. 1 (2019), https://doi.org/10.15367/pj.v5i1.145.

"heroic mambisa to the freedom of Cuba": Anne Fountain, "Questions of Race and Gender: Evangelina Cisneros and the Spanish-Cuban-American War," *Annals: Latin America: Approaching the Millennium*, 1999, 39.

Paulina Ruiz Gonzales

"Were you"; "soft dark"; "slim as a poplar"; "very graceful": Grover Flint, *Marching with Gomez* (Boston: Lamson, Wolffe and Company, 1898), 87.

"a shower of Mauser"; "Viva Cuba": Flint, *Marching with Gomez*, 86.

"I would not": Flint, *Marching with Gomez*, 88.

"A Woman Bravely": "A Woman Bravely Fighting for Cuba," *San Francisco Examiner*, June 7, 1896.

"The Cuban Joan of Arc"; "Cuban tigress"; "will fight"; "ready to avenge"; "dead shot"; "envied by"; "greeted with": "The Cuban Joan of Arc," *Great Falls (MT) Tribune*, June 19, 1898.

... style of newspaper . . . : "U.S. Diplomacy and Yellow Journalism, 1895–1898," Office of the Historian, https://history.state.gov/milestones/1866-1898/yellow-journalism.

"plain unvarnished": Flint, *Marching with Gomez*, xxix.

"heads the spirit"; "risen among": "The Cuban Joan of Arc," *Great Falls (MT) Tribune*, June 19, 1898.

"interesting stories"; "sharing the hardship"; "only one": Flint, *Marching with Gomez*, 88.

"full of intense": Display ad, *Werner's Magazine*, August 1898, iv.

"Our kinfolk"; "What another"; "No snarling": "Recitation and Declamation," *Werner's Magazine*, September 1898, 41.

"Out, machete"; "Ah, here comes": "Recitation and Declamation," *Werner's Magazine*, September 1898, 42.

"A dramatic setting": "Miss Rodeffer's Class Recital," *Salida (CO) Mail*, June 6, 1899.

"appropriate stage"; "thoroughly appreciative": "Musician and Literary," *Salida (CO) Mail*, June 9, 1899.

Teresa Magbanua

"The insurgents will have": "Tension Great," *Madison (SD) Daily Leader*, October 17, 1899.

Born in Iloilo province: Demy P. Sonza, *Illustrious Ilongos* (Iloilo City, Philippines: Iloilo Provincial Historical Committee, 1972), 147.

"energetic": Christine Doran, "Women in the Philippine Revolution," *Philippine Studies*, Third Quarter 1998, 368.

". . . earning a degree . . .": Sonza, *Illustrious Ilongos*, 147.

"militant underground . . .": Jones, *Honor in the Dust*, 43.

"In 1898 two of . . .": Sonza, *Illustrious Ilongos*, 148.

"You know very well"; "in the Battle of Barrio Yating": Gregorio F. Zaide, "The Visayan Joan of Arc," *Philippines Free Press*, November 26, 1938; Sonza, *Illustrious Ilongos*, 148.

"wolves": Leon Wolff, "The Sham Battle of Manila," *American Heritage* (December 1960): 5.

. . . fifteen thousand . . . : Jones, *Honor in the Dust*, 97.

"somewhat disturbed"; "It appears": "The Fall of Iloilo," *Semi-Weekly New Era* (Lancaster, PA), December 31, 1898.

"It was a sight"; "It is no fun": "Melvin's Soldier Boy," *Melvin (IL) Transcript*, April 28, 1899.

"much of the city": Jones, *Honor in the Dust*, 207.

four hundred Americans: Cecilia Locsin-Nava, "Teresa Magbanua: Woman Warrior," *Review of Women's Studies* 6, no. 1 (1996): 63.

"shell and shrapnel"; "almost sixty-three"; "persistent attacks": "Battle Near Iloilo," *Salt Lake Tribune*, March 22, 1899.

"much of the countryside"; "Throughout the summer": Jones, *Honor in the Dust*, 208.

"attack any": Locsin-Nava, "Teresa Magbanua: Woman Warrior," 63.

It was in October 1899: "Tension Great," *Madison (SD) Daily Leader*, October 17, 1899.

"It has never been": "With US Troops at Jaro," *Boston Globe*, December 23, 1899.

"In the summer of 1900"; "the pervasive reach": Jones, *Honor in the Dust*, 208.

"The situation of the island": Jones, *Honor in the Dust*, 209.

CHAPTER 4

Introduction

". . . we considered"; "massing together"; "men dealing": "Women Gather from Afar," *Omaha Daily Bee*, June 28, 1899.

"On us war": "Letter from President of General Federation of Women's Clubs," *Star-Gazette* (Elmira, NY), April 1, 1898.

An Iowa paper: "Case of Big Head," *Gazette* (Cedar Rapids, IA), April 6, 1898.

"I've already given": "Two Women of Chicago," *News-Palladium* (Benton Harbor, MI), April 2, 1898.

As one newspaper: "Mrs. Henrotin's Letter," *Woman's Exponent* (Salt Lake City, UT), May 1, 1898.

"I will most": "No Parisian Luxuries," *Burlington (VT) Free Press*, May 10, 1898.

"we plead that"; "We think it": "Women's Council on War," *Woman's Exponent* (Salt Lake City, UT), May 15, 1898.

"giving aid": "National Enemies," *Salt Lake Tribune*, June 18, 1899.

"not by becoming": "The National Council of Women," *Woman's Exponent* (Salt Lake City, UT), November 1, 1898.

Charlotte Smith

"A Yankee battleship"; "fading to"; "close pursuit": "An Incident of the War," *Cheyenne (OK) Sunbeam*, July 22, 1898; "An Incident of the War," *Chester (VT) Advertiser*, July 30, 1898; "An Incident of the War," *Miltonian* (Milton, PA), July 1, 1898.

"corrupting": "Washington Letter," *Watchman and Southron* (Sumter, SC), August 15, 1882.

"great lever"; "I found here": "Mrs. Charlotte Smith: An Open Letter to the Press of the Country," *National Republican* (Washington, DC), March 14, 1885.

"a bad character,": "In Congress To-day," *Critic* (Washington, DC), July 5, 1888.

"morals, restraint": "Charlotte Smith's Petition," *Critic* (Washington, DC), August 29, 1890.

"I was afraid": "Colored Woman Inventor," *Woman Inventor* (April 1890): 2.

"certain portions": "The Blushing Bloomers," *Mexico (MO) Weekly Ledger*, January 10, 1895.

"women who"; "evil associations"; "opportunities for"; "more to"; "the devil's": "War on the Bike," *Los Angeles Herald*, July 3, 1896.

"old maids": "A Woman's Daily," *Times* (Shreveport, LA), March 18, 1898.

"Why our"; "The idea"; "angel of peace": "Angel of Peace," *Evening Star* (Washington, DC), April 6, 1898.

"a poor"; "fled in terror"; "the working": "War Very Shortly," *Kansas City (MO) Journal*, April 10, 1898.

When the Washington, D.C. *Evening*; "There are so"; "There are ten": "Angel of Peace," *Evening Star* (Washington, DC), April 6, 1898.

"Mrs. Smith has": "A Woman's Daily," *Times* (Shreveport, LA), March 18, 1898.

"not the place": "Quiet False Rumors," *Evening Star* (Washington, DC), May 25, 1898.

A Pennsylvania; "A War"; "treat with": Display ad, *Miners Journal*, May 9, 1898.

"national military-naval"; "nominal fee": "Insurance for Soldiers," *Washington Post*, June 18, 1898.

"in order that": "To Put It in the Deed," *Baltimore Sun*, November 22, 1899.

"deserved a home": "A Home for Schley," *Baltimore Sun*, November 18, 1899.

"any possible wiles": "To Put It in the Deed," *Baltimore Sun*, November 22, 1899.

"the gift house"; "secure in": No title, *Twice-a-Week Messenger* (Owensboro, KY), November 25, 1899.

"We wonder where": No title, *Fair Haven (VT) Era*, January 11, 1900.

"Why I never": "More Mud Thrown by Foes," *Pittsburgh Press*, August 17, 1901.

According to the paper: "The Schley House Fund," *Charlotte (NC) News*, March 26, 1900.

"There is no excuse": "Hero Unearthed by Roosevelt," *Our Southern Home* (Livingston, AL), February 26, 1902.

"in the interest of": "Insurance for Soldiers," *Washington Post*, June 18, 1898.

"Here comes"; "Yes, and I'll": "Advocate of Woman's Rights," *Indianapolis Journal*, June 23, 1900.

Lucy Parsons

"Ah, the shame": "Mrs. Parsons Makes a Speech," *Chicago Tribune*, July 17, 1899.

Born into: Jacqueline Jones, *Goddess of Anarchy: The Life and Times of Lucy Parsons, American Radical* (New York: Basic Books, 2017), ix.

She credited fictitious Mexican: Jones, *Goddess of Anarchy*, xiii.

And a Mexican-Indian ancestry: Tera W. Hunter, review of *Goddess of Anarchy*, by Jacqueline Jones, *Washington Post*, January 12, 2018, https://

www.washingtonpost.com/outlook/latina-heroine-or-black-radical-the
-complicated-story-of-lucy-parsons/2018/01/10/2126da90-dead-11e7
-8679-a9728984779c_story.html; Emily England, "Searching for Lucy
Parsons: A Racial Riddle," *Black Perspectives*, March 22, 2015, https://
www.aaihs.org/searching-for-lucy-parsons-a-racial-riddle; Natalia Molina,
How Race Is Made in America (Berkeley: University of California Press,
2014), 5.

"a slaughterer": Jones, *Goddess of Anarchy*, 172.

"parasitic capitalist class"; "sent the working"; "relics from": Carolyn Ashbaugh, *Lucy Parsons: An American Revolutionary* (Chicago: Haymarket
Books, 1976), 32.

"stayed at": Ashbaugh, *Lucy Parsons*, 31.

"Go through": Lucy Parsons, "I Am an Anarchist," in *Lift Every Voice:
African American Oratory, 1787–1900*, ed. Philip S. Foner and Robert
James Branham (Tuscaloosa: University of Alabama Press, 1998), 655.

"Liberty": "Why She Is an Anarchist," *Chicago Record*, November 28,
1898.

"I can't tell": "Lucy Parsons Is Mild," *Sunday Inter Ocean*, August 12, 1900.

"I would rather": "Lucy Parsons Called Down," *Journal and Tribune*
(Knoxville, TN), November 12, 1895.

"anarchistic tirade"; "loud howls"; "foreigners"; "wade in gore"; "spent
enough": "Chicago Distress," *Fort Scott (KS) Dispatch*, August 24, 1898.

"We know that": "Revolt of the Bees," *Industrial Freedom*, July 23, 1898.

"tendency toward": "The Professor and Aguinaldo," *Inter Ocean*, April 28,
1899.

"Treason!" "Traitors!"; "crusade in"; "the emblem"; "criminal aggression";
"invaders"; "We deplore": "Call a Halt on the War Policy," *Chicago Tribune*, May 1, 1899.

Inter Ocean newspaper speculated: "Will Praise Rebels," *Inter Ocean*, July 16, 1899.

"Cuba has been"; "fight the trusts"; "Suppose you"; "Every stripe": "Mrs. Parsons Makes a Speech," *Chicago Tribune*, July 17, 1899.

Upon his arrival: Ashbaugh, *Lucy Parsons*, 208.

"The story": "Deny Story of a Row," *Inter Ocean*, August 3, 1900.

"We are getting": "Reds in Chicago," *Star Tribune* (Minneapolis, MN), August 14, 1901.

"Oh, I don't care": "Lucy Parsons Is Mild," *Inter Ocean*, August 12, 1900.

"Lucy Parsons wasn't": Ashbaugh, *Lucy Parsons*, 10.

Constancia Poblete

The guiding: "Peace League of Manila," *New-York Tribune*, July 1, 1901.

"armed only with faith"; "what armed force": Rosa L. Sevilla de Alvero, "The Filipino Woman in War and in Peace," in *Gems of Philippine Oratory*, by Austin Craig (Manila: University of Manila, 1924), 71.

"It is the"; "Though great": "Women's Dept.," *Newport (RI) Mercury*, May 25, 1901.

"for the purpose": "The Woman's Peace League," *Semi-Weekly Spokesman-Review* (Spokane, WA), February 10, 1901.

". . . it did not touch": Mrs. William Howard Taft, *Recollections of Full Years* (New York: Dodd, Mead, 1914), 31.

"Enough of war"; "Join hands": "Another Factor in the Consummation of Peace in the Philippines," *Ottumwa (IA) Tri-Weekly Courier*, April 9, 1901.

"If the women will come": Alice Byram Condict, *Old Glory and the Gospel in the Philippines: Notes Gathered during Professional and Missionary Work* (Chicago: F. H. Revell Company, 1901), 81.

"La Liga Femenina"; "We rejoiced": Byram Condict, *Old Glory and the Gospel in the Philippines*, 83.

"90 percent"; "Even so": "Aguinaldo Interviewed," *Evening Herald* (Ottawa, KS), April 3, 1901.

"Your son was"; "He sank slowly": "Details of Death of Lieut. Robert Bean," *Journal and Tribune* (Knoxville, TN), December 16, 1901.

"scour and burn"; "for final extermination."; "Samar island": "Are Burning It Up," *Iola (KS) Weekly Record*, December 20, 1901.

"Insurrection at End on the Isle of Samar"; "Governor Taft looks": *Lincoln (NE) Evening News*, March 20, 1902.

"While I have": "Malvar Pleased," *Ottumwa (IA) Tri-Weekly Courier*, June 12, 1902.

"If the Filipino": "Public Opinion," *Journal and Tribune* (Knoxville, TN), December 15, 1901.

". . . became the mouthpiece": Gretchen Bloom, "Gender and Women in Development: Relevant in the Philippines?" GENESYS Project, prepared for Office of Women in Development, Bureau of Research and Development, Agency for International Development (Washington, DC: The Futures Group International, October 1992), 132.

"urged women to": Tingting Cojuangco, "Women Who Made Our Nation Proud," *Philstar Global*, March 13, 2005.

Jessie Agnes Schley

"Spartan women used": "Jessie's Ideas Odd," *Saint Paul (MN) Globe*, September 25, 1898.

"Miss Schley Is Guilty": "Miss Schley Is Guilty by Her Mission," *Chicago Tribune*, July 26, 1898.

"poorest and unfortunate"; "compelled to work for a living": "Milwaukee Woman to See Christina in Behalf of Peace," *Chicago Tribune*, July 21, 1898.

"While praying the thought"; "I was elected a committee": "Jessie's Ideas Odd," *Saint Paul (MN) Globe*, September 25, 1898.

"self-appointed dove of peace": "Miss Schley's Peace Commission," *Chicago Daily Tribune*, September 24, 1898.

"meddlesome"; "delegate from . . ."; "unnecessary"; "undesired": "Personal," *New York Times*, August 2, 1898.

"hysterical young"; "not only Quixotic"; "criminal": "The Peace Working Schleys," *Los Angeles Herald*, August 3, 1898.

"try her hand": "Miss Schley's Mission," *Marshfield News and Wisconsin Hub*, July 28, 1898.

"rebellious girl": "Aus Spanien's Hauptstadt," *Der Deutsche Correspondent*, July 25, 1898.

"I do not endorse": "Efforts for Peace," *The Peacemaker and Court of Arbitration* (Providence, RI: Universal Peace Union, August 1898), 29.

"Joan d'Arc of the peace cause": "Jessie Schley," *The Peacemaker and Court of Arbitration*, 78.

They went so far: "Miss Schley Is Guilty of Treason by Her Mission," *Chicago Tribune*, July 26, 1898.

"carries on any verbal": *Federal Statutes Annotated* (New York: Edward Thompson Company, 1918), 422.

"mission of mercy"; "trying to save life": *Advocate of Peace* (Boston: American Peace Society, August 27, 1898), 205.

"neither the queen regent": "Queen Won't Receive Her," *Kansas City (MO) Journal*, July 26, 1898.

"I had never written"; "audacious forgery": "Jessie Schley," 80.

"It shows how the press": "Jessie Schley," 79.

In early August": "Miss Schley Sees the Queen," *Chicago Tribune*, August 4, 1898.

Finally, Jessie offered: "Jessie Schley Claims Credit," *Chicago Tribune*, November 20, 1898.

"visiting and conferring"; "prominent officials": "Miss Jessie Schley Takes the Credit for Ending the Late Spanish War," *Times* (Philadelphia, PA), November 20, 1898.

"who littered the streets": "Now Bent on Relief Work," *Courier-Journal* (Louisville, KY), September 7, 1898.

"celebrity"; "monomaniac"; "Instead of being the slim"; "You know I brought"; "went away"; "finally said": "Miss Schley at Havana," *Evening Star* (Washington, DC), September 17, 1898.

"retire to the sylvan": "Miss Schley's Peace Commission," *Chicago Daily Tribune*, September 24, 1898.

"venting her indignation"; "This government": "Says Peace Is Her Work," *Chicago Tribune*, October 4, 1898.

CHAPTER 5

Introduction

"I was determined": "The Romance of the Only Woman War Correspondent," *St. Paul (MN) Globe*, June 1, 1904.

"positively absurd": *The Story of Our Wonderful Victories Told by Dewey, Schley, Wheeler, and Other Heroes: A True History of Our War with Spain by the Officers and Men of Our Army and Navy . . . Reminiscences of Life in Camp, Field and Hospital, Soul-Stirring Poems and Songs of the War, with a Full Description of Our New Possessions* (New York: American Book and Bible House, 1899), 506.

"After all"; "Why it's foolish": "The Romance of the Only Woman War Correspondent," *St. Paul (MN) Globe*, June 1, 1904.

"As the 'State of Texas'": Elsie Reasoner, "What a Young Girl Saw at Siboney," *McClure's*, October 1898, 538.

"Soon after"; "Quickly and skillfully": "Story of a Kansas Girl," *Atchison (KS) Daily Champion*, August 9, 1898.

"I was present": "The Romance of the Only Woman War Correspondent," *St. Paul (MN) Globe*, June 1, 1904.

"I had read": *The Story of Our Wonderful Victories Told by Dewey, Schley, Wheeler, and Other Heroes*, 506.

"I was near": *The Story of Our Wonderful Victories Told by Dewey, Schley, Wheeler, and Other Heroes*, 507.

"I was not exactly"; "not bad": Teresa Dean, "A Woman in Camp," *Frank Leslie's Weekly*, July 28, 1898, page not identified.

"The hearse": Teresa Dean, "The Pitiful Side of War," *Frank Leslie's Weekly*, August 5, 1898.

"In the United States"; I have shut": Gonzalo de Quesada and Henry Davenport Northrop, *Cuba's Great Struggle for Freedom* (Washington, DC: J. R. Jones, 1898), 225.

"Well, drive in"; "We don't want": Kate Masterson, "A Visit to a Dynamite Factory," *Democrat and Chronicle* (Rochester, NY), November 9, 1896.

"There is no more pathetic": Kate Masterson, "Cuba's Children on the Battle-Field," *Democrat and Chronicle* (Rochester, NY), March 11, 1898.

"The average man"; "Remember the mange": Margherita Arlina Hamm, "Needs of Our Soldiers," *Los Angeles Herald*, August 28, 1898.

"The conclusion": "The Philippines," *Salt Lake Tribune*, March 30, 1899.

"Our troops were"; "drop a tear"; "He may have": Margherita Arlina Hamm, "Strange Sights and Scenes Witnessed in Porto Rico," *Buffalo (NY) Sunday Morning News*, October 2, 1898.

"Plucky Woman": Bessie Dow Bates, "Plucky Woman War Correspondent," *Logansport Pharos-Tribune* (Logansport, IN), June 17, 1899.

"The First Woman": "The First Woman War Correspondent to Go to the Front," *Times* (Shreveport, LA), July 13, 1898.

"The swish"; "Time was": Charles B. Brown, "A Woman's Odyssey: The War Correspondence of Ann Benjamin," *Journalism Quarterly*, Fall 1969, 522.

"A lady war correspondent!": "Mrs. Blake Watkins," *New York Times*, July 3, 1898.

Anna Northend Benjamin

"The quarters of the mules"; "like the tenement"; "triple-deckers": Anna Northend Benjamin, "Putting the Stalls and Bunks in the Transports at Port Tampa, *Frank Leslie's Weekly*, June 16, 1898, page not identified.

"Haven't you been"; "Oh, we had some"; "We stole"; "their fame"; "Teddy's Terrors": Anna Northend Benjamin, "The Truth about Army Rations," *Frank Leslie's Weekly*, June 30, 1898, page not identified.

"Most of them"; "There are some"; "The other ships": Anna Northend Benjamin, "The Darker Side of War, *Frank Leslie's Weekly*, August 4, 1898, page not identified.

"Were the cabins": Brown, "A Woman's Odyssey," 525.

"It is a fine harbor": Anna Northend Benjamin, "A Woman's Point of View," *Frank Leslie's Weekly*, August 18, 1898, page not identified.

"The last mines: Brown, "A Woman's Odyssey," 526.

"It is literally": Benjamin, "A Woman's Point of View," page not identified.

"woe-begone war"; "We glided into": Anna Northend Benjamin, "Santiago after the Surrender," *The Outlook*, September 3, 1898, 21.

"We had been coming": Benjamin, "Santiago after the Surrender," 23.

"on the brink"; "The wealthiest citizens"; "a surging mass"; "Standing there": Anna Northend Benjamin, "A Woman's Visit to Santiago," *Frank Leslie's Weekly*, August 25, 1898, page not identified.

"tracked and beaten"; "in every way inferior"; "Filipinos at times"; "Concentration for any"; "coolies"; "native jabbering": Anna Northend Benjamin, "Consul William Tells of Talks with Aguinaldo," *San Francisco Chronicle*, September 16, 1899.

"I was the only woman"; "I was forced": Brown, "A Woman's Odyssey," 528; "An Interesting Journey," *New-York Tribune*, August 5, 1900.

"Filipino bullets": Anna N. Benjamin, "Cleaning Up Manila," *Independence (KS) Daily Reporter*, December 20, 1899.

"full-fledged"; "It was a dangerous": Anna Northend Benjamin, "An Echo from El Caney," *Columbian* (Bloomsburg, PA), December 28, 1899.

Muriel Bailey

"It seems strange"; "Within even": Muriel Bailey, "At Home with Aguinaldo," *Overland Monthly* (San Francisco: Samuel Carson, 1899), 258.

"shining example": Bailey, "At Home with Aguinaldo," 256.

"short and slender"; "It could be": Bailey, "At Home with Aguinaldo," 257.

people were forced: O'Toole, *The Spanish War*, 56.

"And you"; "No, I have"; "absolute independence"; "I do not"; "nothing but sullen"; "as I sat"; "I have been": Bailey, "At Home with Aguinaldo," 258.

"It does make"; "It fills you": Muriel Bailey, "In the Trenches before Caloocan with the Utah Battery Boys," *San Francisco Examiner*, April 3, 1899.

"I have seen"; "I have heard"; "We carried our pistols; "grim and"; "And then I"; "Six miles of"; "They say that women"; "It was a Mauser"; "Not dead yet"; "I ducked"; "the errands of destruction"; "I could not": Muriel Bailey, "On the Fighting Lines," *Unionville (MO) Republican*, April 26, 1899.

"In the Trenches"; "The fortune of"; "He is liable"; "expressions not learned"; "But then"; "Now and then": Muriel Bailey, "In the Trenches before Caloocan with the Utah Battery Boys." *San Francisco Examiner*, April 3, 1899.

"lonely singing": Muriel Bailey, "On the Fighting Lines," *Unionville (MO) Republican*, April 26, 1899.

"fussy, pompous": Jones, *Honor in the Dust*, 98.

"Some things wanted"; "Oh, yes!"; "Two weeks"; "the matter well"; "waited anxiously"; "Women know"; "We all know": Muriel Bailey, "The Way General Otis Has His Being and Distributes Canned Goods in the Philippines," *San Francisco Examiner*, October 29, 1899.

Fannie Brigham Ward

"Words fail": Fannie Brigham Ward, "The Story of Cuba's Woes," *New Era* (Lancaster, PA), March 26, 1898.

"Fannie B. Ward Among"; "How Valeriano Weyler"; "A Tale of"; "Fancy being"; "extermination"; "Nobody in the hospital"; "While we stood": Fannie B. Ward, "A Tale of Horrors," *Daily New Era* (Lancaster, PA), February 21, 1898.

"with the big head"; "the first human emotion"; "I believed that": Fannie Brigham Ward, "The Story of Cuba's Woes." *New Era* (Lancaster, PA), March 26, 1898.

"I have seen": Fannie B. Ward, "A Tale of Horrors," *Daily New Era* (Lancaster, PA), February 21, 1898.

"Every train that": Fannie Brigham Ward, "The Story of Cuba's Woes," *New Era* (Lancaster, PA), March 26, 1898.

"I find"; "undersized"; "The Spaniards"; "pounce": Fannie Brigham Ward, "Cuba on the Eve of War," *New Era* (Lancaster, PA), April 13, 1898.

"The American soldiers"; "It is not safe": Stephen Crane, "About Cuban Soldiers," *Missoulian* (Missoula, MT), July 22, 1898.

"At first nobody"; "Maceo, the mulatto"; "transformed into"; "They fought": "The Cuban Women," *Wheeling (WV) Daily Intelligencer*, May 14, 1898.

"Spanish bullets"; "eventually cost": Fannie Brigham Ward, "Dangerous Cuba," *New Haven (CT) Morning Journal and Courier*, July 1, 1898.

"to encounter"; "Decayed fruit"; "The wonder"; "Men are dying"; "The Sternbergian theory"; "Surgeon-General Sternberg announced"; "Thus hundreds": Fannie Brigham Ward, "Santiago de Cuba in War Time," *New Haven (CT) Morning Journal and Courier*, August 25, 1898.

"No wonder Spain"; "Heaven knows": Fannie Brigham Ward, "Sugar Making in Cuba," *New Haven (CT) Morning Journal and Courier*, April 26, 1898.

"Speculators have"; "A man with"; "It seems a pity": Fannie Brigham Ward, "The Queen of the Antilles," *New Era* (Lancaster, PA), April 30, 1898.

"Soon as hostilities": Fannie Brigham Ward, "Dangerous Cuba," *New Haven (CT) Morning Journal and Courier*, July 1, 1898.

"done what few"; "from which"; "vigorous style"; "too masculine": "Mrs. Fannie B. Ward," *New Era* (Lancaster, PA), July 30, 1898.

"All my life": Alice Fahs, *Out on Assignment: Newspaper Women and the Making of Modern Public Space* (Chapel Hill: University of North Carolina Press, 2011), 250.

CHAPTER 6

Introduction

". . . women as well": Bell Merrill Draper, "Woman's Work in the War," in *The American-Spanish War: A History by the War Leaders* (London: Chas. C. Haskell & Son, 1899), 452.

"In New York by 1898": Vicki L. Ruiz and Virginia Sánchez Korrol, eds., *Latinas in the United States* (Bloomington: Indiana University Press, 2006), 182.

"We do not have": Annie Laurie Woods, "Women Who Work for Cuba," *Sunday Leader* (Wilkes-Barre, PA), May 15, 1898.

"to abstain"; "to employ": "The Total Abstinence Pledge Card," *Kansas Issue*, December 1, 1898.

"A number of women": Mary E. Leonard, "For Sick Soldiers," *Edwardsville (IL) Intelligencer*, August 30, 1899.

"We deeply deplore": "Philippine Policy and Canteen Decision Denounced by the W.C.T.U.," *Star* (Reynoldsville, PA), November 1, 1899.

"cease at once": "Protest of Women Against Imperialism," *San Francisco Call*, May 31, 1899.

Paulina Pedroso

"El dia de la Patria": Gary R. Mormino and George E. Pozzetta, *The Immigrant World of Ybor City* (Gainesville: University Press of Florida, 1998), 80.

"create an interracial": Nancy Hewitt, "Paulina Pedroso and Las Patriotas of Tampa," in *Spanish Pathways in Florida, 1492–1992*, ed. Ann Henderson and Gary Mormino (Sarasota, FL: Pineapple Press, 1991), location 2193 in Kindle book.

whom he had first met: Susan D. Greenbaum, *More Than Black* (Gainesville: University Press of Florida, 2002), 74.

"You are going": Greenbaum, *More Than Black*, 75.

"civilian camp": Hewitt, "Paulina Pedroso and Las Patriotas of Tampa," location 2169 in Kindle book.

"Gentlemen, if any": Mike Morgan, "Moment with Morgan," *Tampa (FL) Times*, November 24, 1956.

doorman at a Havana: Hewitt, "Paulina Pedroso and Las Patriotas of Tampa," location 2321 in Kindle book.

"aged mammy"; "gave all she": "One of Cuba's Heroines," *Buffalo (NY) Times*, June 16, 1913.

"bronze woman": Alex Sommers and the Tampa Historical Team, "Paulina Pedroso," *Tampa Historical*, accessed April 24, 2020, https://tampa historical.org/items/show/119.

Ellen Hardin Walworth

"I found a body": Thomas Dunphy, *Remarkable Trials of All Countries*, vol. 2 (New York: S. S. Peloubet & Company, 1882), 145.

"My father treated"; "the family persecutor": "Some Trials," *Brooklyn (NY) Daily Eagle*, December 28, 1882.

"I had been subjected": Dunphy, *Remarkable Trials of All Countries*, 148.

"I can do nothing": "Mother and Son," *New Northwest* (Portland, OR), October 31, 1873.

"In view of the crisis"; "As patriotic women": "Nurses Will Be Needed," *Wichita* (KS) *Daily Eagle*, April 4, 1898.

"Men are organizing": "Troops at Attention," *Evening Times* (Washington, DC), April 26, 1898.

"allegiance to the United": "Prominent Women Interested in Relief for Men in War Service," *Chicago Tribune*, May 24, 1898.

"little better than"; "It is rather": "Cold Welcome to Wounded," *New York Times*, August 14, 1898.

"With a carelessness": Mary E. Leonard, "For Sick Soldiers," *Edwardsville (IL) Intelligencer*, August 30, 1898.

". . . things still appear": "Gate City at Montauk," *New York Times*, August 14, 1898.

". . . the business of": Women's National War Relief Association, *Women's National War Relief Association: Organized for the Emergency of the Spanish-American War* (New York: Printed by order of the Board of Directors, 1899), 76, https://www.loc.gov/item/99003434.

"the mother of the camp": Mary E. Leonard, "For Sick Soldiers," *Edwardsville (IL) Intelligencer*, August 30, 1898.

"Her work was"; "Miss Walworth saved": "A Nurse Dies of Typhoid," *New York Times*, October 19, 1898.

"I was one"; "Never a doubt has"; "the warning note"; "We're burying": "A Kentucky Heroine," *Courier-Journal* (Louisville, KY), August 20, 1899.

". . . there has been": "The National War Relief Association," *Courier-News* (Bridgewater, NJ), September 20, 1898.

"Except for the boundless": Women's National War Relief Association, *Women's National War Relief Association*, 82.

Laura Drake Gill

"The care and education": New York State Legislature, Senate, *Documents of the Senate of the State of New York*, vol. 7 (Albany, NY: James B. Lyon, 1900), 705.

". . . I desire"; "Sternberg Speaks": *Logansport (IN) Pharos-Tribune*, September 6, 1898.

"The Americans have": "Mexico's Spanish Paper," *Hanover (KS) Democrat*, March 31, 1899.

"The suffering which": "Orphans in Cuba," *Muncie (IN) Daily Herald*, March 14, 1899.

"mere little skeletons"; "whether it was"; "at least 250"; "I wish that I might"; "The need is urgent"; "if the children": "The Cuban Orphan Fund," *New York Times*, June 11, 1899.

"a friend of the cause"; "anonymously": "Cuban Orphan Fund," *Brooklyn (NY) Daily Eagle*, July 30, 1899.

"This will make": "Reforming Cuba," *Pittsburgh Press*, July 23, 1899.

"Young, self reliant"; "unattractive and laborious": "Down in Cuba," *Marion (OH) Star*, May 2, 1900.

"see the city by night": "Cubans in Cambridge," *Lawrence (MA) Daily Journal*, July 28, 1900.

Clemencia Lopez

"Gen. Bell Tired": "The Rigors of War," *Emporia (KS) Daily Republican*, January 21, 1902.

"Gen. Bell Herding": "General Bell Herding Natives in Towns and He Will Carry on a Policy of Confiscation," *Osage Journal* (Pawhuska, OK), January 3, 1902.

"Gen. Bell Driving": "Gen. Bell Driving Filipinos in Batangas Like Sheep," *St. Mary's Star* (St. Mary's, KS), January 9, 1902.

"leaving the field"; "the bodies floating": "Insurgents Used Bolos," *Fort Scott (KS) Weekly Monitor*, April 28, 1900.

"The wealthy": "Death for All Traitors," *Woodford County Journal* (Eureka, IL), January 23, 1902.

"the arrest of": "Filipinos in Flight," *Ottawa (KS) Daily Republican*, January 6, 1902.

"he does not think"; "no injustice was done": "Girl Appeals to Roosevelt," *Wichita (KS) Daily Eagle*, May 24, 1902.

"little brown brothers": "The Philippine War—Suppressing an Insurrection," https://www.nps.gov/prsf/learn/historyculture/the-philippine-
war-suppressing-an-insurrection.htm.

according to a president: Zinn, *A People's History of the United States*, 228.

"It is certain"; "The Filipinos have": "Manila Advice to Sixto Lopez,"
Honolulu Advertiser, November 1, 1901.

"one of benevolent"; "the strong arm": Karl Irving Faust and Peter Mac-
Queen, *Campaigning in the Philippines* (San Francisco: The Hicks-Judd
Company Publishers, 1899), 118.

At Wellesley Clemencia: Laura R. Prieto, "A Delicate Subject: Clemencia López, Civilized Womanhood, and the Politics of Anti-Imperialism,"
Journal of the Gilded Age and Progressive Era 12, no. 2 (2013): 228.

"spent some of": The Twentieth Century Club, *A Farewell Luncheon in
Honor of Senorita Clemencia Lopez* (Boston: The Arakelyan Press, 1904),
10.

"We have found": The Twentieth Century Club, *A Farewell Luncheon in
Honor of Senorita Clemencia Lopez*, 17.

It was hoped that Clemencia: Prieto, "A Delicate Subject," 209.

"I believe that"; "I should like to"; "I should have reason": Florence Col-
lins Porter, ed., "Chats about Women and Women's Clubs," *Los Angeles
Herald*, June 29, 1902.

"The very badness": "Charges 1,000,000 Lives to Americans, *Boston Post*,
May 14, 1903.

"I think that": "Only True Way," *Boston Globe*, May 14, 1903.

"Let us continue"; "Who would imagine"; "ascertain the real situation";
". . . the Filipinos have no natural": "Charges 1,000,000 Lives to Americans," *Boston Post*, May 14, 1903.

"The Boston anti's": "Roosevelt and Expansion," *Statesman Journal* (Salem,
OR), May 22, 1903.

"One of the great": The Twentieth Century Club, *A Farewell Luncheon in Honor of Senorita Clemencia Lopez*, 18.

"Pious fraud": The Twentieth Century Club, *A Farewell Luncheon in Honor of Senorita Clemencia Lopez*, 19.

"Which boasts of"; "conduct business"; "foreign soldiery"; "a christian civilization": The Twentieth Century Club, *A Farewell Luncheon in Honor of Senorita Clemencia Lopez*, 26.

"She has told us": The Twentieth Century Club, *A Farewell Luncheon in Honor of Senorita Clemencia Lopez*, 2.

"I beg our": The Twentieth Century Club, *A Farewell Luncheon in Honor of Senorita Clemencia Lopez*, 8.

"The doctrine that": The Twentieth Century Club, *A Farewell Luncheon in Honor of Senorita Clemencia Lopez*, 29.

"In the struggle": The Twentieth Century Club, *A Farewell Luncheon in Honor of Senorita Clemencia Lopez*, 30.

"Now it is brown"; "I have found": The Twentieth Century Club, *A Farewell Luncheon in Honor of Senorita Clemencia Lopez*, 10.

"A picture full": The Twentieth Century Club, *A Farewell Luncheon in Honor of Senorita Clemencia Lopez*, 11.

"We were indignant": The Twentieth Century Club, *A Farewell Luncheon in Honor of Senorita Clemencia Lopez*, 25.

"more influence": "The American Women Are Better Than the Soldiers," *Detroit Free Press*, January 30, 1902.

President Roosevelt appointed: Jones, *Honor in the Dust*, 354.

Clemencia carried on her fight: Prieto, "A Delicate Subject," 232.

"committed to social service"; They called for reform: Prieto, "A Delicate Subject," 231.

CHAPTER 7

Introduction

To Pay the Tax: Sidney A. Witherbee, ed., *Spanish American War Songs* (Detroit: Sidney A. Witherbee, Publisher, 1898), 30.

"capable of crushing": "War Taxes," *Scranton (PA) Tribune*, April 21, 1898.

"The Chewing": "The Chewing Gum Tax," *Buffalo (NY) Times*, April 29, 1898.

"As every war furnished": "Our War Songs," *Wichita (KS) Daily Eagle*, April 26, 1898.

"To the Women": Ella Randall Pearce, "To the Women of America," *Salt Lake Herald*, May 29, 1898.

"A Song of '98": Witherbee, *Spanish American War Songs*, 56.

"The Soldiers' Saying": Witherbee, *Spanish American War Songs*, 39.

"Manila, May 1, 1898": "Witherbee, *Spanish American War Songs*, 215.

"When I say": "Song Business Is Dead," *Anaconda (MT) Standard*, July 5, 1898.

"Fire upon this": "The Great Spanish American War Drama," *Madison (KS) Star*, January 6, 1899.

"the loves and losses"; "palpitating vibration"; "of fife and drum"; "weeping and laughter": "Cuban War Drama," *Pittsburg (KS) Kansan*, March 24, 1898.

"picturesque lover": "Grand Theater," *Boston Globe*, May 10, 1898.

"hilariously illustrating"; "creating a comic": "Grand Opera House," *Oshkosh (WI) Northwestern*, December 2, 1899.

"It's a right novel"; "Either the doll"; "At first sight": "Stories of the Stage," *Buffalo (NY) Times*, July 10, 1898.

"joke rollicking"; "with a Wall Street-broker"; "Oh don't go"; business interests": "Washington Letter," *El Paso (TX) Herald,* June 9, 1898.

"the greatest wonder": No title. *Hope (KS) Dispatch,* October 13, 1898.

"We strive to please": "Local News," *Hope (KS) Dispatch,* January 13, 1898.

"The conquest of Spanish"; "There is also": "Gossip of the Theater: What the Play Folks Are Doing," *Washington Post,* August 28, 1898.

"Art, great as it is": "Battle Pictures," *Kansas City (MO) Star,* February 19, 1899.

Frances Benjamin Johnston

"pure white striped": Frances Benjamin Johnston, "Some White House Orchids," *Demorest's Family Magazine,* June 1895, 436.

"cut and enameled": Frances Benjamin Johnston, "Some Homes under the Administration," *Demorest's Family Magazine,* December 1890, 72.

Her father's position: Victoria Olsen, "Victorian Womanhood, in All Its Guises," *Smithsonian Magazine,* May 2010, https://www.smithsonianmag .com/history/victorian-womanhood-in-all-its-guises-14265506.

"Our Washington": "The Norsemen," *Sun* (Baltimore, MD), August 30, 1876.

"Photography as a profession"; "Good common sense": Frances Benjamin Johnston, "What a Woman Can Do with a Camera," *Ladies' Home Journal,* September 1897, 6.

"fitted up in artistic": "Washington Women with Brains and Business," *Washington (DC) Times,* April 21, 1895.

"Court photographer": "Eve Up to Date," *Times-Democrat* (New Orleans, LA), March 22, 1899.

Frances worked for George: Maria Ausherman, "Frances Benjamin Johnston's Legacy in Black and White," *Journal of Heritage Stewardship,* Summer 2007, https://www.nps.gov/crmjournal/Summer2007/article1.html.

"modest, courteous gentleman": "The First Photograph," *Evening Star* (Washington, DC), October 7, 1899.

"a piece of energetic work": "The Week," *Harper's Bazaar*, September 16, 1899, 774.

"They are like fine": "Washington Women with Brains and Business," *Washington (DC) Times*, April 21, 1895.

Jean Mawson

". . . a girl of more": "The World of Sounds," *Boston Home Journal*, April 22, 1899, 14.

". . . still young and pretty": "Jean Mawson in 'A Daughter of Cuba' at the Academy of Music," *Washington Post*, April 23, 1899.

". . . graceful as a fawn": "Amusements," *Grand Rapids (MI) Herald*, April 28, 1893.

"You care"; "I too can": Joshua Polster, *Stages of Engagement: US Theatre and Performance 1898–1949* (New York: Routledge, 2016), 23.

"plenty of atmosphere"; "will belch forth": "Academy—'A Daughter of Cuba,'" *Times* (Washington, DC), April 23, 1899.

". . . insight into human nature": "Jean Mawson in 'A Daughter of Cuba' at the Academy of Music," *Washington Post*, April 23, 1899.

"fine flow of wit"; "alternately bring": "Academy—'A Daughter of Cuba,'" *Times* (Washington, DC), April 23, 1899.

"pure and wholesome"; "filled with human": "A Great Play To-night," *Morning Call* (Allentown, PA), October 1, 1898.

"a dismal failure"; "long, tedious"; "the almost unanimous"; "about which"; "barely passable"; "example of": "Academy of Music," *Evening Star* (Washington, DC), April 25, 1899.

"charming"; "wounded, fever-stricken"; "a story in their": "A Great Play To-night," *Morning Call* (Allentown, PA), October 1, 1898.

Georgiana "Georgie" Franck Greenleaf

"Almost by the time"; "air reek"; "worst possible"; "The saloonkeeper sneaked": "The Saloons of Manila," *Outlook* (Independence, KS), March 21, 1900.

"counter-attraction to the saloon": "Soldiers' Library and Reading Room at Manila," *Los Angeles Times*, October 4, 1900.

"The undertaking was"; "work and perseverance": "Manila Transformed by Women," *Brooklyn (NY) Daily Eagle*, March 3, 1901.

"We need financial"; "but we cannot do": "Manila Library Fund," *Los Angeles Times*, June 24, 1900.

"There is not an hour": "Books for Soldiers," *New-York Tribune*, September 9, 1900.

"natives would hardly": Bernadette Cheryl Beredo, "Import of the Archive: American Colonial Bureaucracy in the Philippines, 1898–1916" (doctoral dissertation, University of Hawaii, May 2011), 81.

Later the library became: "National Library of the Philippines: History," http://web.nlp.gov.ph/nlp/?q=node/190.

"given by the"; "We have a large airy": *Papers and Proceedings of the Twenty-Seventh General Meeting of the American Library Association Held at Portland, Ore. July 4–7, 1905* (Chicago: The Association, 1905), 141.

"At one time": "American Library," *Evening Star* (Washington, DC), May 25, 1900.

CHAPTER 8

Introduction

"As a rule": "The Cuban Women," *Wheeling (WV) Daily Intelligencer*, May 14, 1898.

"I listened to their": Louis A. Pérez Jr., *To Die in Cuba* (Chapel Hill: University of North Carolina Press, 2012), 114.

"Be cheerful": "Today in Philippine History," The Kahimyang Project, https://kahimyang.com/kauswagan/articles/1475/today-in-philippine -history-july-18-1875-marina-dizon-was-born-in-trozo-in-manila.

The legendary Melchora Aquino: "Melchora Aquino (1812–1919)," https://www.Encyclopedia.com.

"success in"; "every Cuban woman": "Women Are Good Spies," *Kansas City (MO) Journal*, June 12, 1898.

Patrocinio Gamboa

"rebellious nature": Sonza, *Illustrious Ilongos*, 65.

"Insurrection is the": "Marcelo Hilario Del Pilar," Your Dictionary.com, https://biography.yourdictionary.com/marcelo-hilario-del-pilar.

"newly constituted"; "will be a free": "Iloilo Before the Surrender," *St. Louis (MO) Globe-Democrat*, January 18, 1899.

"I do not ask"; "People said throughout": "Patrocinio Gamboa 1865–1953 Revolutionary 'Heroine of Jaro,'" http://www.oocities.org/sinupan/gam boapat.htm.

". . . in 2015 a marker . . .": "NHCP Unveils Historical Marker for Ilonga Heroine," Philippine News Agency, April 30, 2015.

Magdalena Peñarredonda Doley

The two-hundred yard: Philip S. Foner, *The Spanish-Cuban-American War and the Birth of American Imperialism*, vol. 1, *1895–1898* (London: Monthly Review Press, 1972), 33–34.

cut her long hair; a captain in the Spanish army: Herminia del Portal, "Las Mambisas: Magdelena Peñarredonda," *Bohemia*, December 13, 1942, 12.

Somehow, maybe from: Prados-Torreira, *Mambisas*, 114.

"El Ponton": Del Portal, "Las Mambisas," 12.

Magdalena married; "a young lady"; "an older man": Del Portal, "Las Mambisas," 60.

El Criollo: "Heronia Cubana," *El Mundo Ilustrado*, April 26, 1903, 7; Del Portal, "Las Mambisas," 60.

Underwear, writing supplies: Prados-Torreira, *Mambisas*, 116.

concealed in her petticoats: Del Portal, "Las Mambisas," 60.

In addition to conveying: Prados-Torreira, *Mambisas*, 115.

"Sometimes, with a gesture"; betrayed by someone: Del Portal, "Las Mambisas," 60.

She sometimes used: Del Portal, "Las Mambisas," 64.

fifty or sixty pounds; "He rang a bell": "While Commissions Dally," *Washington (DC) Times*, September 16, 1898.

"They only stop": Lillian Guerra, *The Myth of José Martí: Conflicting Nationalisms in Early Twentieth-Century Cuba* (Chapel Hill: University of North Carolina Press, 2005), 60.

At one point, she: Lillian Guerra, *The Myth of José Martí*, 94.

"I have witnessed": Prados-Torreira, *Mambisas*, 124.

Selected Bibliography

Abbot, Willis J. *Watching the World Go By*. Boston: Little, Brown, 1933.

Andersen, Eleanor. "Helpless Martyr or Hardened Mambisa: Race, Gender, and Agency in the Cisneros Affair." *Perceptions* 5, no. 1 (2019). https://doi.org/10.15367/pj .v5i1.145.

Ashbaugh, Carolyn. *Lucy Parsons: An American Revolutionary*. Chicago: Haymarket Books, 2012.

Betancourt Cosio Y Cisneros, Evangelina. *The Story of Evangelina Cisneros*. New York: Continental Publishing Company, 1898.

Bonsal, Stephen. "The Night after San Juan: Stories of the Wounded on the Field and in the Hospital." *McClure's*, December 1898, 118–28. https://babel.hathitrust.org/cgi/ pt?id=mdp.39015030656113&view=1up&seq=132.

Brown, Charles B. "A Woman's Odyssey: The War Correspondence of Anna Benjamin." *Journalism Quarterly* 46, issue 3 (September 1, 1969): 522–30.

Campbell, W. Joseph. "Not a Hoax: New Evidence in the *New York Journal*'s Rescue of Evangelina Cisneros." *American Journalism* 19, no. 4 (Fall 2002).

Egbert, Nelly Young. *List of Books in the American Circulating Library of Manila*. Manila: Bureau of Printing, 1907.

Espinosa, Mariola. "The Question of Racial Immunity to Yellow Fever in History and Historiography." *Social Science History* 30, no. 3–4 (Fall/Winter 2014): 437–53.

Eyot, Canning, ed. *The Story of the Lopez Family: A Page from the History of the War in the Philippines*. Boston: James H. West Co., 1904.

Fahs, Alice. *Out on Assignment: Newspaper Women and the Making of Modern Public Space*. Chapel Hill: University of North Carolina Press, 2011.

Flint, Grover. *Marching with Gomez*. Boston: Lamson, Wolffe and Company, 1898.

Foner, Philip S. *The Spanish-Cuban-American War and the Birth of American Imperialism*. Vol. 1, *1895–1898*. London: Monthly Review Press, 1972.

Fountain, Anne. "Questions of Race and Gender: Evangelina Cisneros and the Spanish-Cuban-American War." *SECOLAS Annals* (1999): 36–43.

Funtecha, Henry F. "The Iloilo Fiasco." *Philippine Quarterly of Culture and Society* 14, no. 2 (1986): 75–85.

Graf, Mercedes. "All the Women Were Valiant." *Prologue: The Journal of the National Archives* 46: 24–34.

Greenbaum, Susan D. *More Than Black: Afro-Cubans in Tampa*. Gainesville: University Press of Florida, 2002.

Hewitt, Nancy. "Paulina Pedroso and Las Patriotas of Tampa." In *Spanish Pathways in Florida, 1492–1992*, edited by Ann Henderson and Gary Mormino, 258–79. Englewood, FL: Pineapple Press, 1991.

Jefferson, Robert F., Jr. *Brothers in Valor*. Guilford, CT: Lyons Press, 2019.

Jones, Gregg. *Honor in the Dust*. New York: New American Library, 2012.

Jones, Jacqueline. *Goddess of Anarchy*. New York: Basic Books, 2017.

"Journal of Esther Voorhees Hasson," *Henry Ware Lawton Papers, 1849–1930*. Library of Congress. http://hdl.loc.gov/loc.mss/eadmss.ms009261.

Kinzer, Stephen. *The True Flag: Theodore Roosevelt, Mark Twain, and the Birth of American Empire*. New York: Henry Holt and Co., 2017.

Lopez, Victoria. "I Am Woman," *Philippine Tatler*, August 2014, 156–58.

Lyndall Dunbar, Virginia. *A Cuban Amazon*. Cincinnati, OH: The Editor Publishing Company, 1897.

McAllister Linn, Brian. *The Philippine War, 1899–1902*. Lawrence: University Press of Kansas, 2000.

McKee, Syrena. "The American Library in Manila, P.I." *Bulletin of the American Library Association*. 2, no. 5 (September 1908): 254–57.

Merrill Draper, Bell. "Woman's Work in the War." In *The American-Spanish War: A History by the War Leaders*. London: Chas. C. Haskell & Son, 1899.

Mormino, Gary R., and George E. Pozzetta. *The Immigrant World of Ybor City*. Gainesville: University Press of Florida, 1998.

Murphy, Erin L. *No Middle Ground*. Lanham, MD: Lexington Books, 2019.

Musicant, Ivan. *Empire by Default: The Spanish-American War and the Dawn of the American Century*. New York: Henry Holt and Co., 1998.

O'Toole, G. J. A. *The Spanish War: An American Epic—1898*. New York: Norton, 1984.

PBS. *Crucible of Empire: The Spanish-American War*. http://www.pbs.org/crucible.

Porter, Edwin S. *Sampson-Schley Controversy*. Parts 1–2. New York: Edison Manufacturing Co., 1901. Video. https://www.loc.gov/item/00694297.

Prados-Torreira, Teresa. *Mambisas: Rebel Women in Nineteenth-Century Cuba*. Gainesville: University Press of Florida, 2005.

Prieto, Laura R. "A Delicate Subject: Clemencia López, Civilized Womanhood, and the Politics of Anti-Imperialism." *Journal of the Gilded Age and Progressive Era* 12, no. 2 (2013): 199–233. https://www.jstor.org/stable/43902949.

Sarnecky, Mary T. *A History of the U.S. Army Nurse Corps*. Philadelphia: University of Pennsylvania Press, 1999.

Sixth Annual Report of the Philippine Commission, 1905, Part 4, 398–400, 639–46.

Sonza, Demy P. *Illustrious Ilongos*. Iloilo City, Philippines: Iloilo Provincial Historical Committee, 1972.

Stoner, Lynn. "Militant Heroines and the Consecration of the Patriarchal State: The Glorification of Loyalty, Combat, and National Suicide in the Making of Cuban National Identity." *Cuban Studies* 34 (2003): 71–96.

The Story of the Lopez Family: A Page from the History of the War in the Philippines. Edited by Canning Eyot. Boston: James H. West Co., 1904.

Tendrich Frank, Lisa, ed. *An Encyclopedia of American Women at War*. Santa Barbara, CA: ABC-CLIO, 2013.

Williams, Kayla. *It's My Country Too: Women's Military Stories from the American Revolution to Afghanistan*. Edited by Bell Jerri and Crow Tracy. Lincoln: University of Nebraska Press, 2017. http://www.jstor.org/stable/j.ctt1q8jj0f.

Wolff, Leon. *Little Brown Brother: How the United States Purchased and Pacified the Philippine Islands at the Century's Turn.* N.p.: History Book Club, 2006.

Women's National War Relief Association. *Women's National War Relief Association: Organized for the Emergency of the Spanish-American War; Report, March 1898 to January 1899.* New York: Printed by order of the Board of Directors, 1899.